CANADIAN INTELLECTUAL PROPERTY: THE POLITICS OF INNOVATING INSTITUTIONS AND INTERESTS

Defining and regulating 'intellectual property' is a growing industry for information brokers, economists, and the legal profession. While other authors have documented the intellectual property (IP) market and its laws (copyright, patents, and trademarks), Bruce Doern and Markus Sharaput are the first Canadian political scientists to provide an integrated political and institutional analysis. The authors delve into the politics of big business and protectionism, lobbies in the healthcare industry, the significance of an emerging IP framework, pressures for equitable dissemination, and internal pressures within government, all of which influence Canada's intellectual property policy and its implementation.

Among the conclusions advanced by Doern and Sharaput is that the main impetus for change in Canada has come ultimately from American corporate and political forces seeking to strengthen IP protection at the expense of IP dissemination. The authors show that although such pressures were initially resisted, with the advent of the innovative economy they became an entrenched part of the Canadian IP debate. Intellectual property user and dissemination-oriented interests are emerging in new ways that will undoubtedly change the politics of IP in the first decade of the twenty-first century.

G. BRUCE DOERN is a professor in the School of Public Administration at Carleton University and holds a joint chair in Public Policy in the Department of Politics at Exeter University. At present he is involved in the Carleton Research Unit on Innovation, Science, and Environment (CRUISE).

MARKUS SHARAPUT is completing his doctoral studies in political science at York University. He graduated with his MA in political economy from Carleton University, where his research focused on the pharmaceutical industry.

D1475830

CANADIAN INTELLECTUAL PROPERTY

The Politics of Innovating Institutions and Interests

160 404

G. Bruce Doern and Markus Sharaput

UNIVERSITY OF TORONTO PRESS
Toronto Buffalo London

© University of Toronto Press Incorporated 2000
Toronto Buffalo London
Printed in Canada

ISBN 0-8020-4473-5 (cloth)
ISBN 0-8020-8255-6 (paper)

Printed on acid-free paper

Canadian Cataloguing in Publication Data

Doern, G. Bruce, 1942–

Canadian intellectual property : the politics of innovating
institutions and interests

Includes bibliographical references and index.
ISBN 0-8020-4473-5 (bound)   ISBN 0-8020-8255-6 (pbk.)

1. Intellectual property – Canada.   2. Intellectual property –
Government policy – Canada.   I. Sharaput, Markus.   II. Title.

KE2779.D63 2000   352.749'0971   C99-933016-0
KF2979.D63 2000

University of Toronto Press acknowledges the financial assistance to its
publishing program of the Canada Council for the Arts and the Ontario
Arts Council.

University of Toronto Press acknowledges the financial support for its publishing activities of the Government of Canada through the Book Publishing
Industry Development Program (BPIDP).

In loving memory of
Christina Doern Harvey, 1908–1999

For my family

Contents

Preface

Research for this book has been a genuine joint voyage of discovery for both of us over the past three years. There was good and varied work to draw upon concerning intellectual property (IP) from legal scholars, and there was, of course, a vast and overwhelming array of technical literature and government reports on specific Canadian IP agencies. A special window into IP matters was supplied by the pharmaceutical industry, both through its own position papers and the periodic federal policy reviews that have centred on this crucial feature of IP in Canada. There was a burgeoning international literature, largely by economists but also by lawyers, on the trade-related aspects of intellectual property. In our own discipline, there was literature on the interest-group politics of sectors such as the pharmaceutical industry and patents, but remarkably little on the core Canadian intellectual property regime. There was no basic mapping of the array of institutions that came even close to adequately dealing with the structure and interplay among national bodies within Canada, and between Canada and international agencies and institutions, let alone with the underlying cluster of political interests and interest groups in the IP field.

This book is an effort to partially fill this gap by providing a basic institutional perspective. The key Canadian IP institutions and interests are examined in a very basic manner, as well as in the broader context of a changing industrial-trade-innovation policy agenda and a general effort to cope with, and profit from, the knowledge-based economy.

The analysis is based first on the literature cited and on related agency documents and reports. It is based secondarily on over seventy interviews carried out with officials, experts, and practitioners in the key Canadian IP agencies, the IP professions, and IP-related firms, interest groups, and non-governmental organizations in Canada and abroad.

We are indebted to John de la Mothe, Wallace Clement, and Jeremy Richardson for helpful comments on earlier draft chapters or aspects of this work. The comments of two anonymous reviewers were also immensely helpful. Doug Kuntze and Lisa Power at the Canadian Intellectual Property Office were especially supportive in getting this work started and in nurturing it along the way with timely advice and encouragement. We also wish to thank the many persons in the key Canadian IP agencies, the IP professions, and IP-related industries who kindly gave us their time and insights, some of whom have also commented on earlier drafts of this book or on particular chapters. Gratitude is also owed to Marie Blythe and Jeff Roy for excellent research assistance at early stages of the work. The above persons have certainly made this a better product, but they bear no responsibility for any remaining errors or weaknesses in the analysis. These are our responsibility alone.

Special thanks are also due to several institutions which provided research funding and support along the way, including the Social Sciences and Humanities Research Council of Canada, the School of Public Administration and the Institute of Political Economy at Carleton University, the Carleton Research Unit on Innovation, Science and Environment (CRUISE), the Politics Department at the University of Exeter, and the Canadian Intellectual Property Office.

G. Bruce Doern and Markus Sharaput
July 1999

CANADIAN INTELLECTUAL PROPERTY

Introduction

Creations of the mind and inventions are given protection by the state as intellectual property (IP) in exchange for disseminating such creativity to society so that others may create and innovate to an even greater extent. Intellectual property policy and institutions in Canada and elsewhere are thus centred on a crucial trade-off between protecting IP and disseminating IP. But the nature and point of that trade-off has been changing over the last twenty years in ways that require us to understand Canadian IP through the politics of innovating institutions and interests.

This book examines IP and innovating institutions and interests from three overall vantage points. Its focus is on Canadian IP institutions whose very purpose is to encourage invention and innovation through laws, policies, and decisions that both protect IP and disseminate it. It deals with IP institutions, an array of governmental departments and agencies as well as private interests which are themselves being compelled to innovate in the global economy and in the face of pressures to change the nature of governance in many policy fields. And it deals with IP institutions and policies that are embedded in a larger transformation of microeconomic policy from an era of industrial policy to one centred on innovation policy, and, more broadly, to changing conceptions of national versus international innovation and access by Canadians to an international community of innovation.

These three vantage points for looking at Canadian IP are necessary to come to grips with where and how the IP trade-off is being renegotiated. For many, IP is a crucial element of prosperity in a knowledge-based economy, an economy in which competitive success in the production of goods is increasingly dependent on the development of information and services anchored in research and knowledge. For others IP is a kind of perverse new protectionism and a United States–led effort at the globalization of property, a substitute, in effect, for other earlier or declining forms of trade protection such as the tariff and industrial subsidies. At yet another level, it may be seen, in even a populist context, as a needed, though less understood, form of protection. Author Margaret Atwood is a Canadian cultural icon – indeed, industry – who deserves copyright protection, as will many unknown authors whose first books are only a sketch in their mind's eye. Tim Horton's has a trademark that gives recognition and protection to business acumen. The doughnut empire is better known than its namesake's former hockey prowess. Banting and Best, the discoverers of insulin, received patent protection and are now cited as icons in the advertising and lobbying material with which Monsanto aims at garnering political support for its role as an innovator in the field of modern health miracle products, which need IP protection. Even more broadly, the emergence of the Internet suggests to some that intellectual property rights will be virtually unenforceable and thereby there is being established a greater community ownership or free ownership of information and ideas. IP issues also raise vital economic, social, and moral issues in the patenting of life forms, and in matters regarding biodiversity.

The ultimate context for, and cause of, this rise in the importance of IP is global change in general (de la Mothe and Paquet 1996; Bellamy and Taylor 1998; Weiss 1998; Leadbeater 1999). The key features of such change are well known but are also bewilderingly complex and interdependent: the globalization of production and the massive increases in the mobility of capital; the digitalization of computer and telecommunications, which escalates the formation of information- and service-based economies and societies; the demise of the Soviet Union and the transformation of Eastern Europe; the entrenchment of free trade and the formation of competing trading blocs as well as competing countries; the obvious interdependence of environmental ecosystems in a shrinking world; and, last but not least, the reinvention of government, as governments that are caught up in change seek to influence and guide it in less bureaucratic and more innovative and democratic ways.

The state as an even broader institution than the government of the day is itself simultaneously a creator, grantor, enforcer, and user of intellectual property. Government laboratories such as the National Research Council invent products and processes and obtain IP rights.

The state grants patents. The courts and customs agencies enforce IP rights. Governments use IP, including copyrighted studies, books, and publications. In matters of IP, as in other policy domains, the state is not a neutral player. Its interdepartmental and institutional politics help define IP policies and implementation and are in turn influenced by changing interest-group coalitions and policy communities.

These compelling global forces also change the nature of public policy formation, and indeed transform the boundaries and focal points of policy fields and their political and economic constituencies. Science and technology policies writ large shift from a once simpler and even exclusive focus on R & D spending to a concern for whether a country is adept at establishing and using IP rights (Wallerstein, Mogee, and Schoen 1993; Jasanoff 1998). New technologies in materials, biotechnology, computer software, and other fields are produced through varied and complex inter-firm and business-university alliances and partnerships. Innovation policies and actions, rather than industrial policies, are increasingly seen as the motive force behind competitive success, though the latter have not totally disappeared. More and more policies are cast as trade policies or as trade-related policies, and hence realms of policy-making power inside and outside the state change (Doern, Pal, and Tomlin 1996). In addition, trade policy hegemony is seen as being driven by the global economic power of the United States, but it also raises new problems in the relations between the developed and developing world (Hoekman and Kostecki 1995).

Canadian IP policy and institutions have been so obscurely buried in the layers of other policy and institutional topsoil that there is not even a basic map of the core Canadian policy institutions and interests. This is not true of most other policy fields such as macroeconomic, social, health, or environmental policy, where institutional guideposts are available to interested readers and practitioners. This is the analytical gap in the IP policy and institutional domain which this book seeks to begin to fill.

Purpose, Scope, and Main Arguments

The purpose of the book is to describe and assess Canadian intellectual property institutions as focal points for innovation in the knowledge economy of the new Millennium. Written and researched from the disciplinary perspectives of political science and public administration, the book seeks to complement the analyses of economists and legal scholars and practitioners who have tilled the IP soil more extensively in Canada, but not with any real focus on the breadth of IP institutions and interests actually in place or on institutional politics.

Intellectual property and its main constituent parts – patents, trademarks, copyright, and designs – have not been properly examined in the authors' home disciplines of political science and public administration. Analysis has been at best tangential, not only on policy but even more with respect to institutions. Political analysis tends to focus on particular interest-group sectors in patent policy, such as the chemicals industry, pharmaceuticals, and biotechnology (Campbell and Pal 1994). These are important perspectives which we build on, but the intellectual property policy and institutional arena itself is still treated in these analyses, at best, as contextual and secondary.

The book is best seen as focusing on a middle level of institutional analysis, for reasons which are set out below. It essentially brings together a quite standard mix of analytical concepts and issues, which, for the most part, have been derived from examining policy and regulatory institutions. But one caveat about this approach must be made especially clear. Any examination of institutions must be set in a context of policy issues and debates; changes to this policy context, however, make up only one of the three forms of institutional innovation to be examined. Thus, while a middle-level focus on changing IP institutions means that policy issues must be engaged, they are secondary in the overall scope and structure of the book.[1]

This book tries to keep the focus on the core Canadian policy, regulatory, and operational bodies that reside at the centre of IP institutions but around which many of the global changes are occurring. For the most part, this means that we also have to set analytical priorities on the

---

1 If this book were focused on IP *policy*, a different structure of analysis would be needed, and it would have to deal much more thoroughly than this book does with crucial policy debates on the interplay between IP policy and trade, the Internet, competition, and environmental policy (Bhat 1996; Chartrand 1996; Anderman 1998; Gallini and Trebilcock 1996). Some attention to institutions would undoubtedly be a part of such an alternative policy-focused book, but their consideration would have to become secondary simply to make possible the proper examination of the array of policy concerns. It is also the case that the IP institutions that would emerge in a policy-focused study would be different; for example, it would be necessary to take more of a look at each of industry, foreign policy, telecommunications, and the health and environment policy departments of governments and their clusters of interests.

four main areas of IP as an operational system of protecting and disseminating intellectual property. Thus, throughout the book, we look first and most at patents, then at trademarks, and then at copyright. We do not examine the issue of designs. Trade secrets are a further aspect of intellectual property that does not receive attention.

In part these choices and rankings are driven by the mandates, cultures, and politics of the core IP agencies. In a core entity such as the Canadian Intellectual Property Office (CIPO), both patents and trademarks are central. In recent transformations, however, patents, and the patent registration process, have been granted greater prestige. In part, this has been a result of the long-term 'rhythms' or cycles of patent versus trademark use in their respective business constituencies and policy and service delivery communities. In addition, the privileged position of patents has been driven in part by their greater capacity for reconciliation with the contextual preferences of the time. Patents are examined through a registration process that involves scientific and technical judgment and competence, qualities which are much in favour in the new 'innovative economy.' Trademark registration, in contrast, is currently viewed as a process involving judgments that are closer to artistic, rather than technical, expertise.

Copyright aspects are in one sense only a third-priority concern in our institutional focus. This is because copyright institutions are different, as will be made clear, partly because they typically do not centre on a registration process. But in another sense, copyright aspects assume a far higher priority concern. Copyright issues and politics are arguably the main driving force in international IP politics and hence are crucial to understanding how and why, during the 1990s, international IP agencies have undergone changes that, in turn, have affected Canada's system of IP governance.

All of this means that the book devotes more analytical attention to the patent aspects and that trademarks and copyright receive second-order emphasis. But all three elements must be covered to some reasonable extent if we are to understand Canada's IP institutions in a basic way.

Five key arguments or themes are advanced in our analysis of Canadian IP institutions and their historical evolution, especially during the last twenty years. The first argument is that, despite over seventy years of debate and linkage to international IP treaties and rules, IP in Canada has only very recently emerged from political obscurity in national economic and political debate. Thus we first argue that IP policies and issues have remained in the backwaters of political and economic debate, in part, because the keys to Canadian prosperity and the preferred policies and policy levers were seen historically to reside in other realms, be they a reliance on natural resource–driven growth, Keynesian macroeconomic policy, tariffs, subsidies, and R & D spending, or any number of particular policy initiatives. In the 1990s, IP has ridden the conceptual coat-tails of innovation policy to greater political-economic prominence, but innovation policy, as we will show, is hardly a beacon of clarity as the new Millennium begins.

The second argument to emerge from an institutional and political focus is that the main impetus for change in Canada has come ultimately from U.S. corporate and political forces seeking to strengthen IP protection at the expense of IP dissemination. The analysis will show that Canada initially resisted such pressures but then ultimately adopted them as being in the national interest in the new innovation age. In an overall sense, Canada has become more of a policy-taker than a policy-maker on matters of IP. The greater emphasis on the IP protection function, especially for patents and copyright, is undoubtedly being driven mainly by U.S. industry lobbies with IP protection interests, backed both by an American government that sees such industries as areas where U.S. economic advantage can be maximized and by U.S. political power in international trade and economic relations.

The third argument is that within the federal government, despite the proliferation of agency and departmental stakeholders, and the increased institutional complexity of IP policy, IP policy has increasingly been dominated by a consolidation of power by trade policy agencies. IP policy now is concentrated in Industry Canada and the Department of Foreign Affairs and International Trade (DFAIT), where IP protection and trade-related IP norms are all-pervasive. They, along with CIPO, have become ever more powerful vis-à-vis departments such as Health Canada and Canadian Heritage and their ministers.

A fourth theme is that despite the claim that IP is becoming one integrated policy field with beneficial 'framework'-oriented non-discriminatory features, institutional evidence suggests that it is still driven overwhelmingly by sectoral politics centred especially in the pharmaceutical and biotechnology industries. Thus its claims to being a framework policy must remain suspect.

Finally, we also argue that the dominance of the protection function in IP institutional politics and interest-group relations seriously underplays the importance of other emerging interests for whom IP dissemination is crucial but whose voice has not yet been found in the IP policy process, in part because of their inherent political weaknesses as IP users but also because of the complex nature of how innovation is viewed in practical terms. The analysis will argue, for example, that both small business and universities, as more dispersed IP dissemination interests, show considerable diversity at the level of the individual firm or university as to how they view IP, and as to where in the menu of innovation-promoting activities and policies they place IP. It will also be evident from the analysis that the more one probes the interests themselves as simple aggregates (small business, universities), the more it is necessary to recognize that they themselves are composed of sub-interests who have benefits and costs to trade off on both the protection and dissemination sides of the IP coin. Universities, for example, are also only beginning to come to grips with their role as both creators and users of IP.

To deal with these arguments and themes, several analytical tasks are essential. First, we have to examine the changing roles, cultures, and interdependent relations of entities such as the Canadian Intellectual Property Office (CIPO), Industry Canada, the Department of Foreign Affairs and International Trade, Canadian Heritage, and the Copyright Board of Canada. Though this book deals with IP as a whole, it is a moot point as to the degree to which the above institutional mélange allows a truly integrated IP policy field with which one can deal, as opposed to a series of separate component realms for patents, trademarks, and copyright.

Another essential task is to identify the core interests involved in the protection versus dissemination trade-offs, the changes in the power structure among such interests, and the role of representational politics for different interests in IP policy institutions. We also have to look at the diverse interplay among interest groups, key firms, and collective associations that range from the pharmaceutical industry and biotechnology lobbies, the IP professions and computer firms, to organizations representing authors, universities, and public health coalitions.

We also have to appreciate how IP has evolved historically at the international level. Three stages of overall development are usually portrayed (Drahos 1996; Marlin Bennett 1995; Merges 1990). The first stage is a territorial or national stage, in which there were no international rules or regimes. Beginning in the latter part of the nineteenth century, an international regime emerged centred on the Paris and Berne conventions. It was still territorially based but extended the rights of creators through treaties. The most recent stage, which has elevated IP to its present state of political-economic centrality, began in the mid-1980s, with a U.S.-led attempt to globalize intellectual property through the formation of a common IP regime. We return to various aspects of these stages in several of the chapters that follow.

Finally, we also have attempted to understand the issues related to Canada's developing a greater culture of invention and innovation and what they suggest about the meaning of innovation in a full economic and social context. This requires a discussion about innovation in firms as new products and processes are generated; innovation *in* a national economy as opposed to Canada's *access to* a world of innovation; and social and institutional innovation in such diverse realms as health care and universities, where IP changes have established new values and ways of doing things relative to an emerging more *propertied* world.

Through a focus on the five central arguments and themes, the book seeks to provide a clearer analytical journey for those interested in how Canadian IP institutions function as political and governmental bodies and sets of interests.

An Institutional Approach

This book does not present an elaborate discussion of the vast theoretical literature concerning institutions, bureaucracies, and complex organizations. Though it employs an institutional perspective, including a linkage to international bodies and institutions, its larger purpose is to provide an initial useful middle-level way of understanding Canada's IP institutions, and therefore the institutional politics which result from interactions among key IP agencies and their interests. Nonetheless, it is important to consider briefly how institutions have been viewed conceptually since we seek to derive insights about Canada's IP agencies from several of the strands of institutional analysis.

A governing institution can be thought of as an entrenched set of values or rules, and hence it is structured by the external and internal constraints of the organization or body involved, including its culture of operation (Ostrom 1990; Peters 1999). But institutions are also historical constructs. Early formative choices have a pervasive influence over later decisions. Regulatory bodies such as an IP agency can and do change, but not without overcoming these internal features, which may be seen as valued features by some interests and inertia by others. Other structuralist conceptualizations of government institutions highlight even more fundamental veto points or constraints on how subsets of public policy or institutional change are made or are allowed to be made (Searing 1991; March 1996; Lowndes 1996).

Institutional analysis by economists has tended to focus on institutions as aggregates of individual preferences, and hence the reform of regulators and regulations is seen to turn on either getting rid of unproductive rules or redesigning them with the appropriate new mix of incentives that will produce more efficient outcomes (Ogus 1994). A more holistic notion of institutions as prior or larger sets of beliefs or views of the public interest tends to be eschewed and indeed is a suspect concept among mainstream economists. There are, however, more recent strands of institutional analysis by economists that are broader and more in line with how political scientists and many practitioners have always seen governing institutions (Yarbrough and Yarbrough 1990; North 1990; de la Mothe and Paquet 1996). In short, they focus on a more historical evolutionary form of economics, analyse systems of trust and cooperation, and seek to locate the core structure of individual incentives in larger sets of complex relationships.

As a regulatory body within the federal government, an IP agency such as CIPO needs to be examined with several institutional elements fully in mind as derived from basic regulatory and other literature (Doern, Hill, Prince, and Schultz 1999). In this book, we look at several such elements: the core rhythms of activity and organizational culture central to the basic regulatory existence of an agency, in short, its production cycle surrounding applications for patents and trademarks; the larger mix of functions that any such body plays, such as related service and advisory roles; the financing of the organization; the political saliency of the organization and its policy field within its ministry and the government as a whole; and its relationship to 1990s government-wide reforms, particularly those centred on the reinvention of government and the so-called New Public Management, the latter propelled by political-managerial theory and ideology but also by the communications revolution centred on the Internet (Ferlie et al. 1996; Aucoin 1997; Campbell 1996). A central feature of these governmental and managerial reforms has been to make governmental agencies more conscious of their diverse customers and users, and more entrepreneurial towards meeting their needs (Ferlie et al. 1996).

With regard to all the elements above, we are interested in how they constitute a reasonably accurate picture of the 'internal' organization as such, but we also seek to extend these features outwards to encompass institutional politics among federal IP departments and agencies. And institutional analysis necessarily looks at core relations affecting its main interests, stakeholders, or policy communities. Institutional analysis thus necessarily involves the institutional politics that result from interests and their changing positions and configurations.

It must quickly be added that the analysis of such interests in this book is a general one, focused on the cluster of interests that surround particular bodies or that interact around the protection versus dissemination functions of IP in Canada. Nonetheless, we trace changing developments in interest coalitions and policy communities that include the following: the IP professions (patent and trademark agents); big business; multinational and Canadian drug companies; health coalitions; small business; universities as complex sets of interests of faculty, students, and administration; and the ubiquitous Internet interests of the information society.

Structure and Organization

The book is organized into two main parts, the first dealing with history and context and the second with Canada's IP institutions as functioning political and operational entities interacting with each other and with their sets of political interests. In Part I the basic historical context for IP institutions and policies is set. Chapter 1 supplies an account of the main components of intellectual property and the nature of the central policy trade-offs between the protection and dissemination of IP. It also takes an initial inventory of the key governmental players in IP and of the private stakeholders and policy communities. Chapter 2 provides a longer-term historical context for the evolution of IP in Canada, focusing on five main features and events, which begin with early laws at the time of Confederation and extend through periodic policy reviews to changes in the later 1960s regarding pharma-patents and the historical formation and development of the IP professions. Chapter 3 provides a needed complementary look at how IP policy has evolved in relation to medium-term industrial policies and efforts in the 1990s, influenced by the emergence of the knowledge-based economy, to recast Canadian industrial policy. Chapter 4 sets out the evolving and recent context of global and international pressures, including the basic nature and influence of such international IP institutions as the World Intellectual Property Organization (WIPO) and the

World Trade Organization (WTO), and, most crucially of all, pressures from American IP institutions and business interests. Taken together, the first four chapters also flesh out more completely why the five main arguments previewed above are central to the book.

Part II of the book then explores these arguments by looking more closely into Canadian IP institutions and institutional politics 'in action,' as partially integrated and partially separate bodies and sets of players and interests. Chapter 5 focuses on the patent and trademark regulatory and registration process centred in the Canadian Intellectual Property Office (CIPO) of Industry Canada. Chapter 6 centres on the very different world of copyright institutions, where jurisdiction is divided between two ministries, and where the politics of the Copyright Act of 1997 reveal the presence of divisions among cultural producers and other business and educational users of copyrighted products.

In chapters 7, 8, and 9, attention shifts to a closer look at the way interests align around the two functional aspects of the IP trade-off, especially in the realm of patents. Chapter 7 focuses on IP protection and the key interests which coalesce around it, especially big business and the IP or patent agent and trademark agent professions. Chapter 8 zeroes in on what is undoubtedly the core politics of IP change in Canada, namely that centred on the pharmaceutical and biotechnology industries and on related issues in health care and innovation. Chapter 9 then examines the IP dissemination function and the much more dispersed sets of user interests that revolve around it, including universities and related knowledge-based institutions.

Lastly, in chapter 10 conclusions are offered, centred around a final discussion of the five main arguments set out above but also on other related matters that emerge from the cumulative analytical journey.

PART ONE

IP Institutions and Policy: Setting the Context

1. Key IP Policy Trade-offs and Institutions: An Initial Profile

An understanding of Canada's intellectual property policy and institutional realm must start with a basic profile of its main components, the basic policy trade-offs inherent in the field, and its core and secondary institutions, players, and interests. This chapter is very much of a stocktaking nature, but all the more necessary since there is such a limited understanding of the Canadian IP policy system as a whole. In later chapters, we build on this basic profile by giving a more detailed treatment of the dynamics and subtleties of this important policy field, especially in the context of economic globalization, but also in relation to the potential differences that arise in the transformation from a goods-oriented to a knowledge-based and service-oriented economy.

The Main Components of IP

Intellectual property is traditionally divided into two fields, 'industrial property' and 'copyright.' Industrial property includes protection by means of patents, trademarks, and industrial designs. Copyright gives authors and other creators of works of the mind, such as literature, music, and art, rights to authorize or prohibit, for a certain period of time, certain uses made of their works. So-called neighbouring rights also supply rights to performers, such as singers and musicians.

Stated somewhat more specifically, the four elements of intellectual property can be defined, in layperson terms, as follows (though in any jurisdiction detailed definitional reference must be made to the particular provisions of the law and practice):

- A *patent* is a monopoly right 'granted for inventions relating to new technologies. An invention can be a product, manufacture or composition of matter, an apparatus, a method or process or an improvement on any of these' (Baldwin 1997, 51). The monopoly right provides inventors 'with the right to exclude others from making, using or selling their invention for 20 years from the date of filing a patent application' (Baldwin 1997, 51).

- A *trademark* is 'a word, a symbol, a design, or a combination of these, used to distinguish the wares or services of one person or organization from those of others in the marketplace' (CIPO 1994a, 5).
- A *copyright* is a right to prevent copying of literary, artistic, and musical works. It arises automatically without a period of waiting for registration but does not give a complete monopoly in the way that patents do (Bainbridge 1994). A copyright does not protect the underlying ideas or concepts themselves but rather protects the way an author or artist expresses an idea or concept. Other rights exist that are related to or 'neighbouring on' copyright and typically include the rights of performing artists, producers of phonograms, and broadcasting organizations (WIPO 1995e, 165).
- A *design* right is a means of 'protection for designs for industrial products' (Jacob and Alexander 1993, 15). In some countries, an unregistered design right arises, like a copyright, without any need for application or registration, and it does not give a complete monopoly. More typically, however, a design must be registered. In essence, a design protects the appearance of articles but not the way they work.

Each of the above broad working definitions also inherently begs the question of whether there is, in practice, a functioning *intellectual property* policy field as opposed to separate realms of patent, trademark, copyright, and design policy, each marching to the beat of different political-economic drummers. To some extent, they are separate fields because of the different characteristics, situations, interests, and traditions in each area. But there is no doubt that political, technological, and economic pressure is also causing governments to fashion policy for the IP field as a whole, particularly given that modern economies are said to be increasingly knowledge-based.

The Central IP Policy Trade-offs

The central policy trade-off in IP as a whole is between that of protect-

ing creations and inventions of the mind and disseminating such creations for the broader good of society. Within the context of a nation
state, economists express the need for the state to determine such trade-
offs because of the presence of a public good. Thus, in the first instance,
the new intellectual creation is a public good because one person's
consuming of it does not diminish anyone else's capacity to consume it
(Maskus 1995). Private markets could not easily prevent such con-
sumption. Moreover, because such private actors could not appropriate
the gains to themselves, they would have only limited incentives to
innovate or create. Society would be worse off because secrecy would
be encouraged and there would be an under-supply of such ideas,
creations, and innovations. This creates the case for state intervention,
but it does not in itself make the case for *how far* to intervene or *what
instruments* to use to intervene (Trebilcock and Howse 1995).

If, at the other extreme, the state intervenes and gives the creators
and owners of intellectual property full control, then it is creating
monopoly economic power, with resultant higher prices, economic
inefficiencies in general, and a lessened exchange and use of the innovations themselves. Hence, there emerges the search for a regulatory or
interventionist balance – in short, a set of trade-offs between two principles or policy rationales that are both seen to be, in this sense, 'in the
public interest.'

Within nations that have advanced IP policies, the tendency has been
to characterize such policies as being framework-oriented in that the
pressure is to define one overall trade-off rather than create special ones
for different industrial sectors such as computers or pharmaceuticals.
But in theory and in practice such varied sectoral trade-offs are also
possible, and they certainly drive key aspects of the politics of IP
(Trebilcock and Howse 1995).

When the core IP policy trade-offs are conceived *among* nations, it
follows that country-to-country differences in policy could be justified
depending upon whether a country's policy-makers saw their nation as
being directly 'innovating' or as being mainly engaged in 'imitation.'
Thus, in theory, there is 'nothing suspect or unreasonable with the
preference of many developing countries for a relatively lax system of
intellectual property rights' (Trebilcock and Howse 1995, 251). For example, Japan practised such an imitation strategy with great success in
the immediate post–Second World War decades (Okimoto 1989). Developing countries could gain considerably in terms of consumer welfare,
and hence a battle has long been present over what the optimum global

policy might be. Canada, too (see chapters 2 and 8), has faced these dilemmas, as evidenced by the debates over compulsory licensing and over generic versus patented medicines.

Clearly, such trade-offs in an international context are not the product of some set of benign processes of economic calculation or inevitability. The political interests of nation states or regional blocs, and political interests within countries, both help determine where and how a trade-off will be made and how it will be continuously adapted.

There is little doubt that IP rights and the nature of the core trade-offs have moved to a higher plane on the international global economic and regulatory-trade agenda. Many developing countries have devised IP policies that have provided quite short periods of patent protection (Siebeck 1990). Canada for some time had such a policy regarding pharmaceutical drugs (Campbell and Pal 1994). In recent trade debates and negotiations, the United States and, somewhat more belatedly, the European Union have led the fight for both more stringent IP policies and policy enforcement. Concern about lax enforcement to deal with pirated products such as videos and recordings is a major concern.

All of this political pressure was also fuelled by a general recognition that the knowledge-based economy of the modern era is a different kind of economy from those of the past in that now intellectual property rights are especially crucial, but not unambiguously so (Renko 1987; Maskus 1995). Thus, both ideas about fairness and views of global versus national or regional economic welfare are at the centre of the international and national expression of the IP policy trade-offs. Such trade-offs, however, must be made through a complex set of national and international agencies and institutions, which are in turn pressured by business interests, the IP professions, varied users of IP, and national governments.

The protection role is central to the existence of the Canadian core intellectual property institutions being examined in this book. They exist to establish rights to intellectual property. The protection role centres on five issues or processes: (1) the quality and efficiency of pendency performance or of the central processes of granting patents and registering trademarks, particularly the patent examination process; (2) issues and debates regarding the length and quality of patent protection and IP protection in general; (3) national and international enforcement and compliance issues, especially in the context of copyright; (4) the role of big business in giving focus to the protection function; and (5) the role of the IP professions (patent agents and trademark agents) as intermediary interests between IP applicants and the IP agencies but whose primary interest is also in the protection function.

The IP dissemination role, as a whole, is both an old and new role for Canada's IP institutions. The oldest IP dissemination role is that of making available to IP users in the economy the current information held in the stock of patents, nationally and globally. A second or more recent variation on this role arises when CIPO and Industry Canada see opportunities, through computer information technologies, to make available to business new value-added kinds of commercially useful information from IP information held by the government. A third kind of IP dissemination arises in the form of efforts to expand awareness of IP among those parts of Canada's economy, and society, in general, which have not yet sought IP rights, so that more firms will use the IP systems and contribute to a more innovative economy. In some instances, such efforts can be seen as campaigns to produce an IP culture within the Canadian economy.

The IP dissemination role as a whole attracts a different and much more dispersed array of interests than does the protection role, in that small and medium-sized businesses, individual inventors, universities, R & D organizations, and fast-forming knowledge networks and consulting firms are involved. This does not mean that big business and the IP professions have no stake in the dissemination roles. They are also major users of IP information. Rather, what happens is that an inherently wider set of interests coalesce around these roles. The dissemination role as a whole is more diffuse than the protection role, and so are the interests.

As the discussion of policy trade-offs suggests, it is useful in an overall sense to distinguish between a core set of Canadian IP institutions and non-core or secondary set of players. As later chapters will show, this is not always a distinction one can consistently maintain, but it is certainly valid for our initial stocktaking purposes.

In policy and regulatory terms, the following are the core IP institutions and interests: the Canadian Intellectual Property Office (CIPO); Industry Canada; Canadian Heritage; Foreign Affairs and International Trade Canada; big business; and the IP professions. As suggested above, these core players centre around the protection function, but by no means exclusively.

The secondary set of institutions and interests include the following: other federal departments and agencies, such as the Patented Medicines Prices Review Board, Health Canada, and Agriculture and Agri-Food Canada (and their regulatory units), whose clientele may have major or periodic concerns about IP; provincial governments; small and medium-sized business; university, educational, library, and research institutions; and individual inventors or creators.

The two sets of institutions and interests are profiled very briefly below. We also profile international institutions, which nominally are not national or Canadian IP players but whose influence is growing enormously in both the core and secondary realms as sketched above. A more complete analysis of international influences, including crucial U.S. influences, is found in chapter 4, and in other chapters as well.

Core IP Institutions and Interests

The Canadian Intellectual Property Office (CIPO)

CIPO's mission is to 'accelerate Canada's economic development by encouraging the utilization of the IP system and the exploitation of IP information' (CIPO 1994, i). Its operations entail the 'establishment of principles, policies, and procedures that enable clients to obtain intellectual property protection.' It is the focal point for the regulation and management of Canada's intellectual property system. Associated now with Industry Canada but formerly, until 1993, a part of the Department of Consumer and Corporate Affairs, CIPO is a Special Operating Agency (SOA), financed by a revolving fund, and hence has special management powers and financial flexibility designed to make it a better and more service-conscious organization. CIPO's mandate deals with patents and trademarks as well as with other realms of intellectual property such as copyrights, industrial designs, and integrated circuit topographies.

CIPO itself must be differentiated from the role of the Commissioner of Patents and Registrar of Trademarks, currently Sheila Batchelor. The Chief Executive Officer (CEO) of CIPO, she is also the Commissioner and the Registrar. In the latter capacities, she is a statutory person, whereas in her role as CEO, which is her Industry Canada administrative title, she is a regular senior public servant. Her role as a statutory person is important because all of the regulatory powers reside in this legally defined role. This is to ensure that decisions on patents and trademarks are based on independent objective judgments and not on political considerations. In other respects, however, as CEO of CIPO, she is within the jurisdiction of her minister and department in the normal way. For example, if legislative policy changes were being considered to the Patent Act, they would ultimately be the responsibility of the Minister, although it is possible for the Commissioner to comment on amendments to the legislation for the Minister's consideration and approval.

Industry Canada

Industry Canada is the department to which CIPO is accountable and within whose broad policy mandate it must function. Industry Canada, as the lead microeconomic policy department, is to provide leadership in three primary areas:

- as 'the government's principal advisor on the national micro-economic policy agenda – helping create a business environment in which firms can meet the challenges of the knowledge-based economy';
- as the setter and enforcer of modern market-place rules and the provider of the services to give them effect; and
- as a promoter of sector development 'by providing services to the private sector to assist in increasing the competitive capacity of industry' (Industry Canada 1995, 2).

This mandate, though basically established with the 1993 reorganization, became even more compelling after the federal government's 1994 program review resulted in a 42.5 per cent cut in Industry Canada's budget (Industry Canada 1995, 3).

Industry Canada's corporate governance branch also houses a policy group that deals with intellectual property policy. Industry Canada has the lead role in IP policy and legislation in the areas of patents, trademarks, and designs but must share the policy lead role with Canadian Heritage in respect of copyright policy. It is also of considerable importance to note that the overall portfolio of the Minister of Industry includes bodies such as the National Research Council (NRC), whose laboratories and institutes patent numerous inventions every year. Industry Canada also has the lead responsibility for federal science policy and hence for policies affecting other federal departmental science laboratories, most of which also hold patents or license inventions to private firms. Industry Canada has also been the chief advocate of the innovation policy approach and its focus on the commercialization of government laboratories.

Canadian Heritage

The Department of Canadian Heritage has a broad heritage and cultural policy mandate that includes citizenship and Canadian identity, cultural development and heritage, and national parks. It is in its cultural mandate that the department has a shared policy role in aspects of intellectual property. The policy role is quite direct in key aspects of copyright policy. As chapter 6 will show in greater detail, changes to copyright law and policy involve the Heritage Canada minister and ministry officials because of policy responsibilities for the broadcasting industry, including cable television. The Canadian Radio-television and Telecommunications Commission (CRTC) also reports to Parliament through the Heritage Canada minister, whereas other aspects of telecommunications policy are the responsibility of Industry Canada. Recent policy development regarding the information highway has also involved Heritage Canada in a direct way.

The key political reality for copyright policy is that an array of interest groups representing performers, writers, and other creators in the arts coalesce mainly around Heritage Canada and see it as their voice in copyright policy. Crucial federal-provincial aspects of copyright policy can also arise, especially regarding Quebec, whose traditions share some of the historical views originating in France about copyright as a moral right rather than as only an economic property right.

Foreign Affairs and International Trade Canada

The Department of Foreign Affairs and International Trade Canada (DFAIT) has emerged in the 1990s as a key intellectual property policy player. It has historically always had a role in Canadian membership in key IP international treaties (see more below). But DFAIT's role has especially emerged in the trade negotiations regarding the Free Trade Agreement (FTA), the North America Free Trade Agreement (NAFTA), and the World Trade Organization (WTO). Patent issues, especially regarding the pharmaceutical industry, were a key backdrop to the FTA negotiations, and then IP issues as a whole became even more centrally involved in NAFTA and the WTO. The latter involved the negotiation of the agreement on Trade Related Intellectual Property (TRIPs).

IP policy has also involved bilateral and hemispheric matters centred on the IP policy power and intentions of the United States and the U.S. Patent and Trademarks Office. These issues extend to the possibility of establishing a North American IP office.

Big Business
'Big business' is an inexact category, but normally in Canadian political discourse it is reflected in the lobbying power and positions of bodies such as the Business Council on National Issues (BCNI) and the Alliance of Manufacturers and Exporters. These core lobbies have certainly applied pressure regarding trade, business framework, and IP laws in an overall sense and regarding patent policy, in particular. However, in the IP field, big business pressure has especially been led by sectoral interest groups such as the Pharmaceutical Manufacturers' Association of Canada (PMAC) and, more recently, by biotechnology firms and groups. In the mid-to-late 1990s, telecommunications firms, computer companies, and the major banks have also been active, as they have come to see the economic value of intellectual property rights.

The IP Professions
The IP professions of patent and trademark agents are lesser-known key players in the IP regulatory system, and their interests are represented primarily by the Patent and Trademark Institute of Canada (PTIC). The 950-member organization describes itself as being interested 'in promoting the protection of intellectual property in Canada and abroad within the context of enhancing Canada's economic prospects as a sovereign nation and fostering cooperation between Canada and its trading partners around the world' (Patent and Trademark Institute of Canada 1991, 1). More particularly, the objects of the PTIC include the following:

a) to form a united and representative group of specialists practicing in the field of intellectual property;
b) to promote the efficient administration and development of laws and practice for the protection of intellectual property in Canada;
c) to promote and maintain high standards of training and ethics among its members; and
d) to disseminate to the public useful knowledge relating to the protection of intellectual property. (Patent and Trademark Institute of Canada 1991, 1)

The PTIC includes foreign members practising in the field of intellectual property in their own countries. Such members do not have voting rights within the PTIC.

With respect to the broad values of the PTIC as the main institutional embodiment of the IP professions, one can certainly discern an overall strong desire to promote a proper and efficiently functioning intellectual property regime. Within this overall value statement, there is a strong emphasis on the 'protection' side of the intellectual property public interest trade-off. The sharing/dissemination half of the intellectual property equation is given secondary emphasis. This should not be surprising since agents are primarily in business to serve their clients, who are seeking such protection.

The IP professions are, however, more than just the PTIC. The institutes individual members are also independent economic entities who conduct their professional practice through small boutique agent firms, large and small law firms, a few large R & D corporations with in-house agents, and firms/practices with varying mixtures of patent and trademark clientele. Some practices deal almost exclusively with work for foreign (mainly U.S.) applicants and are often closer to 'post-office' – like processing operations. Others are more complex, deal with Canadian inventors and trademark applicants, and hence embrace the full cycle of advice and regulatory involvement.

Secondary IP Institutions and Interests

It is an inherent feature of the secondary IP institution that one must describe them in much more general and even tentative terms. They are an array of actual or potential players that are often users or producers of IP, but are also partially regulators of IP themselves.

Other Federal Departments and Agencies
Other federal departments and agencies with a secondary IP interest include Health Canada, the Patented Medicines Prices Review Board, Justice Canada, and departments with their own R & D laboratories. Health Canada has a direct interest in health-care costs, which are in turn linked to the costs and efficacy of drugs and to the issue of patented versus generic drugs. It also – along with other federal departments, such as Agriculture and Agri-Food Canada (in matters of plant breeders' rights) and Environment Canada – regulates biotechnology products, which are also tied to issues of patenting.

The Patented Medicines Prices Review Board (PMPRB) is a small independent agency established under the 1987 amendments to the Patent Act. Its mandate is to ensure that the prices of patented medicines sold in Canada are not excessive. It also reports to Parliament on pharmaceutical price trends and research and development commitments.

Justice Canada has an overall involvement in IP arising in part from the government's own obligations as a producer and user of intellectual property, especially copyright. Department of Justice lawyers are also involved in broad legal issues of intellectual property. Justice Canada has a small Intellectual Property Secretariat, which, among other things, has co-sponsored symposia on digital technology and copyright.

An array of federal departments and agencies have their own laboratories. Scientists in the these agencies (e.g., the National Research Council, Agriculture and Agri-Food Canada, Natural Resources Canada, Health Canada, and Environment Canada) may produce patentable products and processes for which IP rights are an issue. However, they are also agencies under pressure to push the innovation process outwards from their labs to the private sector, and therefore the question of IP ownership has become an issue.

Provincial Governments

The role of provincial governments in IP matters is undoubtedly more indirect than the federal role as a whole, but it certainly can arise in a variety of ways. Provincial jurisdiction over health-care delivery means that the issue of patented versus generic medicines is crucial to provincial health ministries and provincial treasuries. Particular provinces may have industrial policy concerns if key firms or industrial sectors that use IP are located in their territories. Such concerns certainly arise with respect to the concentration of pharmaceutical manufacturers in Quebec (in Montreal), and of generic drug manufacturers in Ontario (in Toronto).

The provinces (and local governments) will also have IP interests arising out of their roles regarding education and libraries. But these latter interests are best highlighted as separate institutions in the IP policy process.

Educational and Research Institutions

Bodies as diverse as universities, community colleges, schools, and libraries have a significant IP interest. For some it is as a direct user with financial and budgetary interest in copyright issues and the way that these affect the availability and cost of teaching and research material. The increasing use of the Internet also raises important copyright concerns. For universities, IP interests also extend to their own faculty members' and students' production of patentable and copyright material. Patents, in particular, including partnership arrangements with business firms, also raise important issues about the ownership of research and its full and free circulation in the interests of preserving academic freedom and exchange.

Small and Medium-Sized Business

When discussed at the national level, the main lobby for small and medium-sized business is usually thought to be the Canadian Federation of Independent Business (CFIB). But other lobbies include such bodies as the Canadian Advanced Technology Association (CATA) and smaller sectoral bodies with overall R & D interests. In the IP field per se, it is more difficult to pinpoint how and when small and medium-sized businesses are mobilized or interested. Chapter 9 will deal more fully with these kinds of micro-politics of IP, but two points warrant an initial mention.

First, it is thought that small and medium-sized businesses are those that most need to be persuaded to become IP users, by informing them about the value of IP. If more firms could be so persuaded, Canada would come closer to fostering an IP and innovation business culture. Second, small and medium-sized firms are interested in the innovation process but define it, not surprisingly, in very broad ways. Thus, this set of interests, more than any other, brings out some of the practical links between innovation as a diffuse process and intellectual property as specific rights.

The Individual Inventor

Finally, we draw attention to the individual inventor or author and creator. The individual Canadian as inventor is the ultimate mythical client for an IP agency and even the ultimate *raison d'être* for patent regimes in some general populist sense, especially in the United States. Mythical interests are always partially real, indeed vitally real. Many accounts of economic and social history give proper place to path-breaking inventions by individuals that created whole new industries (Diebold 1990; Flatow 1992). In Canada, Bombardier began as a small inventor, became a small business, and is now a multinational (Brown 1967a, 1967b).

Relative to other IP interests in the current secondary list, this interest is perhaps the most dispersed. Except for the United States and Japan, most national IP agencies search in vain for an organization that might speak for it. However, individual inventors can at times attract political attention by going to the media and/or by lobbying their elected representatives about the need to help the creative individual.

The inventor tinkering away in a garage evokes one image. But there are also individual authors/creators who are beavering away at their computer screens, working on their first books. Or an individual author could be a Margaret Atwood or a Pierre Berton, who are mini-industries in their own right.

International IP Agencies
As mentioned above, this account is nominally putting international IP agencies among the secondary set of 'domestic' IP players and influences. However, as chapter 4 and other chapters will show, the key international agencies are also increasingly core institutions for Canada, especially because of the U.S. IP and trade agenda and its mobilization around the World Trade Organization (WTO) and Trade Related Intellectual Property (TRIPs). However, two international agencies, in particular, need an initial profile, the World Intellectual Property Organization (WIPO) and the WTO-TRIPs development.

The World Intellectual Property Organization (WIPO)
Headquartered in Geneva, WIPO is one of sixteen specialized agencies of the United Nations system of organizations. It has 161 member states and was established by the 'Convention Establishing the World Intellectual Property Organization' signed at Stockholm on 14 July 1967. The convention came into force in 1970.

WIPO's lineage, however, is more than a century old in that its functions can be traced to the 1883 Paris Convention for the Protection of Industrial Property and the 1886 Berne Convention for the Protection of Literary and Artistic Works. Both conventions provided for secretariats, which eventually became, under various names, one international bureau. At the centre of WIPO's tasks were the various 'Unions,' fifteen in total, each founded on a multilateral treaty (e.g., the Paris Union, the Berne Union) and each with different numbers of signatory states.

The objectives of WIPO are to:

1) promote the protection of intellectual property throughout the world through cooperation among States, and where appropriate, in collaboration with any other international organization; and
2) to ensure administrative cooperation among the intellectual property Unions. (WIPO 1995e, 7)

Divided into the two main branches of intellectual property, industrial property and copyright, the promotional objective is carried out in a variety of ways. These include WIPO's active encouragement of the development of new international treaties (and hence new Unions) and the harmonization of national legislation. It also includes technical assistance to developing countries, the assembly and dissemination of information, and the provision of services for facilitating the obtaining of protection of inventions, marks, and designs for which protection in several countries is desired.

The World Trade Organization (WTO) and Trade Related
Intellectual Property (TRIPs)
The World Trade Organization owes its existence largely to an aggressive IP and trade policy in the United States in the 1990s. The United States still wanted WIPO to carry out its important functions, but it began looking for other institutions to solve the problems identified in its aggressive trade-in-services and IP agenda. Because that agenda was copyright-centred, the concern was whether other countries had proper copyright rules and, equally important, enforcement provisions against pirating. For this, the United States saw the trade policy arena, and the emerging World Trade Organization and its far more effective dispute settlement capacities, as its preferred venue.

The GATT Uruguay Round's wide-ranging negotiations also enabled more pressure to be put on developing countries because wider kinds of trade-offs could be negotiated, including those things that developing countries might seek in exchange for providing tougher IP regimes (Bradley 1987; Beier and Schricker 1989; Braga 1995).

The TRIPs provisions of the Uruguay Round both consolidate and incorporate older patent and trademark conventions, but they also include the long-sought U.S.-levered provisions on dispute settlement in the IP field (Trebilcock and Howse 1995). We return to these and other international provisions and realities in later chapters.

Conclusions

Few if any policy fields can be compactly described, with boundaries precisely laid out and the structure of interests made totally clear. However, the basic stocktaking which this chapter has provided is always analytically necessary, and is especially needed in the case of the Canadian intellectual property field. Long in existence but essentially coming into the political spotlight only recently, the IP policy and regulatory field is multifaceted.

Its most basic component parts – patents, trademarks, copyrights, and designs – have been sketched out, but by no means fully examined. Indeed, it must remain a partially open question as to the degree to which intellectual property can be fully seen as one policy field versus four (or perhaps more) policy and institutional arenas.

The core policy trade-offs, between IP protection and dissemination, have been introduced and in some respects are simple and basic. But we have yet to see how these play out when put in the context of a more detailed account of the functioning IP institutions and their structure of political interests within and outside the state.

Finally, we have presented an initial stocktaking of an array of core and secondary institutions and interests, including international agencies that are of growing importance. In an overall sense, the core institutions and interests are portrayed as coalescing around the IP protection function, whereas the secondary set of players are clustered more around the IP dissemination function. These are valuable distinctions to make in an initial mapping exercise, but as the analysis proceeds in Part II, we will have to deal with more complex overlaps. However, we need a further phase of context-setting analysis, namely an examination in chapter 2 of IP policy and institutions in a historical context.

2. Scarcely Noticed: Canadian IP Developments from Early Days to the 1970s

The focus of this book is on IP changes in the last twenty years, but aspects of earlier Canadian IP history are crucial in order to understand institutional evolution, policy change, and changing configurations of interests. There are two central themes to this brief historical and contextual account of five IP developments in the period from Confederation to the early 1970s. First, during this period IP developments were scarcely noticed among the higher priorities of Canadian political-economic life. All five changes or episodes examined, including IP changes in the late 1960s, essentially transpired in ways that did not garner high priority or sustained political attention. Second, although it is important to understand IP as a framework-oriented set of ideas, institutions, and interests, it is also crucial to understand that a historical tension exists between IP, in general, and patents, in particular, especially in the case of pharmaceutical patents (a tension which will be further explored in chapters 7 and 8).

In some respects, the low profile of IP up to the 1970s is easily understood in that, for most of this hundred-year period, Canada's economy was still based on natural resources, while national economic policy was still structured around the tariff. Even after the Second World War, despite the emergence of an industrial and manufacturing economy characterized by extensive foreign ownership, issues of R & D or science policy were not extensively debated until the mid-to-late 1960s (Doern 1972). In the government's economic policy toolbox, IP was buried at the bottom, to be ignored while other more promising or more tried and tested instruments were looked for to ensure Canadian prosperity.

The exception to this general case was, unsurprisingly, pharmapatents, which were debated in the late '60s. One of the most significant characteristics of pharmaceutical patent debate has been its durability. In contrast to wider IP discourse, pharmapatents have been subject to periodic public review. This debate did not impinge, however, on the wider discussion of IP, for two reasons. First, pharmapatents have traditionally been dealt with as a special case by lawmakers and regulators. Second, the pharmapatent debate in the 1960s was dominated by the intrusion of health issues into traditional IP discourse.

To a large extent, this has been the result of the unusually complex range of issues associated with pharmapatents. Although governed by the need to balance the same priorities as other patent forms (the dissemination and diffusion of technology balanced against the need to encourage and reward innovation), pharmapatents have been complicated by further sets of issues, such as the need to balance industrial versus health priorities. Pharmapatents have been subject to periodic review, with each policy review iteration responding to previous debate, but also creating the conditions for new debate. They have had a pervasive influence over the policy field they govern, an influence whose scope and effect varied as each new re-regulation of pharmapatents emerged. Ironically, the sector which best illustrates the role of IP as an institutional framework in this period, is also the sector which lends itself least to the role of IP as a general case. It was not until the tension between industrial and health priorities was resolved (in the post-1987 debate) that pharmapatents became the exception which proved the rule.

With the above two themes in mind, the chapter deals with five aspects of Canadian IP history from Confederation to the early 1970s. The first part of the chapter traces the origins and evolution of general IP law. The second looks at important changes in the 1920s, when compulsory licensing raised issues about the protection versus dissemination trade-off. The third part of the chapter traces the origins and evolution of the patent and trademark professions. In various ways, these sections draw out the mainly British, but also sometimes American, influences on Canada's basic patent law and practice and some of the early need to meet IP treaty obligations. The fourth section then looks at two IP policy reviews, the Ilsley Royal Commission in 1960 and the Economic Council of Canada review in 1971, which capture key underlying aspects of Canadian IP activity and policy but which also show their slow meandering journey even through the 1950s and 1960s. Finally, we examine the changes to patent law made in the late 1960s, which centred on pharmaceutical patents.

Early Laws

Canada's patent law predates Confederation in that it originated in Lower Canada with a law passed in 1823, a law modelled on the British Statute of Monopolies of 1624. Following Confederation, this law was superceded by the federal Patent Act of 1869 (Fox 1969). As we will see further below, one of the key features of this law was that it contained 'working provisions,' which essentially meant that a patented invention had to be manufactured in Canada within a three-year period from the date of granting the patent or the patent would be revoked (Economic Council of Canada 1971, 55). While minor amendments occurred, it was not until 1923 that Canada passed a new Patent Act, largely required, as we see further below, by Canada's own adherence to the International Convention for the Protection of Industrial Property. Canada had become a member of this convention when Britain joined in 1883.

Trademark law in Canada essentially begins with the Trademark and Design Act of 1868. The law gave the owner of a registered trademark a more certain protection than could be obtained by an unregistered mark. In 1932, this law was repealed, and trademark provisions were handled through a new Unfair Competition Act. Dissatisfaction with this more general act led to the passage of the Trade Marks Act of 1953. The post–Second World War Canadian economy of foreign-owned branch-plants and buoyant consumerism simply could not be accommodated by an antiquated law governing trademarks.

Canada's copyright law was decidedly British in origins and content. Federal law dates to 1875. The major Canadian Copyright Act of 1921 was essentially modelled on the British law of 1911. A 1936 amendment established a Copyright Appeal Board, but from then until the last decade of the twentieth century there were no major changes. The 1997 changes examined in chapter 6 are therefore a long overdue catch-up exercise, but one that only really caught up to the 1980s. The economy of the 1990s was already well ahead of copyright law.

The 1920s and Compulsory Licensing

In February 1929, Ferdinand Rinfret, Mackenzie King's secretary of state, introduced Bill 7, a piece of legislation which was intended to bring Canada's Patent Act into conformity with an international convention 'for the protection of industrial property' to which Canada agreed at the Hague conference in 1925 (Hansard, *Parliamentary Debates*, 28 Feb. 1929, p. 339). This convention had two key components regarding patents.

First, it required that the patented article should meet the requirements of the public, and second, that it should be manufactured in the country granting the patent. Bill 7 constituted an amendment to the Patent Act to permit challenges to a patent request under either requirement, namely, that the product did not meet the reasonable requirements of the public, or that the patentee had failed to adequately manufacture the invention in Canada (Hansard, 28 Feb. 1929, p. 340). The system of governance established for patents by Bill 7 placed the preponderance of discretionary power into the hands of the Commissioner of Patents. It was the commissioner who evaluated whether or not the patentee had met the requirements noted above, and if it was determined the requirements had not been met, the commissioner could order the patentee to grant a compulsory licence. If the licence was not granted, the commissioner could revoke the patent in question. In other words, while licences were granted by those who held patents, retaining those patents was conditional upon a recognition of the authority of the commissioner.

The 'requirements of the public' to which the bill referred seems to have implied two factors: the speed with which a product was manufactured (or, rather, the speed with which it was begun to be manufactured); and the scope of manufacturing once it began. For example, there seems to have been an expectation that the manufacturer begin within three years of a patent grant – failure to do so being one possible justification for granting a compulsory licence (Hansard, 14 Feb. 1929, p. 433). This three-year period seems to have doubled as the minimum duration of a patent monopoly. The amendments stated that no licence could be granted before three years had expired, dating from the time the patent was granted. This did not imply that a compulsory licence was issued automatically after the three-year grace period. Rather, it implied that a manufacturer had at least three years before a competitor's compulsory licence application was possible.

It should be noted that Bill 7 did not limit its effect to pharmaceuticals; it was a bill which affected patent regulation as a whole. Nor was Bill 7 a complete overhaul of the Patent Act established in 1923. Rather, as Rinfret repeatedly stressed, it was intended strictly to bring Canadian regulation into line with the international treaty (Hansard, 10 Feb. 1929, p. 341).[1] Bill 7 did initiate, however, a policy framework which set the conditions for much of the debate surrounding pharmaceutical patents in this century. The bill made a connection between the Canadian governance of patents and a larger intellectual property regime, and it established the mechanism of the compulsory licence, which would become a major point of contention in later years.

Despite the debate that Bill 7 provisions would later prompt, its initial passage was relatively unproblematic. In part because of the sparse debate over Bill 7, it is relatively difficult to determine the rationale behind the bill, and hence to infer what its architects saw as the role of patents in 1929. Although little is explicit, there did seem to be some subtextual debate. For example, while Secretary of State Rinfret did not explicitly engage the issue beyond his insistence that the bill provided for treaty-obligated changes, the acceptance of these obligations, and the regime they established, provide some sense of how patents were understood, and how it was understood they were to operate.

We can deduce, for example, that patents were supposed to provide an incentive to manufacturers in the form of a governmentally regulated monopoly, with the proviso that the monopoly would be 'responsibly' managed. 'Responsibly,' in this context, seems to imply three things: first, convergence with internationally accepted norms of intellectual property; second, a willingness to manufacture within the context guaranteeing monopoly; third, an actual willingness to manufacture, that is, to make the results of technological or intellectual advances available to the public (rather than, say, using ownership of a patent to prevent the manufacture or exploitation of strategic new techniques). Rinfret defined the reasonable requirements of the public to imply that the public could reasonably buy the article in question, and that it be marketed in sufficient quantities as to be generally available. He de-

---

1 Rinfret stated that while it may have been appropriate to discuss the wider Patent Act, it was not the government's intention to make changes other than those required to meet the requirements of the Hague convention. Although it is always risky to infer too much from such statements, this statement can be interpreted as evidence of the existence of a conceptual regime at the international level, or at least of a conceptual regime which saw the administration of patents in Canada as connected to the international context.

fined reasonable price as one derived by competition.[2] When these 'responsibilities' were not met, in the case of a patented article, he suggested it would be at the discretion of the department to offer a licence to a competitor so as to make the product available to the public at a lower cost (Hansard, 10 Feb. 1929, p. 340).

Other interpretations of the role of patents did exist, and were raised by members of the opposition. J.S. Woodsworth, a labour MP, asked about the dissemination of new industrial processes, and whether the bill made provisions to 'protect the general public' by making the widespread adoption of patented processes viable (Hansard, 10 Feb. 1929, p. 341). In other words, he seems to have been advocating the rapid dissemination of new techniques and technologies, rather than the products they generated. Woodsworth explicitly stated: 'We are interested in investigating new industrial processes' (Hansard, 10 Feb. 1929, p. 341). This prompts the question of who constitutes the 'we' to which he refers, and whether it differs from the larger international community of intellectual property reflected in Bill 7. Another MP questioned why the Patent Act did not demand that goods manufactured by processes patented in Canada be manufactured in Canada.[3] He noted that over 90 per cent of patents granted in Canada were owned by 'aliens.' He further advocated that in those cases in which Canadian manufacturing did not take place, the result should be, not compulsory licensing, but the active revocation of such 'abused' patents (Hansard, 13 Feb. 1929, p. 431). One can infer, therefore, that for such MPs the purpose of issuing a patent included, at least in part, a deliberate attempt to encourage or invite the development of industry (with its co-commitment, the development of jobs), as well as an attempt to encourage and disseminate innovation.

Additional resistance to Bill 7 emerged demanding amendments to the effect that profits could not be expatriated and that a minimum manufacturing period in Canada be a necessary requirement of patent provision (Hansard, 13 Feb. 1929, p. 431). It seems clear that much of the

---

2 Although this obviously raises the question of how one is to determine a price generated by competition under the conditions of a government-regulated patent monopoly.

3 Although failing to manufacture a patented innovation was recognized by both the Hague conference and Bill 7 as a possible legitimation for granting of a compulsory licence, the bill did not make the granting of a patent conditional on manufacture in the granting country.

debate around Bill 7 centred on the issues of where patents fit into a broader field of industrial policy and governance, and what community should be taken into account when formulating such policy. Much of the Opposition's criticism of Bill 7 focused on a perceived failure to make the most of the possibilities inherent in granting a patent. There was an apparent perception that patents could be used as a tool to generate the development of industrial capacity, employment, and general wealth, as well as the development and eventual dissemination of innovation.

Furthermore, the Opposition contended that the Patent Act did not adequately reflect the interests of Canada, that the failure to fully capitalize on the potential of the Patent Act was based in its preoccupation with the wider intellectual property community, rather than the specific interests of Canada and Canadians. This is a repeated theme throughout the debate around Bill 7, with Rinfret stressing that it was the goal of the bill to bring the Canadian Patent Act into international conformity, and responses by various members that the legislation should be changed to reflect the needs of Canadians. It is also one of the earliest examples of a theme that would become central nearly seventy years later, in the debate surrounding Bills C-22 and C-91 (see chapter 8). The 1960s pharmapatent debate, however, would be dominated by two other issues: an evaluation of the compulsory licensing system, and the explicit introduction of issues of health and safety into the debate.

The IP Professions: Origins and Evolution

As chapter 1 has indicated, the Canadian IP professions, consisting of patent and trademark agents, are the crucial intermediaries between the inventor (the individual or the firm) and the patent-granting authority. However, it is instructive to note that the main books or studies published on Canadian intellectual property policy do not refer very much to the professions that make the regulatory system tick (Canada 1960; Economic Council of Canada 1971; Smith 1991). One could scarcely imagine any study of the health-care or law-and-order policy fields that left out the role of doctors or lawyers. The status and origins of the patent and trademark professions are accordingly somewhat more obscure than the above noted legal history or the IP policy reviews examined in the next section, but are nonetheless an important third track of general Canadian IP institutional history.

All professions emerge in some basic sense from the nature of work and the need for certain kinds and standards of knowledge that must be acquired and which other persons in society find valuable and useful, if that standard is maintained (Goode 1969). In this basic way, beginning with the patent system first forged in seventeenth-century England under the Statute of Monopolies, a profession of patent agent developed. Not for the first time did the regulations of government create work for its citizens! The profession developed out of the inherent need of inventors and regulators for experts to draft patent applications.

From their earliest days, the patent and the later trademark professions have been caught in the web of inter-professional relationships (Fédération Internationale des Conseils en Propriété Industrielle 1992). In the United Kingdom, Canada, and elsewhere, the first patent agents were often consulting engineers. Almost inevitably, the work of agents, because of its nature, evolved into a mixed engineering and law profession. In countries such as the United States, the profession has primarily been subsumed within the legal profession.

Trademark agents evolved in a variety of ways. Primarily theirs became a form of work and expertise that naturally evolved out of patent-agency work in that inventors often also needed expertise in protecting the designations of their work. Later, trademark agents became associated with an even wider array of business and corporate work that ranged from forming new companies to advertising products and creating corporate and product images. When describing the differences between patent-agency work and trademark work, professionals who do both see the first as being more in the realm of science and engineering, while the latter is seen as closer to an art or craft whose subtleties and nuances change more frequently. And both involve law and inherently require excellent and precise writing skills.

When considering the more specific history of the professions in Canada, four features are important as a background for the analysis. The first is that the professions in their latent form go back to pre-Confederation days, when each of the prior colonies had their own patent acts (Maybee and Mitchell 1985). The federal Patent Act of 1869 further nurtured the professions in their early days in a small number of engineering and later law firms in Montreal, Toronto, and Ottawa. Hence they became, and remain to this day, largely central Canadian professions, albeit with a growing contingent in the Vancouver area.

A second feature of the evolution of the IP professions is that their gestation consisted of forming a professional body centred on the Patent Institute of Canada (the forerunner to the current PTIC profiled in chapter 1). This was a development that arose partly out of concerns about advertising (Maybee and Mitchell 1985, ch. 3). Patent practitioners were, among the professions, the most prolific advertisers. Many would not join any then-proposed institute because they did not want to comply with its required curbs on advertising, curbs which others felt were needed to differentiate competent and qualified professionals from those who were not.

Further pressure to create a more controlled profession came in the aftermath of the First World War. Industrialization was increasing greatly and with it the volume of patent applications. Changes in the law in 1923 to enable Canada to conform to the Paris Convention for the Protection of Industrial Property also had a profound effect. A new flood of applications emerged from abroad and the Patent Office was ill-equipped to handle them.

For several related reasons, the verdict that 'the profession itself was in disarray' was not at all inaccurate (Maybee and Mitchell 1985, 25). As Maybee and Mitchell point out, 'in 1923 for the first time a register of attorneys had been established. The only requirements were good character and the ability to prepare and file patent applications.' In other words, 'no special education or training was required and those already practicing were virtually automatically put on the register' (Maybee and Mitchell 1985, 25). The Commissioner of Patents had no facilities for assessing the qualifications to practise. At the same time, the commissioner knew that in his own office 'the processing of applications was slow and the examinations cursory' (Maybee and Mitchell 1985, 25). There was also a serious economic concern about the new influx of largely American patents through 'post-office' patent application processes.

As a result, in 1925 a meeting was held to form what became, in 1926, first the Canadian Institute of Patent Solicitors and, in 1935, the Patent Institute of Canada. It was to be an association 'to improve the law and practice relating to patents of invention and promote and maintain high standards in the profession' (Maybee and Mitchell 1985, 25).

A third element of the professions' history in Canada are their strong connection to the professions in Britain. The founding meeting in 1925 to establish an institute was organized by the then manager of the Ottawa office of the English firm of Marks & Clerk. The main model for the professions, albeit necessarily adapted to Canadian circumstances, was the British profession of patent agent, which was, and is, separate from the dual legal professions in the United Kingdom of barrister and solicitor. Trademark agents have their own professional association in Britain, as well. Of particular import in the transference of institutional practice from Britain was the nature of the examination that eventually was established. In Britain, the Chartered Institute of Patent Agents, established in 1882, was given control in 1888 by the Board of Trade of the register of patent agents and hence of the determination of qualifications.

It was transplanted British patent agents who used the rigorous U.K. exam as their model for their test of qualifications in Canada. Many 'Brits' were on the early examining boards. The British influence was also present in the profession and within the Patent Office in Ottawa because, in the late 1960s, a recruitment blitz brought many U.K.-trained patent agents to Canada. This emigration of agents out of Britain was the product of a mixed set of incentives and circumstances. Many saw Canada as a greener pasture. In addition, the Patent Office, because of low civil service salaries, recruited many British agents to become Patent Officer examiners. Some stayed only briefly with the Patent Office and instead joined the profession in Canada, exercising considerable influence within it. The British contingent of agents were predominantly from engineering backgrounds rather than law backgrounds. But by the 1970s and 1980s, the Canadian profession was changing, and much of this change involved relations with, and developments within, the law profession.

Hence the final feature of this brief historical portrait deals with the relationship between patent agents and lawyers, and eventually the lawyer–trademark agent relationship. This evolving relationship is connected, in turn, to the larger post–Second World War changes in the nature of law and of corporations. In the 1940s and 1950s, several large corporations, such as Canadian General Electric and CIL, had established their own patent departments (Maybee and Mitchell 1985, 38–40). The link with law firms specializing in patent practice, or at least having a significant patent practice, had begun even earlier but created an important conflict that came to a head in the late 1940s and early 1950s.

From the mid-1930s to the mid-1940s, the Patent Institute of Canada had tried to persuade the federal government to establish a standard for the registration of patent agents in Canada 'by way of an examination controlled by the Institute' (Maybee and Mitchell 1985, 49). The government supported the concept of an exam, but one administered by the Commissioner of Patents. Interlocked with this lobbying was a growing controversy over the proper title for patent practitioners. At the time, Canadian practitioners, like their American counterparts, were called 'attorneys,' a title which their British counterparts could not use. The Canadian Bar Association and the various provincial law societies wanted this designation to end (Maybee and Mitchell 1985, ch. 7). While the Patent Institute of Canada objected to this demand, it had, in turn, long been pressing for a requirement that would exclude all lawyers who were not trained in patent practice from practising before the Patent Office.

The compromise solution to this battle of qualifications and professional territoriality was that those who had used the designation of 'patent attorney' until 1948 would be allowed to continue to do so, but those engaged from 1948 on had to use the term 'patent agent.' As well, all applicants for registration, including lawyers, had to pass an examination. That examination would be 'set by a board consisting of representatives of the public service and the profession' (Maybee and Mitchell 1985, 51).

In the 1970s and 1980s, the IP professions were influenced by further underlying changes in the economics of legal practice, as well as by general economic and technological developments. Law firms became even more involved in patent and trademark practice when the overall area of intellectual property was seen to be a growth area for legal practice. Furthermore, law firms themselves were transformed, with some becoming mega–law firms engaged in a wide-ranging full-service practice. Smaller 'boutique' patent and trademark firms went through various iterations of sometimes being merged into these larger firms and, at others, splitting off again, with partners leaving to re-establish boutique firms.

Meanwhile, many of the ten or so largest Canadian corporations that had in-house patent offices had contracted out these activities to law firms. All of the above dynamics changed the nature of the business, affected the relationships between lawyers and patent and trademark agents, and altered the perspectives of those whose educational roots were in science and engineering, on the one hand, or law, on the other.

The potential for inter-professional boundary and qualification disputes with the legal profession did not end in 1948. In 1989 the Canadian Bar Association established an intellectual property group, which some members hoped would rival and constrain the patent agent profession. Some of this was directed at new demands that all lawyers be required to take the trademark agent exam before they could practise as trademark agents. The CBA's aggressiveness on these boundary issues is still present but may be somewhat muted by potential problems the law profession could face on some of its other flanks. For example, the rise of supermarket law firms has meant that lawyers are often seen by other professions, such as accountants, as committing territorial sins of their own. In short, playing the qualifications card is a game that more than one can play (Flood and Skordaki 1995).

Periodic Policy Reviews: The 1960 Ilsley Commission and the 1971 Economic Council Review

The low profile of IP developments continued into the 1950s, 1960s, and 1970s. It is illustrated by the work of two policy reviews: the Ilsley Royal Commission's work from 1954 to 1960, and the Economic Council of Canada's work from 1966 to 1971.

The Royal Commission on Patents, Copyright, Trade Marks and Industrial Designs (Ilsley Commission) was appointed in 1954 but did not report until 1960 (in itself an indicator of the leisurely low-priority nature of IP during this period). Revisions to Canadian patent law in 1935 had identified six potential abuses which, if proven, could lead to the revocation of a patent or the grant of a compulsory licence. Partly because of this, the Ilsley Commission was asked to explore whether Canada's patent law gave enough incentives to inventors in a manner that also safeguarded the public interest.

In the end, few of the Ilsley Commission's recommendations were adopted. Its analysis, however, is useful to our initial historical inquiry for a number of reasons: the Ilsley Commission advocated changes to the patent system which echoed those called for by the IP professions; it highlighted the extent of foreign ownership of Canadian patents; and it illustrated the contemporary perspective on IP as an integrated framework.

One of the Ilsley Commission's key recommendations was that Canada's patent system be changed from a 'first to invent' to a 'first to file' system. Canada had historically adopted the 'first to invent' feature of the U.S. system (and was one of only three countries in the world to use such a concept). The Ilsley Commission suggested that a 'first to file' system would be more predictable, in that it would provide incentives to reduce the number of invalid patents, as well as the number of legal challenges to patents. Canada's IP professions had recommended this reform, as well.

A second aspect of the Ilsley Commission's analysis which is worthy of note is that it made more widely known the fact that a very high percentage of Canada's patent applications came from, and were granted to, foreigners. It cited data for the 1930s which showed foreign owner-ship of Canadian patents at over 90 per cent, by far the highest percent-age of patents granted to foreigners among twelve countries (Canada 1960, 13). By the 1950s, the commission's data showed figures that ranged from 92 to 95 per cent. However, despite the evidence that only about 7 per cent of patent applications came from Canadian residents, the Ilsley Commission advocated lessening the role of compulsory licensing within the system. Although the commission did make an exception for such areas as pharmaceuticals (see more below), it argued that Canada's own subset of generally smaller inventors (individuals or small firms) needed the basic protection of patents. It implied that exceptions to patent protection, such as compulsory licensing or work-ing requirements, made the small Canadian inventor vulnerable to bigger firms, including foreign firms (Canada 1960, 15–17).

Finally, the report of the Ilsley Commission is significant in that it illustrates some contemporary attitudes towards IP. While the commis-sion's report 'covered' IP as a whole, it was not 'about IP' as a whole in any integrated sense. It was about each IP realm separately, and it was quite legally oriented, perhaps because it was headed by a judge and lawyer. On patents, it did begin to discuss a shift in where the IP trade-off should be made, in that it was asked to assess the adequacy of incentives to inventors and it found that more incentives were needed. But its tilt in this direction was mild, and it is not clear that anyone was listening, given that Canadian economic policy-makers in 1960 were focused on other matters and other visions of economic prosperity.

The second policy review carried out in this period was that of the Economic Council of Canada. In 1971 the Economic Council of Canada issued its report on intellectual and industrial property, which was in turn the product of a three-part reference given to the Council by the federal government in 1966 (Economic Council of Canada 1971). The larger reference to the Council dealt with IP as well as consumer policy and competition policy, and thus was one of the first policy reviews to attempt to examine market-place framework law and policy, an even more complex cluster of policies that was being given a home of its own in the then new Department of Consumer and Corporate Affairs (Phidd and Doern 1978).

Read in the present-day context of the new Millennium, the Council's report is quite remarkable in that it casts IP in a conceptual language and framework that was well ahead of its time. It explicitly ties IP to innovation policy and to information and knowledge as a driver of economic growth (Economic Council of Canada 1971, ch. 2). The Council, whose mandate as an economic policy advisory body was to focus on medium and longer-term economic development issues, stressed that 'in order for its economy to grow and develop satisfactorily, a society must be innovative; to be innovative, it must be well-informed, and to be well-informed, it must be good at the production, distribution and use of knowledge' (Economic Council of Canada 1971, 10).

Information and knowledge are then discussed quite extensively in the report and are linked to learning in the broadest social and consumer contexts. The general characteristics of information are also examined. Information is complex, costly, valuable, destroyable, is not depleted by use, involves complex systems of feedback, is exchangeable, is often given away, and is often governed by externalities (Economic Council of Canada 1971, 18–27). IP is then linked economically and socially by the Council to this larger information and learning system.

A further historical point brought out in the study is the strong shift from patents granted to individual inventors to those granted to corporations. In 1908, 97.3 per cent of patents granted to Canadian residents went to independent inventors, and only 2.7 per cent went to corporations. By 1968, 63.5 per cent went to corporations, and 36.5 per cent went to independent inventors (Economic Council of Canada 1971, 47). The Council study reconfirmed the historic Canadian pattern in that, in the late 1960s, about 95 per cent of patents granted in Canada still went to foreigners. It also drew attention to the sluggish processes through which firms had to obtain approval from patent holders to license products (Economic Council of Canada 1971, 64–8).

Again, these historical trends produced different mixes of potential policy prescription and choice. The trend to corporate invention (also revealed above in the discussion of the IP professions) could mean that less IP protection was needed in that firms had a stronger overall incentive to patent and innovate than individuals had. The sluggish licensing regime might be fine for some aspects of Canadian development, but it created difficulties for areas such as medicines and drugs.

The Council made few if any recommendations in its IP report. Instead its IP conclusions dealt with broader themes around the reference as a whole given to it by the government. Thus it linked its views back to the broad importance of consumers, to market-place frameworks (consumer, competition, and IP policies), and to information and knowledge as crucial underpinnings to the Canadian economy.

Released in 1971, the Council's review, in its views and treatment, integrated the components of IP more than any previous review. The report itself, however, as well as IP in general, was still overshadowed by the larger issues of the late 1960s and early 1970s (Phidd and Doern 1978). Indeed, even beyond this period, extending from 1970 to the mid-1980s, it was extremely difficult for the federal government to generate any sustained general political or ministerial interest in any areas of market-place framework policy change. Attempted efforts to modernize legislation on competition, patents, copyright, consumer law, and bankruptcy all floundered in the face of competition from other areas of public policy (Doern 1987). Chapter 3 will show this more clearly and will also show how, in the late 1980s, IP and innovation policy began to have more frequent days in the political sun and in the attention spans of ministers and corporations in Canada.

Patent Policy Change in the 1960s: Pharmaceuticals, Health Costs, and Compulsory Licensing

The final IP development examined in this chapter concerns changes to patent law and policy in the late 1960s, and is centred on the recurring role of pharmaceutical patents as exceptions in the larger field of IP. During this period, Bill C-190 was tabled by the newly formed Department of Consumer and Corporate Affairs under John Turner. The legislation was intended to address specifically the issue of pharmaceutical costs via new mechanisms to encourage competition. Introduced in February 1968, the bill grew out of two royal commissions, the previously examined Ilsley Commission and the Hall Royal Commission on health care, which reported in 1964, as well as a 1967 House of Commons special committee on drug costs and prices.

The key issues surrounding Bill C-190 were those of competition, safety, and price. As Campbell and Pal note, both royal commissions argued that drug prices were too high, an argument supported, in part, by the anecdotal evidence of those who testified before the commissions and, in part, by a comparison of profits in the drug industry to those in the wider manufacturing sector (Campbell and Pal 1994). The Liberal government, in turn, argued that these high prices resulted from the limited competition caused by patent monopolies. Campbell and Pal have suggested that the commissions 'stimulated the political momentum for change and a consensus on the tactic to realize equity' (Campbell and Pal 1994, 32–3) To some extent, this claim is supported by contemporary records, such as the Hansard debates.

It is certainly true that the government claimed Bill C-190 was a product of the royal commission recommendations. In the second reading of the bill on 12 February 1968, John Turner made an extended speech in which he drew on the findings of the two royal commissions and argued that the high cost of pharmaceuticals demanded action (Hansard, 12 Feb. 1968, pp. 6615–33). Although the Opposition was quick to point out that cost and accessibility, the focus of Bill C-190, only constituted one aspect of the commissions' reports, it was this focus on cost which in retrospect makes Bill C-190 significant. By focusing on the cost impact of patent policy, and linking cost to equity, the bill highlighted the health-policy impact of pharmaceutical patent regulation. Turner noted that the roots of public concern over the cost of drugs were obvious: the high cost of medication, coupled with the unpredictability of disease and the reduced capacity of those afflicted to support the costs of treatment, meant that the cost of healthcare could only be assuredly borne by the wealthy. Health itself, he argued, represented an intrinsic social value which should not be determined by wealth alone (Hansard, 12 Feb. 1968, pp. 6615–16). Bill C-190, then, explicitly linked patent policy to the cost of pharmaceuticals, the cost of pharmaceuticals to the accessibility of pharmaceutical care, accessibility to the effective quality of health care, and the quality of health care to the overall quality of life, thereby linking patent policy to the overall quality of life and the 'social good.'

In order to make access to pharmaceuticals more affordable, and hence equitable, Bill C-190 made a small change in how compulsory licences operated. Prior to Bill C-190, compulsory licences could only be issued if the licensed product was manufactured in Canada. Bill C-190 altered this to permit manufacture of pharmaceuticals with imported active components; that is, licences could be issued to manufacturers who imported the 'medical' component of a pharmaceutical product, and who then processed the component into its final dosage form. This, the government argued, would make compulsory licences a more viable option, would introduce greater price competition, and would thereby lower the cost of pharmaceuticals.

In response to the 'partial policy' criticisms noted above, however, Turner was also quick to point out that Bill C-190 was part of a larger attempt to lower drug costs. This 'larger attempt' consisted of a five-step process. First, the government would remove the sales tax on pharmaceuticals and reduce the customs duty due from 20 per cent to 15 per cent. Furthermore, it would narrow the application of the dumping duty to imports. Presumably, this was meant to facilitate the growth of import competition, without seriously endangering the operation of the existing patent-holding firms. Step two of the process was Bill C-190, 'proposed to stimulate price competition among sellers of patented and trademarked drugs through reducing protection against imports which is provided by the Patent and Trade Marks Acts' (Hansard, 12 Feb. 1968, 6623). Third, the government would establish an information program for the 'medical profession' about drug properties and prices, ensuring that prescribing physicians would know the difference in price between demonstratively equivalent drugs. Fourth, the government would take steps to strengthen the industry sector which manufactured and sold lower-price prescription drugs. Fifth, the federal government would consult with the provinces to tackle the cost of pharmaceutical distribution (Hansard, 12 Feb. 1968, p. 6623).[4]

As part of an explicit reassessment of the role and impact of pharmapatent policy in a broader context, 'patent rationality' was discussed to a much larger extent in the debate around Bill C-190 than it was around Bill 7. For example, Turner acknowledged that in the case of the pharmaceutical industry, patents and patent regulations formed one of the defining structural features, that patent policy governed the operational logic of the industry. He noted that the drug industry operated within a given economic framework, to which members of the drug industry responded rationally. He pointed out, however, that this framework was established by Parliament, and was subject to review. When Parliament was not satisfied with the results of operating within a given framework, it had the option of altering the 'ground rules.' In other words, the bill was presented as a deliberate attempt to alter the rules of the game, to reconstitute the pharmaceutical industry by changing how the patents which defined the industry were to operate (Turner, in Hansard, 12 Feb. 1968, p. 6622).

Turner argued that under the system of regulation prior to Bill C-190 there existed little incentive for price competition. The demand for drugs was generally governed by two sources: doctors' prescriptions

---

4 Foreshadowing the still-repeated call for a federally administered national drug program.

and institutional purchases. While institutional buyers, through the sheer volume of their purchases, could generate a degree of price competition, Turner argued that under ordinary circumstances physicians were not price conscious. They might not know the prices of different brands of drugs and therefore gave the factor of price little consideration when prescribing a drug. As a result, there existed little opportunity for the consumer to switch to something else if the price seemed unreasonable. The onus was placed on a sick, and often worried, consumer to comparison shop, in those cases where opportunities for comparison existed.

There existed little encouragement for price competition at the level of producers, as well. The interaction of a number of regulatory instruments, such as the Patent Act, the Trade Marks Act, the customs tariff, and the requirements of the Food and Drug Act, meant that competition between drug companies was competition between monopoly producers of different drugs, rather than competition between manufacturers of the same pharmaceutical products. Turner argued that it was not surprising in these circumstances that the major drug firms had not, on the whole, found price competition necessary. Patents prevented entry by competitors into the production of individual drugs. This, in turn, prevented the sort of head-to-head competition which encouraged a reduction of price. Patent holders had substituted for price competition the development of minor differences in the product and vigorous sales promotion of these small differences. In fact, Turner suggested, this limited form of competition tended to raise the cost of the product. The more producers depended on advertising to compete, the higher the cost of such advertising and, hence, the higher the cost of the product. Turner noted that evidence presented by the Pharmaceutical Manufacturers Association of Canada[5] to the commissions showed that advertising costs roughly equalled those of manufacturing (Hansard, 12 Feb. 1968, 6623).

Even in cases in which price competition did exist, advertising conducted by the major firms tended, by its sheer magnitude to obscure the existence of their smaller competitors. As Turner put it, 'in the case of patented drugs, no price competition need ever develop during the life of the patent' (Hansard, 12 Feb. 1968, p. 6622). This seems a somewhat revealing statement, given that the restriction of competition is one of the main purposes of a patent. Patent restrictions ensured that a

---

5 Or the PMAC, a group representing brand-name drug manufacturers.

manufacturer had a period of time, free of competition, in which to recoup the expenses generated in producing a new product or technique. Turner argued, however, that pharmaceutical patents had traditionally been treated differently by the Canadian government.

It was in articulating this difference that Turner revealed the patent rationality underlying Bill C-190.[6] He noted that the 'Patent Act creates a temporary monopoly in the patented product or process for the inventor with the object of encouraging invention, change and innovation and of making the fruits of that invention available in due course to the public at large. The granting of a patent to the inventor or his assignee gives him the power to prevent others from making, using or selling the patented product or process for a certain period of years' (Hansard, 12 Feb. 1968, p. 6623). In a way similar to the interpretation of patents expressed in the 1920s, in Bill C-190 patents were interpreted as a trade of a temporary monopoly, enforceable through government mechanisms, in return for the distribution of the new technology and/or its specific products.

Turner noted, however, that under Canadian law patents relating to food and drugs had been placed in a special category, a practice dating back to the formation of the Patent Act in 1923. In the first place, the Act provided that in the case of an invention relating to a substance prepared or manufactured by a chemical process and intended for food or medicine, the patent did not include the product itself unless prepared by the patented process. In other words, food and drug patents were process patents, and anyone could import or produce the product, as long as it was not made by the patented process (Hansard, 12 Feb. 1968, p. 6624).

In addition, provision had already been made in reference to food and drugs to ensure as rapid a diffusion of the patented process as was possible. This, of course, was the compulsory licence. When an application was made for such a licence, it was to be granted, unless the Commissioner of Patents saw good reason to the contrary. The commis-

---

6 The existence of the bill itself indicates to some extent that patent rationality was different in the case of pharmaceuticals, insofar as the bill's limited effect isolated pharmaceuticals as a special case. Turned noted that despite a general review of patents, trademarks, and copyright in 1966, drug regulation was a particular matter that could be dealt with without tinkering with general patent law (Hansard, 14 Feb. 1968, p. 6744). This can be contrasted with arguments put forward in the '90s-era debate to the effect that pharmaceuticals were an industrial commodity like any other and, as such, subject to common regulation.

sioner, in so doing, fixed the amount of royalties payable by the licensee for the use of the patent, an amount determined by balancing, on the one hand, the desirability of making the food or medicine available to the public at the lowest possible price, against, on the other, giving to the inventor due reward for the research leading to the invention. Patent regulation for pharmaceuticals was unique, in this sense, because the question of technological diffusion was complicated by notions of *equitable* access. The results of new pharmaceutical technology were not just to be made available, but to be made available to all. 'Reasonable accessibility' (one of the criteria of responsible patent ownership in the 1920s), in this case, seems to have implied universal (or near-universal) accessibility (Hansard, 14 Feb. 1968, p. 6743).

This willingness to extend compulsory licences constitutes a break with the interpretation of the role of the Commissioner of Patents as articulated in 1928. While, in 1928, the commissioner could grant a compulsory licence if, in the opinion of the commissioner, the responsibilities of patent ownership had not been met (i.e., if a reason could be found to justify the licence), by 1968, licences were only *not* granted if a justifiable reason could be found. As Turner himself noted, by 1968, the 'full privileges of patent protection' were not being granted to drugs. Turner claimed that this was, at least in part, the result of Parliament's deciding that the immediate welfare and interest of the general public was paramount and that the private interests of industry, as well as whatever inducement to research the patent would represent, were to be subordinated to the public interest (Hansard, 12. Feb. 1968, p. 6624). Pharmaceutical patent regulation, then, complicated by notions of equity and access, was explicitly recognized as being governed by more than strictly industrial priorities.

Despite this limitation of patent rights in the interest of the public, Turner was careful to point out that patent holders still held an abbreviated monopoly in practice. Before any drug could be sold, it was required to undergo a battery of safety and efficacy tests, with the (successful) results to be submitted to the Food and Drugs Directorate (FDD). If the FDD was satisfied with the results, it would issue a notice of compliance, which enabled the sale of the drug. Once on the market, a drug retained the status of a 'new' drug until sold in sufficient quantity and for a sufficient time to establish that it had no unforeseen side-effects. While a product retained the status of a new drug, no other person or firm was permitted to sell it unless they had submitted similar evidence to the FDD and received a notice of compliance. Because of the time taken up in this process, a new drug usually remained classified as such for a minimum of five years. Thus, in practice, the holder of a patent on a new drug enjoyed an effective monopoly for at least five years (Hansard, 12 Feb. 1968, p. 6630).

Curiously, Turner did not seem to expect the emergence of a domestic import industry in Canada in response to the changes Bill C-190 made in the Patent Act. Rather, he seemed to anticipate that the threat of importation would lower prices. For example, Turner suggested that Bill C-190's impact would be on price, not market share. By creating conditions for price competition (from licensed manufacturers), the formulators of Bill C-190 seemed to hope to redirect the competitive energies of manufacturers, with prices being lowered as much from reduction of advertising as through actual price competition (Hansard, 12 Feb. 1968, p. 6630). To some extent, this was explained by another MP, H.C. Harley (who chaired the 1967 special committee on drug prices). Harley noted that while the legislation made it possible to import active components for processing into final dosage form in Canada, it recommended the importation of products in dosage form (Hansard, 12 Feb. 1968, p. 6651). Presumably, it was the potential of this importation practice which was to encourage the lowering of pharmaceutical prices.

Given Turner's comments on the source of demand for pharmaceuticals, it seems clear that the dynamics of Bill C-190 depended on physicians being aware of the lower costs implied by the importation amendment and, perhaps more importantly, pharmaceutical manufacturers being aware that physicians possessed this knowledge. It is not surprising, therefore, to find that the policy implied by Bill C-190 included mechanisms for informing physicians of their alternatives, specifically, the 'information program for the medical profession' noted above. To that end, the Food and Drugs Directorate made plans to periodically publish a bulletin for the medical profession that presented detailed information on drug properties, action, and prices (Hansard, 12 Feb. 1968, 6623). The dissemination of new technology, then, was to be a far more active process in 1968 than it was in the 1920s.

In the 1960s, pharmapatent change was thus marked by a deliberate attempt to shape how the pharmaceutical industry was to operate. Unlike the 1920s, which were characterized by industrial discourse, an attempt to limit monopolistic excesses, and the maintenance of a balance between those who granted and received patents, pharmapatent debate in the 1960s acknowledged the role pharmaceuticals played in maintaining the health of Canadians. As a result, pharmapatent change was driven by an explicit desire to shape how the industry functioned, in such a way that the perceived health needs of Canadians were met. This theme, and the debates it prompted, would return in the 1990s era of pharmaceutical patent debate, accompanied by the tensions, first explored in the 1920s, between the demands of international treaty and those of domestic need. It would also raise the issue of just what innovation means in the changed contexts of the 1990s.

Conclusions

Canada's Patent Act dates back to 1869, and other IP laws on trade-marks and copyright also have a long history that begins in the latter part of the nineteenth century. This chapter has briefly examined five IP developments or episodes in the period from Confederation to the early 1970s as necessary precursors to the analysis as a whole.

Two themes have been stressed in the chapter. The first is that these developments were scarcely noticed among the larger priorities of Canadian political-economic life. All five changes essentially transpired in ways that did not garner high-priority or sustained political attention in large part because, for most of this hundred-year period, Canada's economy was still a natural resource–based economy and national economic policy was still structured around the tariff or other later policy instruments such as subsidies. The second theme is that although IP as a framework-oriented set of ideas, institutions, and interests is important to understand, there has always been a special historical tension between patents and IP, in general, and pharmaceutical patents, in particular.

The legal history shows a long lineage of basic laws, grounded largely in British legal traditions but also with some U.S. features, including a 'first to invent' system. It also discloses a distinct pattern of IP issues being very episodic, with long periods between major changes in the law. Propelled partly by international obligations, the changes in the 1920s stressed the broader public interest notions of the IP trade-off, in that it was focused on ensuring that innovations were used and made available, in part through compulsory licensing.

The evolution of the patent and trademark professions reveals a more subtle part of Canadian IP institutional history. The nature of the intermediary function emerges as the IP professions evolve out of British roots, but the chapter also shows how the nature of relationships changed as large firms altered the sources of their IP advice, and as both professional and business tensions emerged with lawyers. In later chapters, we pick up further strands of the symbiotic links between business and the IP professions as the core interests that anchor the protection function.

The policy reviews of the Ilsley Commission and the Economic Council of Canada show gradual post–Second World War changes in thinking through to the end of the 1960s. Both show that most patents in Canada were (and are still) filed by foreigners, and they portray the change among Canadian patent holders from largely independent persons to corporations. Gradual shifts in thinking are discussed in these reviews concerning what the right balance is for Canada between protection and dissemination, and just how much protection is needed. The role of compulsory licensing is always a part of this discussion, but there are mixed views about the value of this provision for Canada's IP trade-offs as a whole. The Economic Council's 1971 report is remarkably ahead of its time in its discussion of IP as a central feature of innovation and even of an information economy. But not much change results from these reviews, largely because IP is still not at all central to the economic priorities of government.

Patent changes in the late 1960s show the special importance of pharmapatents. The forces promoting change were becoming more noticed and more complex, but the underlying factor was the issue of price and competition in a monopoly drug industry increasingly linked to concerns about health care. The special nature of pharmapatents is central because it raises the question of the extent to which IP policy is genuinely a framework-oriented kind of policy or a form of de facto sectoral policy. It also raises the issues of what innovation means in different times and contexts. The more recent transformation during the 1980s and 1990s from traditional industrial policy to innovation policy is now necessarily the subject of a second historical profile.

3. IP, Industrial Policy, and Innovation in the Knowledge Economy

The necessary complement to the institutional stocktaking and histori-cal context set out on chapters 1 and 2 is to develop a sense of how the IP policy field has evolved and been situated in the larger debates on industrial policy and innovation policy in Canada. This policy history also needs to differentiate between how these IP–industrial policy links might fit with a goods economy compared to a more knowledge-based economy. To maintain a focus on IP in this larger setting of policies and ideas, the chapter is organized into five sections. First, we look briefly at Canada's IP record, including the assertion that Canada lacks an inno-vation culture. Second, we examine IP policy in the context of tradi-tional industrial policies, those that more or less characterized the period from the 1960s to the mid-1980s. Next, we look at IP policy in the context of what some now cast more broadly as policies for innovation informed by views regarding concepts of national systems of innovation. These policies and ideas have emerged in the last decade and are more explicitly cast in terms of the knowledge-based economy. The fourth section profiles several recent and current IP policy controversies, not only because of their importance but also as a further illustration of how IP and IP-related issues have periodically arrived on the policy and political agenda, but never for long or in strictly IP terms alone. These controversies include the following issues: IP and biodiversity; the patenting of life forms and biotechnology; IP and the information high-way, and IP and competition policy. Conclusions then follow.

Canada's IP Record in a Knowledge Economy

Chapter 2 has already shown a historical trend in which more than

90 per cent of patents granted in Canada have been granted to foreign residents or firms. This suggests strongly that Canada has been a borrower of inventions from abroad and has lacked an innovative culture. Writings on Canadian inventors contradict this view somewhat in that Canada has produced its fair share of inventors, who include Alexander Graham Bell, William Stephenson, and J. Armand Bombardier, to name only a few (Carpenter 1990; Brown 1967a; 1967b). However, these accounts also show how such inventors had to struggle for recognition. As J.J. Brown lamented in his 1967 book, 'by and large, our past treatment of inventors has been contemptible. Not only have we allowed them to be robbed blind by both business and government ... but unlike other nations, we have never even accorded them social recognition, which costs nothing. No Canadian inventor has ever been honoured for his work by the public at large' (Brown 1967a, 8). Canada is not the only country for which one could make this lament.

This notion of invention speaks, of course, to individual inventors, and the obvious comparison is with the United States, whose Constitution enshrines invention and the useful arts and whose popular capitalist culture celebrates inventors and innovators as icons of their age, from Thomas Edison to Bill Gates. But, as chapter 2 has shown, in Canada, as elsewhere, patent filing has become increasingly a corporate affair, and thus judgments concerning the existence of an IP culture or an innovation culture are more complex.

It is impossible to speak of any country having an overall IP record as such, that is, one that could be based on comparative data for all of patents, trademarks, and copyright. The closest recent measures are drawn typically from comparative data on patent filings. John Baldwin's study at Statistics Canada supplies a basic comparative picture of where Canada stands in these international league tables (Baldwin 1997).

Patent filings by both residents and non-residents in 1992 as a percentage of total population are Baldwin's first measure. Comparing OECD member countries with populations of over 15 million persons, Canada had about 1.54 patent filings per 1000 inhabitants. This puts Canada behind Japan and the Netherlands but 'equal to or ahead of the other large members of the OECD' (Baldwin 1997, 13). The OECD total figure is 1.49, and the EC's total is 1.17.

To obtain a useful picture of patents filed by residents, the Baldwin study uses patent filings by a country's residents in the United States. This approach is used to reduce the problem of comparing filings in countries with different standards in patenting. The other feature of this indicator is that filings are expressed as a percentage of the number of research and development scientists and engineers. With these data, Canada has 6.2 patents filed per research scientist and finds itself in the middle of the comparative OECD pack (Baldwin 1997, 13).

Baldwin is careful to stress that neither of these kinds of data allow us to evaluate the relative innovativeness of Canada compared to other countries. As we have seen, it has often been suggested that Canada is an IP or innovative laggard. This portrait has come from a variety of mini-pictures of Canada's economic past and of selective policy indicators, including the previously mentioned fact that over 90 per cent of patents in Canada are granted to foreigners. At the broadest level, this picture has simply arisen from the fact that Canada has lived off its natural resources and has not, until now, had to live off its wits. The Macdonald Royal Commission of the mid-1980s conveyed this picture but was hardly the first to do so (Canada 1985). Another element emerges from the fact that Canada has permitted extensive foreign ownership of its economy and thus developed a branch-plant economy with limited R & D performed in Canada by such firms. Canada's lower-than-average R & D spending as a percentage of GDP was also a commonly cited part of the laggard picture.

As the brief history in the next section of Canada's industrial policy shows, IP was not a priority for national policy-makers and hence there is certainly something to the laggard image. But these features were also cast over a period when a goods-trading economy was the dominant assumption and reality (Gera and Mang 1998). What is different, then, when one adds the new realities of a so-called knowledge-based economy? Some key policy aspects of the knowledge economy and of innovation policies are traced below, but we need first to appreciate some of the suggested dilemmas of dealing with a knowledge economy.

Economists lead the way in the theoretical discussion of these changes, with thinking that takes many forms and organizing concepts. First, at one level, some economists caution against assuming that growth is now more knowledge-based than in the past (Howitt 1996). They point to frequent earlier periods when new dominant technologies and organizational innovations (e.g., textiles, agriculture, autos) were analysed as being crucial determinants of growth.

But many are turning their attention to a re-examination of growth theory, with a focus on endogenous growth. This is because earlier simpler aggregate growth theory treated knowledge and technology much as though they were 'just another good, capable of being accumulated like capital and aggregated with the same precision (or lack of precision) as capital' (Howitt 1996, 9). Endogenous growth theory has questioned and researched the way in which knowledge is different from goods, and hence must be thought about differently in crucial matters of exchange in markets (de la Mothe and Paquet 1996).

At a more aggregate level, other economists have argued that countries must be looked at as national innovation systems whose features range across many policy fields and activities, from systems of human capital formation to levels of competition (Nelson 1993). Business scholars such as Michael Porter have also argued for much more catholic views of what combinations of factors contribute to the competitiveness of nations (Porter 1990).

More concerning the evolution and various strands of this debate will be addressed below. But some cautionary points emerge from this initial consideration of Canada's IP record in the midst of a knowledge economy. With respect to our ultimate focus on IP, it suggests a need to see the IP scorecard as showing a Canadian record that is neither shoddy nor exemplary. It also suggests that IP is but one policy and practical element in the new and quite complex ways in which knowledge economies must be analysed and visualized (Niosi 1999; McFetridge 1996).

However, more of the policy history of both the era of traditional industrial policy and that of the present focus on loosely defined innovation policy needs to be presented in order to lend credence to these cautionary observations.

IP and Traditional Industrial Policy in Canada

It is not an exaggeration to say that during the era cast here as traditional industrial policy, IP policy was scarcely seen as a factor. Chapter 2 has already shown the intermittent and low-priority nature of IP policy reviews or events up to the early 1970s. Canada obviously had IP laws in place and was a signatory to international IP treaties and conventions. For some industries, patents and other kinds of protection were important. But in the overall consciousness of both policymakers and industrial lobbies, IP scarcely even registered. This is because industrial policy was focused on different policy focal points and policy instruments.

For example, in longer historical terms, the tariff was the centrepiece of John A. Macdonald's National Policy and remained focused on building and supporting central Canadian industry (Harris 1993; Eden and Molot 1993) during a long period when there was no GATT.

During the late 1940s, the 1950s, and the 1960s, federal industrial and trade policy supported a more liberal international trade regime, even as it developed programs for various sectoral and infrastructure-based targets of policy, including the 'managed trade' package known as the Auto Pact. This occurred within the context of high but declining tariffs, moderate subsidization, and relatively deep federal budgetary pockets. During the 1970s and early 1980s, while tariffs went down further and some new non-tariff barriers went up (e.g., import quotas, voluntary export restraint agreements), federal industrial policy was cast much more explicitly in terms of regions and sectors (Savoie 1986). As tariff protection went down, expenditure subsidies and industrial policy grants went up, at least as long as federal money was available. The provinces, too, seeking to create regionally vital industries in the name of province-building, played their own spending version of sectoral/regional industrial policy (Tupper 1986). Industrial policy in this period was also characterized by a debate on foreign ownership and the need to screen foreign investment. Indeed, the technologies transferred through such foreign ownership were often depicted as part of a painless way to innovate and to keep up to date with the rest of the world.

There were also periodic concerns and debates about Canada's science and technology policies and overall R & D support. But during this period, policy-makers were far more likely to concern themselves with the volume and nature of R & D spending as a percentage of GNP than they were about rates of patent applications and approvals or rates of diffusion of foreign technology (de la Mothe 2000; Gualtieri 1994; Doern 1972) – or attention focused on the relative generosity of Canada's tax breaks for R & D. It is only recently that IP, in general, and other regulatory aspects of R & D and 'pre-competitive' R & D have begun to receive the attention they deserve.

By the mid-to-late 1980s, as the Canada-U.S. Free Trade Agreement was being negotiated, federal industrial and trade policy shifted into what is now its basic form. When the federal department of Industry, Science and Technology Canada (ISTC) was formed in 1987, it was given a microeconomic mandate that to a greater extent than ever before focused upon international technology-based competitiveness. The Conservative government of Brian Mulroney also announced that its new flagship department for the microeconomy was to base its role much more on good analysis and the dissemination of knowledge than on subsidizing weaker industries or trying to pick winners (Doern 1990). It was also to become, internally within the government, an advocate for industrial competitiveness – in short, a more aggressive horizontal agency.

This focus on a non-subsidizing 'knowledge role' was crystallized even further in the 1993 reorganization that produced the present Industry Canada (Doern 1995c). This period also witnessed a new focus on business framework laws. Such laws on competition policy, intellectual property, corporate governance, and the like have always been a part of domestic policy. However, the new focus, especially following the NAFTA and GATT-WTO agreements of the 1990s, is on how to link and harmonize international framework regimes in these areas to traditional trade policy (Doern 1995b; Hart 1994).

IP and 1990s Innovation Policies

If traditional industrial policy is now not desirable or feasible, just what replaces it? And where do IP policies fit in within this larger rubric? 'Innovation policies' have, in some sense, supplanted traditional industrial policy, but the term is not always clear-cut or easily packaged and sold to various economic and political interests. For example, the Chrétien government made innovation the central concept in its main microeconomic policy paper, *Building a More Innovative Economy* (Industry Canada 1994a; Doern 1995c). The document reflected the need for a knowledge role, but it was also very eclectic about just what this role was and about what processes of continuous innovation meant.

Evolving out of free trade, the globalization of production, and the revolution in telecommunications, computers, and capital and financial mobility, the dominant view inherent in innovation policies was that liberalized markets represented the best overall policies for governments to follow. But within this cluster there continued to be important debates about just what the remaining connections are among a range of fields such as trade, industrial, competition, and intellectual property policies (Ostry 1990, 1993). These debates among economists and various observers and policy practitioners can be grouped around the following related issues: concerns about 'system frictions' and framework laws that affect access to markets; the remaining potential for 'managed trade' or a narrowed range of neo-industrial policies; the role of strategic alliances among firms, especially in the realm of R & D or product innovation; the breakdown of the traditional R & D spectrum; and the role of intellectual property policy in all of the above. In this discussion, we only highlight the issues since there is a significant literature on each.

System Friction and Framework Policies

'System friction' is the term given by economist and former OECD and Canadian senior official Sylvia Ostry to the more evident kind of international friction which, she argued in 1990, was much broader than protectionism (Ostry 1990). The term 'underlined that there were several different market models *among* capitalist economies, the differences stemming from both historical and cultural legacies as well as divergence in a range of domestic policies' (Ostry 1993, 2). These system differences in capitalism influenced the international competitiveness of a firm, which was essentially the product of an 'interaction between the firm's own capabilities and the broad institutional context of its home country' (Ostry 1993, 2). These frictions had to be reduced through harmonization of those policies that affected a firm's innovative capability. Many frictions centred around market-place framework laws such as competition policy, IP, and investment rules. Ostry went on to argue that a key area of focus would have to be on the issue of 'effective market access,' a concept which she acknowledged to be 'soft and even slippery' and which, at its core, was at the blurred boundaries of competition, trade, investment, and 'high tech industrial policy.' Ostry cast her arguments in the context of political realities among 'The Triad' of trading/political blocs, the EU and the U.S.-North America and Japan-Pacific blocs.

Managed Trade

As we have seen, since the early 1980s traditional industrial policy, by which governments subsidized various industrial sectors to promote national economic development, had been severely criticized. Its practice became increasingly less viable both for reasons of budgetary restraints and for fear of trade countervail measures by other countries. But the instinct to practise a more restrained form of industrial policy is still strong. In particular, it emerges under rationales for so-called managed trade. Such rationales refer to a particular set of circumstances in which, it is argued, intervention by governments might pay off for a country's corporations and workers.

The 'managed trade' argument suggests that a country could obtain

economic gains by subsidizing its producers in the development of
new technology products launched for export in situations of imperfect
competition in which monopoly rents or above average returns could
be earned (Brander and Spencer 1983; Krugman 1986). The criticisms of
managed trade centre on the exact presence of these conditions, the
assumptions made about the strategies and expectations of firms, and
the levels of detailed knowledge that governments would have to
possess and, what is more, act precisely on (Richardson 1989).

Laura Tyson, a key Clinton adviser, makes the case for what she calls
a 'cautious activism' in trade policy (Tyson 1993, 13). This is a position
which she argues is '*not* synonymous with protectionism.' She argues
that the several case studies in her research confirm the overall view
that

> technology-intensive industries violate the assumptions of free trade theory
> and the static concepts that are the traditional basis for US trade policy. In
> such industries, costs fall and product quality improves as the scale of
> production increases, the returns to technological advance create benefi-
> cial spillovers for other economic activities, and barriers to entry generate
> market structures rife with first-mover advantages and strategic behav-
> iour. A nation's competitive position in industries with these characteris-
> tics is less a function of its national factor endowments and more a function
> of strategic interactions between its firms and government and between
> them and the firms and governments of other nations. (Tyson 1993, 3)

Biotechnology, key aspects of the information highway, and related
industries are increasingly seen as managed or strategic in this overall
sense, both in the United States and in other countries (Mironesco
1998).

Cooperation in Competition
A third issue in the debate about innovation and the nature of knowledge-based economies is advanced by authors such as Jorde and Teece,
law and business academics respectively (Jorde and Teece 1992). They
argue that 'new intellectual arguments are necessary to understand
how competition takes place in many industries today' (Jorde and
Teece 1992, 579). In an article (as well as books) focusing on the role of
economic thinking in competition policy or antitrust analysis, Jorde
and Teece argue that 'legal scholarship and judicial action (in the U.S.)
have been slow to recognize the primary importance of innovation to

the competitive process' (Jorde and Teece 1992, 579). In particular, mainstream law and economics have failed to appreciate the role of cooperation among many firms and institutions in the overall innovation process, as well as the organizational requirements of innovation.

In a similar vein, Michael Best speaks simply of the need to see the emergence of a 'new competition' centred much more on what he refers to as an 'entrepreneurial firm,' which, while market-based and continuously sensitive to improvement in methods, products, and processes, is inherently a more flexible, social, and cooperative entity (Best 1990). His analysis of everything from Japanese production to small Italian firms and regional cooperative ventures points to something other than the mass-production industrial firms that have dominated the last seventy or so years of capitalist competition and industrial structure (Albert 1993).

Strategic Alliances and Cooperative R & D
A fourth issue, easily evolving from the third, centres on the role of strategic alliances among firms, and hence on policies towards cooperation in research and development. The key question is whether such alliances are a threat to competition or a key manifestation of its socioeconomic nature. Waverman and Khemani's analysis of strategic alliances shows the difficulties (Waverman and Khemani 1993). Before one can even begin to assess their competitive or anti-competitive effects, there are real problems of definition and information. In definitional terms, the problem is one of knowing which 'sub-set of ... inter-firm agreements are meant by "strategic" alliances'? Khemani and Waverman settle on a definition which sees strategic alliances as a 'form of inter-firm agreements or arrangements between independent firms which involve knowledge production or sharing activities aimed at developing products or processes and forms of production. In this regard, the alliance may entail exchange of R & D and/or transfer of various information' (Waverman and Khemani 1993, 2). A key point here is that these alliances are not confined to some arbitrarily defined stage of 'pre-competitive R & D,' but rather involve downstream production and marketing know-how and innovation. This is a vital point because, to the extent that some OECD countries still admit that they practise industrial policy, it is precisely in this R & D realm that they say they will and must practise such policies.

The literature on investment policy suggests that such alliances are growing faster than mergers, but that it is difficult to know not only because of definitional issues but also because the alliances do not need to be announced or registered (Safarian 1993).

The Breakdown of the Traditional R & D Spectrum
A further key element in visualizing innovation is the partial break-down of the earlier post–Second World War model of the spectrum of scientific activity. The broad presumption was that basic or pure re-search, even when curiosity-inspired, broadly drove the *later* applied research and development phases and then led to innovative products. But for at least the last fifteen years, this presumption has been chal-lenged by other evidence and experience which shows that interactions are much more complex, and indeed that causal links are often reversed and much more subtle. In short, the pathways to real innovation are multiple and complex. The new institutional linkages and partnerships between industry and universities are partly forged on the basis of this new understanding of the spectrum of actual R & D and innovative activity. They also create legitimate opposition centred on what this means for the independence of researchers and for science and research as a public good (Lee 1996; Etzkowitz 1996).

The role of science in regulation (and in risk-benefit management) is also linked here because of changes in the sources of scientific informa-tion and linkages of key new industries to systems of regulation by the state (Doern and Reed 2000). It is suggested that the older model and era of science-based regulation was anchored around traditional sources such as epidemiological investigations, toxicological studies, and clini-cal trials. But, more recently and in the context of the risk-benefit management model, other sources and types of scientific information have come into greater use, including the following: biological mark-ers; molecular epidemiology; new toxicological assays; in vitro assays; genetics; structure activity analysis; surveillance; and population health surveys. Almost inevitably, these sources and techniques also break down the traditional boundaries of competence among traditionally defined scientific disciplines and can show up in generational differ-ences among the backgrounds of scientists in government and outside it. This evolution also leads to a far wider sharing, interdependence, and exchange of scientific and professional information and knowledge among experts in Canada and internationally.

R & D Policy and Intellectual Property Regulation
Finally, there is the issue of intellectual property itself in this web of

issues surrounding the knowledge economy. It would be surprising if the issue of regulating intellectual property could escape the above debates, and it cannot. Several analyses show how IP is central to them. In her account of emerging 'system frictions,' Sylvia Ostry clearly places IP in the set of policies now melding into each other. She observed in 1991 that 'convergence in intellectual property would have to involve much more than what is going on in the GATT because it is not simply an issue of having minimum standards within the triad: The question of enforcement is very important' (Ostry 1991, 56). So also is the question of the dissemination of knowledge since, as we have stressed, it is the balance between the two that is increasingly vital.

Perhaps less obvious, but politically crucial, has been the central importance of the political role of industries concerned with abuses of their intellectual property rights. As Geza Feketekuty points out, it was an IP coalition of American businesses that was the most energetic, but somewhat unexpected, advocate of new GATT trade rules in the mid-1980s (Feketekuty 1991). They were interested in extending GATT rules to services and to intellectual property concerns. This U.S. lobby, linked to similar companies elsewhere in the triad, changed the focus of negotiations. As Feketekuty notes, 'intellectual property was not on the initial list of potential negotiating issues identified in 1981 for the new round of multilateral trade negotiations' (Feketekuty 1991, 61), but three years later it was central.

Canada's free trade negotiators in 1986-7 also discovered quickly that the American IP and service lobby was leading the U.S. agenda. Much of the U.S. industries' political energy was directed to the simultaneous battles underway over patents and the pharmaceutical industry, but there is little doubt where the 'new blood' in U.S. pro–free trade politics was coming from, compared to the previous Tokyo Round (Doern and Tomlin 1991; Curtis 1990).

While there is no doubt that intellectual property is a key feature of the debate about the innovation process, this is not the same thing as saying that there is solid empirical analysis about what kinds of intellectual property rules should exist and what effects they have. As economist Keith Maskus has pointed out, 'interest by business persons in foreign IPR systems far outstrips any serious economic analysis of their effects' (Maskus 1991, 120). There are any number of serious issues in what constitutes the optimum trade-off point between the value of protecting a patent versus promoting the social diffusion and adaptation of the invention. Several questions could be posed. How important, in fact, are patents, as opposed to other factors or policies, in inducing innovation? Is it not likely that optimum patent policy would be different in different industrial sectors? If so, it would cease to be 'framework' policy, and IP policy would be more sectoral. There certainly are also highly judgmental issues involved in how strong the patent protection should be. Potential monopoly pricing can occur and produce distortions and social welfare losses, as the debate about the generic drugs issue indicated (Eastman 1985).

The issues about how to characterize the knowledge economy are also important because they all suggest the need for many balancing fulcrums; in short, for quite subtle trade-offs between different kinds of capitalism; between free trade and managed high-technology trade; between cooperation and competition among firms, especially in R & D; and, as intellectual property regimes well know, between protecting ideas and knowledge and disseminating such knowledge. Much of this clustering of thought and practice was also captured by academics who referred to the existence of national systems of innovation (Nelson 1993; Industry Canada 1994a).

However, if innovation policy is now the operative substitute overall umbrella term that replaces past industrial policy, it still lacks clarity and focus. Chapter 2 has shown how even in 1971, the federal Economic Council of Canada's report on IP had a remarkably prescient discussion of innovation, the knowledge economy, and IP (Economic Council of Canada 1971). But it focused on innovation seen in national terms, rather than in the context of what we now refer to as globalization. Later chapters will show how innovation is now increasingly cast in terms of how Canada not only may be innovative itself but also can gain access to a world store of innovation, without which no economy and society can prosper in the new Millennium.

IP and Recent Policy Controversies: Sectoral and Framework Policy Collisions?

The above two portraits suggest a basically stark history for IP. In the era of traditional industrial policy, it was not a sustained factor at any salient political level. In the recent and current era of innovation policies, IP policies rise in importance but are simultaneously embedded in a rather vague set of linked policies and activities that vary among firms and sectors. But there are other portraits that can be painted. IP policy issues and controversies have also emerged, and will again emerge, in sectoral contexts where the particular meanings of innovation will vary and be contested in different ways and by particular clusters of interests. Four of these (biodiversity, the patenting of life forms, the information highway, and competition policy) are profiled briefly below, with most of them also being given further attention in later chapters. We leave aside the key changes in pharmaceuticals and health care since that is the focus of chapter 8.

IP and Biodiversity

The issues of IP and biodiversity can be seen either as a subset of recent trade and trade-environment policies and politics or as an international lead-in to our discussion in the next section of the regulation of biotechnology. Nonetheless there are some separate issues that warrant a section of their own, albeit a brief one. First, it is international politics that is most forcing Canada to take a position on these links. The crucial event and process here is the forging of the Biodiversity Convention at and after the 1992 Rio Earth Summit (Purdue 1995). The process became a North-South economic and social issue.

In the early 1980s, developing countries had been able, through the Food and Agriculture Organization (FAO), to obtain an undertaking which said that all seeds are a common heritage. These included 'inbred elite lines used for breeding by seed companies' (Purdue 1995, 101). Developed countries by the late 1980s had countered this with an agreed FAO interpretation that IP rights were not incompatible with the earlier undertaking. The developed countries shifted their positions somewhat as Rio approached, seeing seeds and plants as natural resources over which nations had sovereign authority.

The resulting Biodiversity Convention speaks of the need for adequate and effective IP protection, and hence in the view of many critics ensures that the WTO-TRIPs agreement will prevail over the biodiversity agreement. Biodiversity is one of many trade and environment tensions, but there are direct IP issues which Canada must deal with both in its own biodiversity and IP laws and in its implementation of international agreements.

IP, the Patenting of Life Forms, and Biotechnology

A second arena of IP-linked policy controversy centres on the patenting of higher life forms (microbial life forms are patentable in Canada) and the broader economic ethical issues inherent in regulating biotechnology. At the time of writing, the situation in Canada is that Canadian law does not allow higher life forms to be patented, whereas U.S. IP law does. There is no strong domestic industry yet pushing for changes in the law, but Canada will have to face these issues since they are on the WTO negotiating agenda.

In the realm of patenting life forms, the most specific decision to at least partly raise these issues was the so-called Harvard Mouse case. The application for a Canadian patent covered an invention entitled 'transgenic animals.' The inventors are Phillip Leder and Timothy A. Stewart, with the application assigned to the President and Fellows of Harvard College. The patent examiner in charge of the case refused to allow twelve of the claims regarding the application. This decision was reviewed by the Patent Appeal Board, and then a decision was made by the Commissioner of Patents confirming the initial examiner's decision under Canadian law (Canadian Intellectual Property Office 1995).

The transgenic mouse could be used as a test vehicle for 'substances suspected of being carcinogenic or for substances thought to confer protection against the development of neoplasms' (Canadian Intellectual Property Office 1995, 1). The Commissioner of Patent's decision drew on various parts of the law, including the Commissioner's duty to consider the public interest. It also turned on what constituted an invention and the degree to which the manufacture or the composition of matter was under the control of the inventor as opposed to the laws of nature.

The Commissioner's decision in effect distinguished between lower and higher life forms, with the lower forms being approved as patentable while the latter were ruled to be unpatentable. He concluded in his 1995 decision that 'the inventors do not have full control over all the resulting characteristics of the resulting mouse since the intervention of man ensures that reproducibility extends only as far as the cancer forming gene' (Canadian Intellectual Property Office 1995, 7).

As the Harvard Mouse case shows, IP issues regarding higher life forms are related to the larger regulation of biotechnology. Biotechnology refers to 'the applied use of living organisms or their components to make or modify products, to improve plants or animals or to develop microorganisms for specific uses' (Industry Canada 1996). Cast in the context of genetic engineering and advanced applications based on recombinant DNA, the biotechnology field raises many concerns about the public interest, commercial regulation, and the nature of risk (House of Commons 1994). And among these concerns may be issues of intellectual property set amidst a quite complex set of existing health, environmental, and safety regulators administering as many as ten regulatory statutes (Doern and Sheehy 1999).

During the 1980s and 1990s, biotechnology has gradually emerged on the national and international policy and economic agenda in three main ways: in federal biotechnology strategies in 1983 and 1998; in an evolving biotechnology regulatory system responding to industry's development of new products and processes; and in periodic controversies about products and scientific developments.

An initial 1983 National Biotechnology Strategy was replaced by the 1998 Canadian Biotechnology Strategy (CBS). The CBS is intended to 'support the responsible development, application, and export of biotechnology products and services' balanced within the context of 'social and ethical considerations' (Canada 1998c, 1). The CBS sets out a policy framework consisting of a vision, guiding principles, and goals that reflect biotechnology's importance both to the economy and to Canada's quality of life. Ten themes 'for concerted action' are identified to be implemented on a partnership basis with stakeholders such as the provinces, industry, academia, consumers, environmental groups, and other interests.

The centrepiece of the CBS is the establishment of the Canadian Biotechnology Advisory Committee (CBAC), an expert panel which will advise ministers on the 'ethical, social, economic, scientific, regulatory and environmental and health aspects of biotechnology' (Canada 1998c, 1). The CBAC will have no role on specific regulatory decisions, but its policy advisory role will include its serving as a forum to give Canadians a voice in an 'open and transparent dialogue on biotechnology issues' (Canada 1998c, 1).

The CBS was devised through a quite elaborate process. Within the federal government, it was forged through a mechanism coordinated by the Minister of Industry, but that included six other ministers whose portfolios had mandates dealing with biotechnology: the Ministers of Agriculture and Agri-Food, Health, Environment, Fisheries and Oceans, Natural Resources, and International Trade. The CBS also involved consultations in which over five thousand individuals participated, encompassing both sectoral interests and round-table discussions in five cities (Canada 1998c, 1998d).

The second way in which biotechnology was emerging was in the gradual fashioning of a biotechnology regulatory system through a Federal Regulatory Framework for Biotechnology (Canada 1998c, 7). Unlike some areas of regulation there is no *single* biotechnology regulator. Hence, a framework of principles was developed to guide the several regulatory bodies and departments which were being called upon to approve biotechnology products and processes. In this sense, the Canadian biotechnology regulatory system has been described as 'relatively new, emerging and institutionally dispersed' (Doern and Sheehy 1999). The core of the biotechnology regulatory system, by deliberate design, is itself a secondary set of arrangements and processes agreed to by several regulatory bodies whose primary regulatory tasks are far broader than biotechnology in that they deal with older established overall health, safety, and environmental regulatory tasks (Canada 1998c).

A third way in which biotechnology has gained a greater public profile is that it has become central to particular policy or regulatory controversies. These range from global scientific issues such as the cloning of Dolly, the sheep, gene prospecting and its links to biodiversity, and the huge human genome research project (Grace 1997; Appleyard 1999; Mironesco 1998). But they also include debates over specific products, such as the one in Canada concerning the regulation of rbST (House of Commons 1994; MacDonald 2000), a biotechnology product that enhances the efficiency of milk production in cows and that has been approved for use in the United States, but has recently been rejected in Canada (*Ottawa Citizen*, 15 Jan. 1999, p. 1).

Underlying all of the above developments are the emergence and growth, both in Canada and globally, of new biotechnology firms, and the consolidation and growth of biotechnology within established pharmaceutical firms (Industry Canada 1997b; Canada 1998e). Thus there is little doubt that biotechnology and its links to IP has a central place in the political economy of Canada as the new Millennium begins.

IP and the Information Highway
A third crucial area where IP issues arise is in the area of digital technology and the information highway (Department of Justice, Industry Canada, and Canadian Heritage 1995; U.S. Information Infrastructure Task Force 1995). Digitalization, fibre optics, and cable are posing fundamental challenges to IP, particularly regarding the creation, reproduction, and dissemination of copyrighted works. Importantly, in this interactive process 'individuals and entities that heretofore have been predominantly consumers of works can now become authors and providers' through such technologies (U.S. Information Infrastructure Task Force 1995, 9).

The related information highway debates have evoked a range of views about just where the IP trade-offs should be made (Brunet 1994). Some argue that copyright protection should be reduced or that, de facto, national sovereignty IP rules simply cannot be effectively applied in the global realm of cyberspace. In addition, the new technologies blur some distinctions between when a creation is a good or product and thus perhaps patentable as opposed to when it is authored information and involves copyright protection.

The choices of IP responses accordingly range from the tough enforcement of existing IP rules, to the need for more flexile regimes precisely to allow the information highway to flourish with a larger sense of information and economic creativity. The question also arises as to whether governments need to enact special separate laws (IP or others) for digital technology.

These and other concerns about IP and digital technology will be brought into our discussion in later chapters on both patents and trademarks as well as copyright.

IP and Competition Policy

Last but not least, we come to the broad links between national and international competition policies and laws, on the one hand, and IP laws, on the other (Gallini and Trebilcock 1996). IP law in the realm of patents creates and endorses monopolies and, in a strict sense, is anti-competitive. Competition law exists to promote competition among firms and economic entities. How then do the laws and institutions of the two realms relate to each other? Which law prevails? Or how are they accommodated or fudged? Space allows us only a few basic observations about these links.

First, it would appear that national IP institutions believe broadly that their realms have precedence and that it is competition law and policy that is 'fenced out' and deemed not in general to apply to situations in which intellectual property rights per se apply. Second, competition laws themselves vary across countries as to whether their main purpose is competition as such or is linked to related economic concepts such as consumer surplus (a stronger norm in the U.S.), economic efficiency (the case in Canada), economic integration (the situation in the EU); or broader public interest or even industrial policy objectives (the situation in the U.K.) (Doern and Wilks 1996). They also vary in their enforcement mechanisms, including whether private actions are possible.

However, in the 1990s, it would appear that concerns about institutional links between each separately desirable area of market-place framework policy are growing. For example, in the U.S. debate about the possible location of the U.S. Patent and Trademark Office (USPTO) if the Department of Commerce were abolished, there was strong opposition in the USPTO to its being located in the Justice Department for fear that it would run headlong into a culture dominated by that department's aggressive anti-trust division. This was certainly an indicator of a larger potential for cases in which IP issues and competition issues would collide under the U.S. system, in which private actions are the norm in anti-trust matters. For example, cases of anti-competitive behaviour have involved situations in which patented products or production processes (themselves protected under IP law) were being extended into anti-competitive actions through the vehicle of licensing arrangements or particular aspects of these arrangements.

In the United States and elsewhere, the more that IP is viewed politically and economically as the 'new protectionism,' with IP becoming the 'high tariff' of the knowledge and information economy, the more that anti-trust cases will be mounted to test the real limits of both sets of laws. 'What' is fenced out of 'where' will be a more fluid, debatable, and contested concept.

To demonstrate a further aspect of these relationships, it is also necessary, as discussed earlier, to look at practices intended to encourage cooperative R & D and technological alliances among firms. Governments in all of the jurisdictions being surveyed have encouraged such alliances and indeed have taken various measures to exempt such activities from the threat of possible anti-trust actions. At the same time, when it comes to obtaining patents for such collaborative work, there are still severe difficulties, in part because fears of anti-trust action still remain and in part because it is genuinely difficult to define property rights and which parties to the alliance should hold them or seek them from IP institutions (Niosi 1995). Given that such alliances are frequently international in nature, the problems presented can be even greater.

Conclusions

This chapter has traced an IP policy history that is important to the broadest understanding of innovating institutions writ large and for the more detailed analysis of IP agencies and interests which follows.

Canada's middling IP record must be seen now in the context of difficult problems in understanding the nature of the modern knowledge-based economy. Canada's IP policy must be seen in the context of its almost complete marginality during the era of traditional industrial policy that characterized most of the 1960s, 1970s, and early 1980s. During this period, IP was not even on the radar screens of key industrial policy-makers in the federal government, except perhaps for the 1969 patent amendments, which introduced compulsory licensing for the importation of pharmaceuticals.

In the recent and current era, cast in this chapter as innovation policy, IP is emerging on the agenda, but not always with a clear-cut sense of just where it actually fits. This is because innovation policies are themselves necessarily eclectic and significantly knowledge-centred, and because it is in fact difficult to map, let alone explain, national systems of innovation. Innovation policies are also centred more on very broad market-place framework policies as a whole, which include IP but go well beyond it.

The analysis also suggests the need to appreciate the way in which IP policy controversies and issues surface in the overall policy agenda. There is a growing frequency to these policy episodes, but they are just that, episodes. Thus, several arenas of controversy are now present, centred in the heart of IP politics, the pharmaceutical and drugs-health industry, but also extending to the other realms introduced above, biodiversity, biotechnology, the information highway, and competition policy. We focus on pharmapatents but will refer again to these other broader IP-related issues, especially in terms of what they might reveal about future IP politics.

4. International Pressures and the Global Politics of IP Institutions

We have already highlighted some of the international pressures that have impinged on Canada's IP policy-making and institutional domains. These general pressures have come in the form of changing global ideas about IP and innovation as a whole, U.S.-led trade policy initiatives, and the impact of trade agreements such as NAFTA and GATT-WTO. We now need to look more closely at these pressures and related aspects of the global politics of IP in order to understand both them and the Canadian situation more clearly.

Such a global focus proceeds in three stages. First, the chapter examines the governance and macro-politics of established international agencies such as the World Intellectual Property Organization (WIPO) and the European Patent Office (EPO), both to exhibit their importance but also to show why, especially in the case of WIPO, the international regimes were viewed with increasing dissatisfaction, especially by the United States. The second section then shifts to a look at the U.S. Patent Office and to domestic U.S. IP political forces, since this is where the core pressure for change is occurring and since Canada has particular bilateral issues regarding the United States. The third section looks at the resulting changing nature of relationships among national and international IP agencies as they separately and jointly try to sort out relationships among themselves that are partly cooperative and partly competitive. These relationships also turn on how the protection versus dissemination trade-offs should be made in a complex and fast changing globalized knowledge economy.

International IP Agencies and Change

The most important point of departure for the 1990s is that international IP bodies such as WIPO, EPO, and the WTO are, in a real sense, also being politically discovered, and paid continuous attention to, for the first time.

The governance of IP international bodies is best seen in two ways: the generic nature of international agencies; and then the basic governance structures and dynamics of WIPO and the EPO. The most basic fact about international agencies is that their governing structures are composed of signatory member *national governments* (Taylor 1993; Taylor and Groom 1988). The national representatives who sit on or attend the governing council or assembly meetings thus bring to the international body both an interest in the body and its success but also a concern for the strategic interests of their own country/government. They also bring the concerns of the home ministry or agency from which they come within a national government.

The typically large membership of international bodies (albeit across a wide range of sizes) also makes their formal decision-making and governing processes slow and unwieldy. Decision-making typically must secure a high degree of consensus. Frustration with these processes and/or the sheer need for action often requires the aggressive action of active coalitions among a smaller subset of member states or from a lead 'hegemonic' member state (Kratochwil and Mansfield 1994). The permanent secretariat of the agency is also a key influence either in slowing down development to reach a broad consensus or, occasionally, through its own leadership's active role (in effect, bureaucratic entrepreneurship and risk taking). The dynamics of the international agency are also affected by whether it has a one member–one vote system or a weighted system of voting favouring the larger or more powerful countries.

In this section, we can only glimpse some of these features, but they can be first seen in the context of WIPO. WIPO is the first of the international agencies in that, even in its modern era, it predates the emergence of the EPO as a regional international body and certainly it predates the mature functioning of the EPO, which really takes shape only in the mid-1980s (Bogsch 1992; World Intellectual Property Organization 1995e).

WIPO is a complex organizational mélange. It is a UN agency but has considerable independence, largely because it has its own independent source of funds. WIPO has a three-level governing structure (General Assembly, Conference, and Coordination Committee). It has upwards of 151 member states, whose interests and priorities vary across the patent, trademark, and copyright realms, and in relation to the priorities that ought to be accorded to its trio of basic functions: norm-setting and advancing the development of IP standards across the world; administering the various 'unions' or IP conventions; and cooperative activity, especially regarding the needs of developing countries.

Since there were and are varying memberships in the different unions, WIPO's meetings can have extremely complicated voting procedures. Its basic financial structure is also reflective of a considerable dispersal of power among member states in that, first, about 80 per cent of its funding comes from fees from private sector applicants for the use of the registration system, especially via the Patent Cooperation Treaty (PCT) (Bogsch 1992). Of the small part of its money (14 per cent) that comes from member states, no one state pays more than a very small share. This means that large countries such as the United States do not obtain a disproportionate influence out of a structure of weighted voting and budget contributions, as is the case in other UN and international bodies (Taylor 1993). There is no weighted voting at WIPO.

All of the above suggests the image and reality of a slow-moving international agency that must, in essence, inch its way along in an increasingly fast-changing world. However, WIPO must also be seen in terms of the continuity of its leadership. From 1973 to 1997 WIPO's Director General was Arpad Bogsch, an American international civil servant, whose personal imprint on the organization is part of the culture of the organization. A tenacious workaholic, Bogsch was involved in virtually every detail of the organization. Nonetheless, he also ensured that it ran as a relatively efficient operational agency, and certainly it was by virtually any UN agency standard. Secondly, Bogsch, with a keen eye on its diverse membership, insisted that its broad overall mandate serve both the needs of the developed and developing world (Bogsch 1992).

If strong leadership and a complex governing structure produced a relatively sound but hierarchical operational agency, it also produced, especially in the 1990s, increasing frustration among key members with its inability to change IP policy in the global economy, especially regarding copyright enforcement issues in developing countries. In this context, the United States, but also the European Union countries, displayed impatience with WIPO and its slow consensus processes and agendas. The politics of copyright policies and laws, increasingly linked to trade negotiations and enforcement mechanisms, were a particular catalyst for change (Abbott 1989; Curtis 1990; Warshovsky 1994). This has been referred to in earlier chapters but in terms of the present focus

on governing structures, the main point to stress is that WIPO's processes were undoubtedly, and understandably, slow, and that it was, like
most IP organizations, mainly an agency concerned with patent and
trademark issues rather than with copyright because the former were at
its operational core.

By definition, the European Patent Office is undoubtedly a less complex international body than WIPO because it is regionally confined to
Europe. Initially, at least, it is of less direct interest to a Canadian-
focused book. However, our interest in it in this chapter is twofold: first,
its importance in its own right on the global stage; and second, its
possible role as a model for any potential 'North American Patent
Office.' The EPO has only eighteen member states and, as its name
implies, is concerned with patents only (European Patent Office 1995).
Without doubt, the key feature of the EPO's governing Administrative
Council is that, in the main, the national representatives that sit on that
council are the heads of national patent (IP) offices. The majority of
these national offices, in turn (see more below), typically report in their
own national governments to industry departments (the German patent office being a significant exception in that it reports to the justice
ministry). The presence, in particular, of the heads of patent agencies
from major countries with patent offices such as the United Kingdom,
Germany, Switzerland, and Sweden is especially important. Such representatives invariably bring a dual set of interests within the Administrative Council, that of their obligation to implement the European
Patent Convention through the EPO, and that of their concern for their
own national patent office, whose functions are partly threatened by
the very existence of the EPO.

The dynamics of the EPO's council and operations are also affected
by the fact that many member states do not have patent offices that
engage in search and substantial examination activities (such as France,
Holland, Italy). All, however, have patent offices which receive patent
applications. Some countries have much less developed cultures and
interests in intellectual property, such as the southern European states
(Spain, Portugal). At the same time, many of the key states across these
ranges of IP interest are extremely concerned about the language in
which commerce is conducted (European Patent Office 1995, 1994).
Hence, issues such as the translation of patents into major European
languages are a key feature of both high politics and such practicalities
as administrative fees, costs, and delivery.

The operational independence of the EPO is reinforced by the fact that it meets all of its budgetary needs through its patent fees. The fact that it is not an agency of the European Union also gives it operational autonomy. But this may be changing for some of the same reasons that we have seen above for changes in the politics of WIPO. In brief, other aspects of intellectual property *are* within the jurisdiction of the EU and its Commission in Brussels. For example, a European (EU) trademark agency has begun operations in Alicante, Spain (Office for Harmonization in the Internal Market 1995). But, more important, copyright policy and key aspects of patent policy in a larger European (EU) sense are a growing policy concern in Brussels. The Directorate Generals in the EU Commission that deal with industry, innovation, and the internal market are increasingly active in discovering the importance of IP writ large.

Canada is a member of WIPO, and Canadian IP interests benefit broadly from its work. It has shared with the United States some of the concerns about the sluggishness of WIPO's decision making and agenda setting, though it clearly does not have the same influence as the United States in WIPO. Canada is also concerned that issues especially relevant to developing countries are not emasculated by a U.S.-driven agenda. With respect to the EPO, Canada is obviously not a member, but it has concerns about Canadian companies seeking European Patent protection. Canada also recognizes the important potential of EPO as a model within the context of the possible U.S. agenda in the late 1990s of leaning towards the establishment of regional IP bodies both in North America and in the Asia-Pacific region.

The U.S. Patent and Trademark Office and U.S. IP Political Forces

From international and regional IP agency realities, we need to turn to the United States itself as both an international and bilateral factor in Canada's IP policy calculations and politics. These IP influences are multidimensional but central among them are the following: the role of the United States as the exemplar of a society and economy with an 'IP culture'; the nature of changes in the U.S. Patent Office and its 'first to invent' as opposed to 'first to file' patent system; and the role of copyright and IP in the U.S. trade and international economic policy agenda.

Regarding the United States as an exemplar of an IP culture, it is instructive first to note that U.S. IP institutions are rooted, in effect, in the United States Constitution. Article I, section 8, asserts the goal central to the creation of intellectual endeavour, namely, 'to promote the progress of science and the useful arts by securing for limited times to authors and inventors the exclusive right to their respective writings and discoveries' (U.S. Patent and Trademark Office 1995, 5). To this constitutional pride of place, one can add the more recent high growth in U.S. patenting activity as well as frequent references to the proverbial claims of 'American know how' in the folklore of American capitalism.

The key institutional features of the United States Patent and Trademark Office (USPTO) are also pertinent. The USPTO's origins can be traced to 1802, when a separate official in the Department of State was placed in charge of patents. As a formal office, the USPTO was established in 1836, and by 1925 it had moved to the Department of Commerce, where it resides today as one of the department's fourteen bureaus. At present a non-commercial federal entity, the USPTO's five thousand employees administer its major functions, namely, the examination and issuance of patents and the examination and registration of trademarks.

A recent review document describes the patent and trademark mission as that of promoting 'industrial and technological progress in the United States' and strengthening the national economy by:

- administering the laws relating to patents and trademarks;
- advising the Secretary of Commerce, the President of the United States, and the Administration on patent, trademark, and copyright protection; and
- advising the Secretary of Commerce, the President of the United States, and the Administration on the trade-related aspects of intellectual property. (U.S. Patent and Trademark Office 1995, 1)

Thus, the USPTO is not the main administrator of copyright law (see more below) but is involved in related policy matters on copyright and on IP as a whole.

The head of the USPTO is an Assistant Secretary of Commerce, who is also the Commissioner of Patents and Trademarks. As head of the office, the Commissioner exercises general supervision over the USPTO and also prescribes the rules, subject to the approval of the Secretary of Commerce, for such matters as the conduct of proceedings within the USPTO and the recognition of attorneys and agents.

In the late 1990s, proposals are being actively pursued to make the USPTO into a semi-independent government-owned corporation. Since 1990, however, the USPTO has already evolved into a quasi–business-

oriented agency. Propelled by the new service ethos in public management circles and by the requirements of the U.S. Government Performance and Results Act of 1993, the USPTO was reorganized in 1994 and
committed itself to numerous actions for meeting customer needs. The
old organizational structure was replaced with a 'process and customer
based' structure (U.S. Patent and Trademark Office 1995, 12).

There is little doubt that the USPTO is, along with Japan's IP agency,
the hub of the world patent system in terms of absolute volume. In
1994, U.S. patent applications exceeded 200,000 and patents issued
exceeded 113,000 (U.S. Patent and Trademark Office 1995, 8). As has
been the case for other IP offices, U.S. concerns centred on reducing the
'pendency rate.' The USPTO faced a steadily increasing volume of
business and a commercial environment in which 'the rapid advance-
ment and innovation of technology today requires a patent protection
system that is swift and adaptable to the needs of individual inventors,
small businesses, and multinational corporations' (U.S. Patent and Trademark Office 1995, 8).

The U.S. debate about corporate status is also rooted in the politics of
the U.S. congressional system. The USPTO had for several years been
adopting many of the features of a service-oriented reinvented government agency (U.S. Patent and Trademark Office 1995). But recently, the
specific idea of converting it into a government corporation has been
included in competing congressional and administration bills. Spurred
on by a Vice President Gore-led general reform of government initiative, in which the USPTO was seen already as an exemplar, the congressional initiatives have also been joined by particular agendas regarding
the USPTO. Big U.S. firms want an independent agency that could run
more efficiently. Smaller inventor groups are suspicious of such moves,
and their voices are heard in congressional offices. And the USPTO has
used the opportunity to point out such questionable financial practices
as the one which requires the USPTO to turn over about 10 per cent of
what it earns in fees to the U.S. Congress, which keeps part of these
revenues for its own projects. To make matters more volatile, the debate
about the USPTO's corporate form has also been embroiled in efforts to
abolish the Department of Commerce, the USPTO's parent department.

Finally, the U.S. influence must be linked to the politics of copyright,
which are centred only partly in the USPTO. Copyright concerns were
at the centre of the U.S. intellectual property agenda of the late 1980s
and 1990s, and an IP agenda was in turn central to the trade-in-services
thrust that motivated the 'aggressive unilateralism' of U.S. foreign eco-

nomic policy in the last decade (Bhagwati and Patrick 1990; Sell 1998). This is not to suggest that patents were not also a key U.S. concern, but it was the copyright issues linked to overall problems of pirating (especially by key developing countries) that became a central part of the U.S. agenda. These areas, in turn, were a part of the larger breakthroughs that the United States sought in trade in services. This U.S pressure to liberalize had begun in the Canada-U.S. free trade negotiations (Doern and Tomlin 1991) but was simultaneously a crucial part of the Uruguay Round negotiations. The pressure for breakthroughs in the service sector also came from within the U.S. business community, from the service industries (Hoekman and Kostecki 1995). Services were also inextricably bound up in the computer and telecommunications revolution, and hence in the emergence of the internet or information highway, where intellectual property issues were extremely complicated and important (Drake 1995; U.S. Information Infrastructure Task Force 1995). It is not difficult to see that these linked issues were bound up in the new debates and strategies about competitiveness and about how nations, in an information/knowledge economy, innovate and continuously learn.

Within the U.S. government, as in other Western countries, this meant that trade policy ministries were driving the agendas. And in the United States there was a direct link between this central fact and the appointment of a copyright expert, Bruce Lehman, to head up the USPTO. Lehman had spent large amounts of his time as the Clinton administration's main IP trade adviser. Within the U.S. administration, it also meant that from the late 1980s the main copyright expertise shifted to the Office of the U.S. Trade Representative, aided by the USPTO, and away from its previous centre, the Register of Copyright, located in the Library of Congress, which is a legislative branch agency rather than an executive agency. The Register of Copyright still retains the important registry function required by U.S. law, but policy and political power on copyrights has clearly shifted.

There is a direct link, then, between the above shifts and strategies and the U.S government's growing dissatisfaction with the previously mentioned slow pace of decision-making within WIPO and the traditional international IP processes. Because it was copyright-centred, the U.S. concern was with whether other countries in the world had proper copyright rules and, equally important, enforcement provisions. For these issues, the United States saw the trade policy arena, and the emerging World Trade Organization (WTO) and its potentially far more effective dispute settlement capacities, as its preferred venue. As mentioned in chapter 1, the TRIPs provisions of the Uruguay Round both consolidate and incorporate older patent and trademark conventions, but they also include the long-sought U.S.-levered provisions on dispute settlement in the IP field (Trebilcock and Howse 1995).

Though this U.S. influence in crucial IP politics is vital to understanding the overall IP institutions of the 1990s, including Canada's, it is important to note that it did not – in any total way – turn the operations of the national and regional/international patent offices on their heads. The latter still had their basic examination/registration jobs to do, even while knowing that IP issues were being raised to levels of unprecedented political and economic priority.

Competing and Cooperating National and International IP Agencies

The third international influence flows from the first two set out above but warrants separate mention because it forces attention to be placed on resultant IP agency interdependencies. National and international IP agencies find themselves in both competing and cooperating postures vis à vis each other (Doern 1999).

Without doubt the most important recent development in basic IP governance is the adoption in all of the key IP nations of new forms of independent corporate governance. Whether cast as executive agencies or special operating agencies, the tendency has been to give the IP agencies a wider range of legal or de facto powers over their finances, personnel, and other operations (Doern 1999). These forms were intended to free the agencies from as many of the government-wide disciplines on finance and personnel as was feasible. Stated more positively, as we will see further in chapter 5, the changes were intended to foster greater efficiency in resource use and management and to facilitate a cultural change so that the IP agencies would be more aware of, and sensitive to, the needs of their *broader* range of clients and customers.

In general, the evidence suggests that the degrees of freedom have been greater in financial realms than in personnel realms. Key national offices are all virtually or totally 100 per cent dependent on fee income, with the larger portion coming from patent fees (filing/examination/granting and maintenance or renewal fees). They are able to carry over funds from one year to the next and can invest in capital improvements. Perhaps the one financial freedom they are denied is the right to set their own fees. This is typically left in the hands of the various treasury ministries and/or with the parent industry ministers, where it is guardedly watched over because of the general sensitivity of fee changes in micro-industrial policy politics and because of the treasury's concerns about 'user fee' policy across the government.

Beyond these general and largely positive preferences for agency status, there are important differences in degree among the national offices. The cases of the United Kingdom and the United States are illustrative of differences in the recent political climate in each country and will help us see why competition and cooperation result as IP agencies calculate their own prospects for growth, contraction, or even survival.

In the U.K. context, the Patent Office became an executive agency in the context of a government that was energetically devoted to transforming virtually the entire British civil service into such forms of organization. But the process went even further. All such agencies are subject to periodic review to determine if they should remain agencies or should potentially even be privatized. The U.K. Patent Office was so appraised in 1994, with at least some voices arguing in front of the Minister of Trade and Industry that it should be entirely privatized. Following a consultant's review, the Minister concluded in December 1994 that it would remain as an executive agency. The point to stress about this U.K. situation is that actual privatization was seriously considered and that the agency is still left under continuous pressure as to whether it will continue to exist, with further uncertainty for agency personnel.

Consider next the relationships between the EPO and a national office such as the U.K. Patent Office (United Kingdom Patent Office 1990). The U.K. Patent Office has sought to improve its performance in the 1990s, propelled both by global forces and by the freedoms and disciplines inherent in being given executive agency status. However, it is the presence and policies of the EPO that most drive the strategies of the U.K. office. Sixty per cent of the U.K. Patent Office's revenue now comes from patents, but, since 1978, the EPO has taken away about 50 per cent of its core patent business. There are advantages, of course, for U.K. businesses (especially big business) if they can obtain a patent from the EPO because it confers wider multi-country coverage within the European countries named in the application. The U.K. Patent Office also obtains, as do other EPO member countries, half of the EPO's renewal fee income.

The EPO's pendency processes and fee structures were partly based on the logic of its start-up period (in the 1970s and early 1980s) and partly on the delicate politics of its relationships with member countries and national patent offices. The EPO's initial fees had to be quite high relative to national offices simply because it did not have a set of existing patents on which it could earn *renewal* fees. If it had renewal fee income, it could have had lower front-end charges. Gradually, it did obtain a stream of renewal fee income, and its fees came down. However, its costs per application are two to three times higher than that of a U.S. national patent resulting from first filing (Industrial R & D Advisory Committee of the European Commission 1996, Appendix 3, 13-14). Care must be taken as to what is included in such cost comparisons, but the EPO's higher costs are largely because (a) there are extensive language translation costs that have to be absorbed; (b) patent applications at the EPO are examined by three examiners rather than one; (c) the EPO has a higher salary and pension system for its international civil servants compared to other national offices; and (d) there are pressures from its members with full national patent offices that the EPO not lower its prices in such a way that it puts remaining national offices out of business.

The EPO relationship with a national office such as the U.K. Patent Office is therefore both a cooperative and competitive one. The U.K. Patent Office must watch carefully, as a fully fee-dependent agency, exactly what the pattern of EPO business is likely to be in the coming years, both in terms of initial and renewal fees.

Both the EPO and national offices in Europe must also be cognizant of the actual and potential influence of U.S. and Japanese patent costs and pressures. The cost of obtaining a patent in the United States is lower that the cost of obtaining a patent from the European Patent Office. However, the United States is aware that in the not-too-distant future there will likely be more direct and real competition in the global offering of patent and IP services. The pressure for change is already coming from big multinational businesses to have a system that is virtually a one-stop harmonized patent process. U.S. studies already indicate that some business surveys of EPO patents indicate, despite or perhaps because of higher EPO costs, that they are of a higher quality (in some aspects of approval) than similar U.S. patent services. But the larger U.S. concerns at present are mainly that EPO costs are too high and that about one-third of EPO filings now come from U.S. firms (American Intellectual Property Law Association 1995). Full harmonization may come, but it has many hurdles to overcome.

However, what looks like bloated costs from one jurisdiction's perspective can simply be the *real politik* when seen from the vantage point of a functioning *international* body like the EPO. The United States and the United Kingdom both function in a national single-language economy. The EPO must function in a political-economic context in which the language of commerce is not a small matter.

The EPO's more expensive and time-consuming process for examinations is partly because of language needs, but also because harmonization had to occur among the different national systems it was replacing or augmenting. There also had to be trust built up in the quality and validity of the judgments reached about applications. A three-examiner process rather than a single examiner process was accordingly adopted. The informal target standard for performance on the cost side is that an EPO patent will cost no more than the cost of obtaining the same patent in three separate member countries.

Just as the United States is eyeing the costs of the EPO patent, so the EPO is aware of its greater costs vis-à-vis U.S. patents. In 1996 an EPO cost study was conducted. It looked at the cost of a defined standard EPO patent (e.g., involving an eight-country coverage and translation into six languages, and other criteria). As a result, as of July 1997, EPO fees have been reduced by 20 per cent. The pressure from big business in Europe is to lower these costs greatly, which means lowering or eliminating some or major aspects of translation costs. Some firms are already shopping around various national offices in Europe to obtain the best costing advantages. Meanwhile, the European patent profession opposes such cost reduction measures, often because, in some member countries, the translation aspects of the business are in fact the bread and butter of the profession's IP-related work.

The EPO has also argued with its member states (and their national IP offices) that it should get a higher proportion (as high as 75 per cent versus the current 50 per cent) of the EPO renewal fees. If it had more renewal fee income, the EPO could reduce its initial fees. This idea has been resisted by member states, especially those with national offices concerned about their own viability in the face of EPO competition.

The foregoing discussion of EPO-U.K. national office relations conveys some of the features of both cooperating and duelling bureaucracies. There is without doubt a good level of cooperation among national and international bodies, but there is also a sense of considerable competition, as well. As harmonization pressures increase and with protection roles 'moving up' to regional IP bodies there is likely to be increased concern about just what the national IP agencies will and should do.

A logical division of labour could be that smaller national bodies would focus on dissemination roles directed at their small and medium-sized enterprises. But it is not clear that one can retain the right kinds of expertise for dissemination activity without retaining the protection role. Moreover, crucial issues arise as to how this arrangement could be financed if fees were gone or seriously reduced. Moreover, national IP professions will likely resist such developments, and, more generally, national governments may support their national offices on nationalistic grounds or because crucial language issues are involved.

A final cautionary point, and inherently a common-sense one, is that with respect to overall structure, there is an obvious need to both appreciate and respect the different dynamics of international bodies, such as WIPO and EPO, compared to national agencies. It is simply a fact of life that because it is nation-states which are the members of the governing bodies of WIPO and the EPO, their decision processes have been and are necessarily different.

Conclusions

Canada's intellectual property policy and institutions have always been influenced by international factors centred in IP treaties and agreements. In the 1990s, however, the extent and nature of external pressures and influences have increased greatly. At their broadest level, these changes emanate from the changed role and importance of bodies such as WIPO and the formation of regional IP bodies such as the EPO.

The chapter has shown, however, that the crucial engine of change has come from the United States, reflecting not only changes in the interest group politics of trade and intellectual property policy but also leadership changes in the USPTO, which have been more copyright-centred. The chapter gives an initial indication of how and why Canada became more of an IP policy-taker than policy-maker, but we need a more complete account of these developments, especially through our focus in chapter 8 on pharmapatents.

Somewhat in between these broad and more concerted causal forces of change have been parallel and reinforcing changes in the nature and structure of IP agencies in key countries. Besides becoming more fee dependent and conscious of comparative pendency efficiency rates and performance, they all have sought to become more service- and dissemination-oriented IP bodies. These developments, in turn, put national offices in a situation of both conflict and cooperation with regional and international bodies in a fast-changing world economy.

PART TWO

Canadian IP Institutions in Action
in a Global Economy

5. CIPO and the Patent and Trademark Regulatory Process

With both the overall institutions and policy issues and the historical and international context set out, we can now proceed to a closer look at Canada's IP institutions and institutional politics in action. We begin with the core regulatory and operational aspects of the patent and trademark regulatory process centred in the role of the Commissioner of Patents and Registrar of Trademarks and of CIPO as an organization. It is within these core institutions that the basic trade-offs occur on a virtual daily basis as applications are made for the protection of intellectual property.

The analysis proceeds in five stages as we look in turn at CIPO as an organization; the Commissioner and Registrar as a statutory person; the basic patent application cycle; the basic trademark application cycle; and CIPO's changing overall view of its clientele.

The Canadian Intellectual Property Office (CIPO)

It is no exaggeration to say that for decades CIPO (and its predecessor bodies) functioned in relative obscurity far away from virtually any political limelight or public attention. Seen by others as a technical operating body and seeing itself in a similar way, CIPO was very much like its corresponding IP regulators in other countries. CIPO is still very much the focal point for the regulation and operational management of Canada's intellectual property system. However, associated now with Industry Canada rather than being a part of the former Department of Consumer and Corporate Affairs, CIPO is also a Special Operating Agency (SOA) and hence has special management powers and financial flexibility designed to make it a better and more service-conscious organization. In this chapter, we are largely, though not exclusively, interested in its role as regulator, which is the way CIPO's main component bodies, the Patent Office and the Trademark Office, still largely see themselves.

In terms of its fundamental values or mission, CIPO's annual reports and business plans stress that it exists to 'accelerate Canada's economic development by encouraging the utilization of the IP system and the exploitation of IP information' (CIPO 1993, i). CIPO statements go on to emphasize that its operations entail the 'establishment of principles, policies, and procedures that enable clients to obtain intellectual property protection' (CIPO 1993, i). In short, CIPO sees its values as being squarely in the middle of the trade-off, the fulcrum, if you like, of the principles and assumptions sketched out more broadly in chapters 1 and 2. It also sees its basic function as being one which 'requires the accumulation of an extensive and diverse information base upon which utility, ingenuity, and originality can be judged' (CIPO 1993, 3). Furthermore, it requires 'assembling and maintaining the expertise to make these judgements, ensuring there is a basis upon which decisions can be made, and disputes resolved, in a fair and equitable manner' (CIPO 1993, 3).

In terms of its interests as an organization, CIPO has at least two characteristics which warrant emphasis. The first is that its mandate deals as well with other realms of intellectual property such as copyright, industrial designs, and integrated circuit topographies. While these are not central to this chapter, they are an important factor in understanding CIPO's interests simply because what CIPO may decide to do or not do on the patent and trademark side of its mandate, in part, depends on policy, resource, and political pressures from its other regulatory mandate areas.

With respect to its interests, a second characteristic of CIPO is simply that it must now – compared to during its earlier history – consider more explicitly its service and IP dissemination roles. Suffice it to say at this point that this also has resource and other implications for its historical regulatory role. In saying this, the intention is not to suggest that CIPO's component bodies did not see themselves at all as being in the service business. Rather, it is to say that the pressures to play an explicit service role are now much greater (see more below).

What must be said about CIPO's overall incentive system, then, is that at the Millennium, it sees itself as a public interest regulator, but one striving to give new emphasis not only to a mixed regulatory and service role but also to an expanded concept of what intellectual property entails.

The Commissioner of Patents and Registrar of Trademarks

It is important in the identification of key players to differentiate CIPO from the role of the Commissioner of Patents and Registrar of Trademarks. The CEO of CIPO, currently Sheila Batchelor, is also the Commissioner and Registrar. In the latter capacity, she is a statutory person, whereas in her role as CEO, which is her Industry Canada administrative title, she is a senior public servant. Her role as a statutory person is important because most of the regulatory powers reside in this legally defined statutory role.

This means that she has an independent role vis-à-vis the Minister and Deputy Minister of Industry Canada. This is to ensure that decisions on patents and trademarks are based on independent objective judgments and not on political considerations. In other respects, however, as CEO of CIPO, she is within the jurisdiction of her Minister and department in the normal way. For example, if legislative policy changes were being considered to the Patent Act, they would be the responsibility of the Minister as advised by his department and by CIPO. The CEO of CIPO is also responsible to her Minister and to the Treasury Board for CIPO's functioning properly within the contractual obligations established for a Special Operating Agency. Under these provisions, for example, CIPO now operates on the basis of a revolving fund, based on its own revenues, which eliminates its dependence on general budgetary appropriations from Parliament.

In functioning as a statutory person, the Commissioner and Registrar is similar in general nature to other regulators of business-framework law, such as the Director of Investigation and Research, who heads the Competition Bureau under the terms of the Competition Act, or the Superintendent of Bankruptcy under the Bankruptcy and Insolvency Act. The Commissioner and Registrar also has powers regarding the regulation and qualifications of patent and trademark agents.

In terms of basic interests and incentive systems, this means that the Commissioner and Registrar has a strong sense of obligation to preserve and defend the independence of the statutory role. But as CEO of CIPO, there is simultaneously a concern for the bundle of values and interests already previously discussed for CIPO, as an *organization*.

However, at the core of CIPO's operating culture are the basic patent and trademark regulatory cycles. It is around and within the application, examination, and approval/rejection processes that CIPO has its core existence. This is also the essential rhythm of business that patent and trademark agents are in. The processes centre on a series of case-driven acts of judgment and bargaining between the regulator (CIPO / the Commissioner / the Registrar / CIPO examiners) and patent and trademark agents representing inventors and originators of intellectual property. In the next two sections, we trace the cycle for patents and then trademarks, in turn, and present some overall data on the case volume that the two CIPO branches handle in the regulatory process.

The Patent Application Cycle

Under the Patent Act, Canadian patents are given to the first inventor to file an application. CIPO's information for potential patent applicants suggests a multi-step sequential process. If an individual inventor calls CIPO's Patent Office, he or she is advised to find a qualified patent agent. If the patent agent is in a larger law firm, the individual first-time inventor/applicant typically meets with a junior articling technically qualified lawyer or a patent agent per se who goes over the invention with the applicant/inventor. A search for prior patents and other publications is then conducted by the lawyer or agent. Since to be patented an invention must demonstrate novelty, utility, and inventive ingenuity, a preliminary search, if it finds a relevant patent, or other disclosure, may simply end the process right then and there. But if the invention is deemed to be new, then the crucial task of the patent agent begins.

The task of preparing a patent application is a process which essentially involves writing a description of the invention and writing claims which 'draw a fence' around the invention in order to define it and so as to distinguish it in a patentable sense from other existing patents and other disclosures. Inevitably, this is a process that involves discussion between the inventor and the patent agent, but it also draws on the agent's own technical knowledge and experience, including patent law and practice requirements.

An application is then formally filed at CIPO's Patent Office, consisting of a written petition, description of the invention and claims, and a fee. At this stage, no patent is guaranteed. At this point, as well, the inventor knows that in eighteen months a notice will be published in CIPO's Patent Office Record disclosing the application, and hence information in it will be available to others. An application is not automatically examined. Examination must be formally requested. If not requested within a five-year period after filing, the application is considered abandoned.

The examination process, once requested, can take two to three years to complete. The application, one of 27,000 filed with CIPO annually (see data below), is classified at filing according to the International Patent Classification system. It then goes to one of CIPO's one hundred patent examiners, who are themselves broadly grouped in scientific/ technical disciplines or according to expertise in mechanical, chemical, or electrical technologies. Their examination of the file involves a search of existing patents and related technologies and information sources, as well as examination of the application for statutory compliance.

There then follows a prosecution stage when something akin to bargaining and negotiation can occur arising out of different professional judgments between the CIPO examiner on behalf of the public interest and patent agent on behalf of the applicant. Some claims in the patent application may have to be redrawn because, in the examiner's view, they define technology which is known to the public and do not meet the tests of novelty, utility, and ingenuity. In effect, these discussions/negotiations are precisely the point at which the boundary is drawn between the inventor's legitimate rights and the public interest; that is, protection is provided in return for sharing the technological information with the public. The patent agent, within limits, tends to press for the maximum protection of the patent fence on behalf of the applicant. The Patent Office examiner must protect the rights of the public but, at the same time, grant the applicant adequate rights in conformity with the law and ensure that new ideas are not unduly hampered.

During this examination phase, the applicant must meet or overcome each objection raised by the examiner. There may also occur at this stage discussions between the patent agent and the inventor about whether it is wise, economical, or prudent to continue. This is also the expensive part of the application process in that the patent agent's fee clock is ticking. Hence, there emerge the often classic debates about whether the costs of the process are too great. Inventors, or at least the small inventor, may at times feel that he or she is being 'strung out' by a procedural conspiracy among lawyers, patent agents, and examiners, all lumped into one category of villain, simply known as the 'system.' Alternatively, patent agents and lawyers see this stage, and the process as a whole, as involving a small cost for the inventor to pay relative to either (a) the future gains to the inventor from a valid patent; or (b) the losses that could be sustained by proceeding with an invention that is not patentable or that results in later infringement suits.

If the patent application is accepted, then the inventor pays a further fee to CIPO. Annual maintenance fees must also be paid both during pendency and after the patent is issued. Ultimate enforcement of patent rights is carried out through private rights enforcement, which involves law suits in the Federal Court of Canada and in provincial courts against persons who infringe patents. CIPO does not have a patent police force, though its examination process is itself a form of scrutiny of the scope of protection granted to individual patents. The full patent cycle also contains a process whereby a granted patent may be re-examined at the request of either the patentee or a third party.

If the patent application is rejected, then a review process is available. The review process is not itself established by statute. Instead, a Patent Appeal Board, made up of senior Patent Office officials, considers the arguments set forth by the patent examiner and the corresponding agent's response, and advises the Commissioner of Patents (see more below). The Commissioner then issues a decision since it is the Commissioner as a statutory person who grants or denies a patent. The Commissioner's negative decision can be appealed to the Federal Court of Canada and ultimately to the Supreme Court of Canada.

The Trademark Application Cycle

A trademark is defined in CIPO publications as 'a word, a symbol, a design, or a combination of these, used to distinguish the wares or services of one person or organization from those of others in the marketplace' (CIPO 1994a, 5). Obtaining a registered trademark, as chapter 1 discussed, and as the above definition implies, is more art than science, and hence even more judgmental than patents. The cycle for trademark applications is simultaneously somewhat simpler (CIPO sets out five steps compared to a patent application's ten) and more subtle. The five-step process, in a general way, follows similar overall processes to those involved with patents.

CIPO, through its Trademarks Office, advises anyone inquiring about registering a trademark to obtain the services of a qualified trademark agent. It must be stressed that trademark rights exist without registration, but most are secured through registration. Then, as with patents, there follows a similar initial process of advice and discussion between the agent and the client/applicant, along with a preliminary search. Of crucial initial importance is that in most instances the trademark must be used in Canada before it can be registered. Thus, by definition, there are many unregistered trademarks used in the market place.

Once an application has been filed along with a $150 fee, the trademark examiners search the trademarks database and other publications to determine if any other registered trademarks come into conflict with the applicant's mark. If there is such conflict, the Trademarks Office immediately advises the applicant. The examination then proceeds through a formal examination/negotiation process as the examiner seeks to ensure compliance with the Trademarks Act and its regulations. All objections from the examiner must be met or overcome. Typically, however, this process is much shorter than for patents, in large part because the judgments needed are less technical.

If all the examiner's objections are met, then a formal publication phase ensues in which CIPO publishes the application in the *Trademarks Journal*, a weekly publication. Publication triggers a potential 'challenge process.' On payment of $250 fee, anyone, within two months of the date of publication, may file a statement of opposition with the Registrar. Challenges are reviewed, in a quite court-like adversarial process, by a Trademarks Opposition Board. This board has delegated authority from the Registrar since it is the latter, as a statutory person, who allows or denies the registration of a trademark. The CIPO documents advise applicants that the whole challenge process 'can take as long as two to four years, sometimes longer' (CIPO 1994a, 14).

Following any challenge process, the Registrar makes his or her final decision, with the parties notified of the final decision and the reasons for it. If there is no opposition or if an opposition is decided in favour of the applicant, the application is then allowed. A Notice of Allowance is sent to the applicant, and, upon payment of a further fee of $200, the trademark is registered. If the application is based on proposed use, a declaration of use is needed before registration. If someone opposing the trademark is unsuccessful in the challenge process, there are avenues of appeal to the Federal Court of Canada.

As is the case with patents, the policing of trademark infringements once a trademark is registered is a private legal matter by way of court injunction and/or damages.

These, then, are the typical application/regulatory cycles for patents and trademarks respectively. To this picture, we need to add more aggregate data and also to comment on what data are typically not published. First, the number of patent applications received in the 1994–5 and 1995–6 fiscal years were 27,883 and 26,629 respectively (CIPO 1996). Patents granted totalled 11,074 and 8,242 for each year. These data are not, however, measures of response time since they contain applications that would have been filed in previous years. For trademark applications received, the figures are 28,567 and 29,528 for the two years respectively, with registrations processed being 15,961 and 14,817 (CIPO 1996). CIPO is working with the IP professions to devise operational and service-delivery indicators and data which are more informative and varied, to match the ways in which such data are invariably interpreted. For example, a faster rate of processing patents may or may not constitute better service since it is the quality of the patent that matters, and this may depend upon an in-depth and longer examination/negotiation process.

Finally, it is also important to re-emphasize from chapter 2 that, of the approximately 27,000 patent applications filed, over 90 per cent are foreign in origin and hence are often more routine patent investigations closer to the post-office end of the activity continuum than the full-service regulatory end displayed above. Only 10 per cent are filed by Canadian firms, which usually then do involve the full-service regulatory cycle. For trademarks, the Canadian versus foreign proportions are the reverse. About 55 per cent originate in Canada and about 45 per cent come from abroad.

There is a further important aspect of the overall patent application process. The above description was for a single national office, but patent processes can also involve those facilitated by the Patent Cooperation Treaty (PCT). Prior to the PCT's coming into force in 1978, the traditional patent system required the filing of individual patent applications for each country for which patent protection was being sought. This was both expensive and time consuming. The PCT does not enable the granting of an international patent since the responsibility for granting patents remains a national responsibility (World Intellectual Property Office 1995d, ch. 20). However, it does establish a system which enables the filing with a patent office (the receiving office) of a single application (the international application) in one language having effect in each of the countries party to the PCT (89 contracting states) which the applicant designates in the application. The receiving office provides a formal examination, and the application is forwarded to one of nine PCT International Search Authorities (ISAs), which conducts an international search and develops a report citing the relevant prior art which should be taken into account in deciding whether the invention is patentable. The report is made available first to the applicant and later it is published. The PCT system also provides for centralized international publication of international applications and the above mentioned reports. It also provides an option for an international preliminary examination.

The application process then shifts to the national phase. The remaining granting procedure is the task of the designated offices, namely, the national offices of, or those acting for, the countries which have been designated in the international application. An international regional authority, such as the European Patent Office, could also act as a single designated office.

The PCT process involves a single set of fees for the preparation and filing of the international application, which are payable in one currency and at one office. National fees are payable later.

CIPO's Changing View of Its Clientele

Both of the above cycles centre on the regulatory role of CIPO and on its IP protection role. However, CIPO has been shifting its focus so as to ensure that it serves a broader clientele with greater emphasis than in the past on IP dissemination. One of the more important indicators of this shift came in the appointment in 1996 of Sheila Batchelor as CEO, Commissioner, and Registrar. A career public servant with varied administrative experience, she is the first person in decades to head CIPO (or its predecessor bodies) who does not have a patent or IP career background. However, the shifting view of CIPO towards its clientele started earlier in the 1990s when her predecessor, Mart Leesti, was in charge.

When CIPO moved to Industry Canada in 1993 from the former Department of Consumer and Corporate Affairs, it was joining a much larger department whose mandate was fixed increasingly on its international competitiveness agenda and on the fact that it would have to carry out this role through its own ability in supplying useful and timely knowledge to business. It would, in short, have to be a service deliverer par excellence. However, at the same time, Industry Canada acquired an entirely new (to it) regulatory and business framework-law role. A key question therefore was how to resolve some of the potential differences of view and habit between being both regulator and service deliverer, particularly because some of the potentially best information it could offer came from its regulatory roles.

CIPO, as we have seen, had already become a Special Operating Agency and thus expected to be more business-like in playing an innovative role itself and in knowing who its clients were. Its clients would be not only those seeking legal protection for their ideas under Canada's intellectual property laws but also other businesses and individuals seeking information and knowledge in the knowledge economy.

However, these demands for a more service-oriented role were not just emerging out of CIPO or Industry Canada mandate imperatives. They were also emerging from government-wide initiatives related to service delivery which we highlighted in chapters 1 and 3. Thus, the important point to stress for CIPO in this context is that the pressure for a new service emphasis, even while it remains primarily a regulator, is coming, in mutually reinforcing ways, from its own international constraints, from the Industry Canada mandate, and from the federal initiatives on service delivery in general.

Thus, CIPO's business plan stresses many of the intertwined and converging developments and ideas examined above. In its discussion of the forces affecting intellectual property, CIPO's views of its new environment first cites the success of the Japanese innovation-centred model of economic development and success, goes on to stress the NAFTA and GATT trade imperatives, and indicates the pressures for harmonization. CIPO states that 'despite fiscal limitations,' government can improve competitiveness 'by granting intellectual property rights and by actively acquiring and disseminating intellectual property information' (CIPO 1994c, 2). CIPO goes on to state that its status as Special Operating Agency exists precisely to help it perform this more active service role. Its SOA 'Charter' from the Treasury Board defines its mandate as the acceleration of Canada's economic development by:

- fostering the utilization of intellectual property systems and the exploitation of intellectual property information;
- encouraging invention, innovation and creativity in Canada;
- administering the intellectual property systems in Canada;
- promoting Canada's international intellectual property interests. (CIPO 1994c, 4)

It is not accidental that words such as 'fostering' and 'encouraging' precede 'administering,' and even that 'administering' is used and not 'regulating.'

The CIPO Business Plan goes on to stress that its SOA status is designed to facilitate an exchange of 'flexibility in return for performance' and that this means, above all, 'the achievement of continuous improvement in the quality and in the delivery of CIPO service' (CIPO 1994c, 9). Accordingly, CIPO has been reorganized to give new emphasis to its clients and to its product lines. Again the language of service rather than regulation is prominent. It is also quite important to reiterate that CIPO is not funded through tax dollars, but rather through client fees, 80 per cent of which are earned from offshore, and most of which are from patents.

Interestingly, the clients of CIPO are seen, in order of listing, as 'current and future creators of intellectual property; the employers of intellectual property – the innovators who capitalize on its economic potential; and agents that facilitate acquisition of intellectual property rights' (CIPO 1994c, 10). Since creators and inventors can come from any part of society, CIPO stresses the need to increase knowledge of intellectual property within Canada's education system. With respect to the second client group, the exploiters of intellectual capital, CIPO indicates that it must do more to identify who they are and what they need. With respect to agents, its 'third client group,' CIPO notes that they are 'by far the most visible client group' and that of paramount importance to them is an intellectual property system administered in a way that 'provides a high presumption of validity – credible and defensible intellectual property rights' (CIPO 1994c, 12).

Conclusions

Any discussion of Canada's IP institutions in action must focus on CIPO and on the role of the Commissioner of Patents and Registrar of Trademarks as a statutory person. CIPO and the statutory regulator have emerged in the 1990s from almost total obscurity as a technical operating agency to an agency now recognized as being very important to Canada's capacity to be both innovative and internationally competitive.

Central to its culture and sense of professionalism are the processes for handling patent and trademark applications, in which the core trade-offs of IP policy are brought to life at a micro case-by-case level. The case process turns on an independent non-political and technical approach to applicants and their claims of innovativeness. At the fulcrum of these assessments are both CIPO's own examiners acting on behalf of the public interest and the IP patent professions acting on behalf of inventors and other business applicants, including small inventors.

The analysis has shown that these core regulatory and IP protection roles are necessarily still dominant, but that CIPO has been actively seeking to broaden its view of its clientele and customers. IP users, small inventors, and small business interests who may not yet even know about their IP rights are a part of this wider clientele. The search for a broader IP dissemination role and for a better service ethos, in general, is being propelled by several external and internal sources, ranging from trade and globalization pressures and Industry Canada's knowledge-based mandate, to government-wide service-delivery imperatives influenced strongly by the ethos of reinvented government and changes in CIPO's own leadership. CIPO is thus seeking to be an innovating institution by itself, reaching out to its full constituency on the dissemination side of the IP trade-off, but the larger forces in its environment are seeking more and more protection.

The portrait of CIPO presented here must nonetheless be considered only a preliminary one. It has focused on the regulatory and protection role. It is only after the analysis of both IP interests and functions in chapters 7 and 9 that we will be able to offer a more complete overall view of CIPO as the core IP regulator in Canada. It must also be reiterated that CIPO has the largest core of IP expertise in the federal government, but that it is not ultimately the main IP policy-maker. As we have seen in chapters 3 and 4, it is Industry Canada and DFAIT that have the crucial policy-making power, with both departments and their ministers influenced more and more by trade imperatives, the IP protection focus, and the innovation policy paradigm.

6. Copyright Institutions and Processes

We now turn to Canadian copyright institutions and processes, an arena of IP that is different in many respects from patents and trademarks, first because it does not have a registration process to ensure protection and second because its core institutions are more pluralistic and dispersed both within the state and among its interest groups and policy communities. As we saw briefly in chapter 1, within the federal government, jurisdiction is shared among the Department of Canadian Heritage, Industry Canada, and Foreign Affairs and International Trade Canada, the latter because of the growing trade policy aspects of copyright and IP. But an array of other smaller but crucial institutions are a part of the copyright policy and regulatory system, including the Copyright Board of Canada and collective associations and other institutions of authors and performers, which are part of a complex quasi–self-regulating regime. The assertion that the structure of copyright interests – producer and user interests – is more dispersed than for patents will be more evident as the analysis proceeds, but, for the moment, this statement simply means that there is no business power in the copyright realm to rival the concentrated influence that the pharmaceutical industry has in the patent realm.

The chapter proceeds in four stages. First, a broad view of the nature of copyright policy and institutions is presented drawn from the larger international experience. Second, a brief history of Canadian copyright policy and law is presented in the context of a discussion of the main federal institutions, and in the initial context of the period from the 1970s until the mid-1980s when it was difficult to get market-place framework law, including copyright law, changed at all. The third section then examines the key provisions of the recently passed Bill

C-32, the Canadian Copyright Act. This is followed in the fourth section by a closer look at the core positions of creator versus user interests and groups.

The General Nature of Copyright Regimes

Copyright regimes have a long history in international and domestic laws and practices, but at their core is the desire to protect the rights of those who create artistic works, be they in the form of books, paintings, poems, sound recordings, films, or other media of communication. What is protected by copyright law and institutions is 'creativity in the choice and arrangement of words, musical notes, colours, shapes and so on,' and the protection is against those who copy such creations (WIPO 1995d, 159). Such protection, however, has some limits. Copyright begins with the creation of the work and typically extends for the life of the author and fifty years after the death of the author (Harris 1995). Of increasing importance in copyright regimes is the protection of rights which are related to or 'neighbouring on' copyright. Such neighbouring rights are typically of three kinds: the rights of performing artists in their performances; the rights of broadcasting organizations in their radio and television programs; and the rights of producers of sound recordings in their sound recordings.

Of crucial importance is the principle that copyright does not protect the ideas that underlie such creations but only the mode of expressing such ideas. The protection aspects of copyright regimes are also influenced by ideas that original authors of works have 'moral rights' as well as economic or property rights. Both rights typically exist in law. However, international global regimes are still influenced by differences in this view. For example, France has been a strong supporter of giving regimes an emphasis on moral rights, whereas countries such as the United States, Canada, and the United Kingdom stress economic rights. Within Canada, similar differences of emphasis have occurred between Quebec creators and the federal government.

The dissemination part of the copyright IP trade-off is that, in the first instance, by providing such protection, creativity will be stimulated and the results will be disseminated widely. This aspect of dissemination clearly has a private-market aspect, but the creativity may be disseminated in other ways, as well. Artistic works are also firmly a part of a country's or people's cultural heritage, and hence dissemination is linked to cultural policy in an overt way. Such norms extend in many countries to the need to protect and disseminate traditional folklore.

Unlike patents and trademarks, there is in most countries no registration process for copyright. Originality must be present, but there is no process for passing 'a test of imaginativeness, of inventiveness' or other sense of quality (WIPO 1995d, 161). Most national copyright laws protect the following works: literary, musical, photographic, and artistic works, maps and technical drawings, motion pictures, and computer programs.

One of the interesting features about copyright regimes, in particular, is that historically there was an international regime before there were very many national regimes. Most international regimes follow on national laws, but in the case of copyright, the reverse has been true. The Rome Convention of 1961 was the centrepiece of this effort at regime building. For example, neighbouring rights were a part of the Rome Convention but only came much later, as we see below, in Canada.

If the rights of a copyright owner are infringed through the unauthorized copying of materials for commercial purposes, such activity is referred to as piracy. Such piracy has always been a part of commerce, but its extent and nature has changed greatly in recent years because of the telecommunications revolution. For example, Philips Electronics has announced that a new CD recorder will go on the market which allows people to record their compact discs as easily as they can cassette tapes (*The Independent*, 26 June 1997, p. 3). The immediate reaction of the phonographic industry is that this development would greatly increase piracy and result in lost revenues and profits for the copyright holders.

The remedies for those whose rights have been infringed are typically based on civil redress. Injunctions are sought through the courts to restrain the continuation of the infringement, and damages are sought. Debate about the efficacy of such compliance and enforcement aspects of copyright regimes has centred not only on international piracy but also on the speed of national remedies and the need for preliminary remedies before it is commercially too late for the copyright holder.

As mentioned above, a further crucial feature of copyright regimes is that they require an elaborate system of self-regulation and collective administration by creators. Workable institutions are needed to enable authors and creators to collect and distribute authors' fees. Authors and creators are typically small and numerous and face users who tend to be larger and more powerful. Moreover, the sites or venues in which creations might be sold or performed can be numerous. A composer, for example, would find it literally impossible to know how often his or her country's hundreds of radio or television stations may have used his or her work. Thus collective administrative organizations are crucial both for authors and publishers and broadcasters (WIPO 1995d, ch. 30; Smith 1988). But other state-run institutions must serve linkage functions in the setting and implementation of fees and royalties. The more complex these become, the more important an entity like the Canadian Copyright Board becomes, as we see further below.

The Canadian Copyright Regime in Recent Historical Context

Like other aspects of IP, copyright regimes are indeed complex, but recent Canadian debates about law and implementation must be set against recent Canadian copyright policy history (Smith 1988; Keyes and Brunet 1977). The current Canadian Copyright Act dates back to 1924 and remained virtually unchanged until 1988, when the first phase of copyright reform culminated in the Copyright Amendment Act (Canada 1960; Economic Council of Canada 1971). The Copyright Act had long been seen to be too antiquated to cope with the technological innovations that were systematically changing the ways in which copyright material could be 'created, disseminated and utilized by the public,' as well as 'the ability of copyright owners to exercise effective control over the use of their material and to get a fair return on their investment' (Hébert 1996, 1).

Copyright reform was given an initial impetus in the late 1950s with the Ilsely Commission's report (Canada 1960), which was followed by a number of studies over the years (Smith 1988). But it was not until the mid-1980s, with the election of the Mulroney government, that any legislative action was taken. As mentioned previously in chapter 2, part of the political problem during the period from the late 1960s until the mid-1980s was that the federal government had difficulty reforming virtually any of its business-framework laws (Doern 1987). Efforts to amend competition, bankruptcy, and intellectual property laws were made on several occasions, but reforms were usually deflected from the top of both Cabinet and Parliamentary agendas. These were not seen as areas in which successive ministers could make their political careers, in part, because they were very technical and, in part, because attention was focused on other aspects of industrial policy, and for performers and authors, on other aspects of cultural policy.

It was the 1984 White Paper on copyright reform, *From Gutenberg to Telidon*, tabled by the Trudeau government and then retabled as a discussion paper by the Mulroney government in January 1985, that created another moment of political attention. The government then referred it to the Sub-Committee on the Revision of Copyright (of the House of Commons Standing Committee on Communications and Culture), which issued its report, *A Charter of Rights for Creators*, in October 1985. Several recommendations in the report were accepted as official government policy in February 1986. The government decided that the needed changes would be made in two separate phases: Bill C-60 comprised the 'first phase' of the planned revisions; 'phase two' would handle those remaining (Hébert 1996, 14).

Bill C-60 was passed in 1988 and was proclaimed into force by 1 February 1989. Characterized as a 'pro-creator' initiative by its sponsoring Minister of Communications, the Honourable Flora MacDonald, the new law, among several changes, provided explicit statutory protection for computer programs; broadened the definition of 'choreographic works' and recognized them as a distinct category of eligible subject matter; expanded and strengthened the moral rights of creators; and abolished the controversial compulsory licence for sound recordings. The law also provided the statutory foundation for the collective exercise of copyright by licensing bodies and set up a distinct regulatory regime that would apply to them. It also restructured the then existing Copyright Appeal Board, as the Copyright Board of Canada. The compliance regime was also improved through increased penalties for infringement (Hébert 1996, 17–18).

The phase two amendments were promised for the year 1988, but were only to emerge almost a decade later with Bill C-32 (see below). Nevertheless, between 1988 and 1996, five other bills amended the Copyright Act, largely because of the impetus of successive trade agreements. The Canada-U.S. Free Trade Agreement Implementation Act of 1988 provided for an amendment that responded to U.S. opposition to the fact that Canadian cable operators were capturing American broadcast signals and channelling them to their subscribers without paying any compensation. The amendment 'created a re-transmission right by replacing the narrower "radio communication right" with a more comprehensive "telecommunication right" (section 3(1) (f)) that would cover all modes of telecommunication' (Hébert 1996, 20–1).

Two other amendments in 1993 were more technical and of a housekeeping nature, but then, that same year, the North American Free

Trade Agreement Implementation Act was also passed. It contained a significant number of largely trade-mandated changes to the Copyright Act. These included the creation of a commercial 'rental right' for computer programs and sound recordings. Other changes largely fulfilled 'the general obligation under Article 1701 that each Party "provide in its territory to the nationals of another Party adequate and effective protection and enforcement of intellectual property rights, while ensuring that measures to enforce intellectual property rights do not themselves become barriers to legitimate trade." In meeting this obligation, each Party was required, among other things, to give effect to the substantive provisions of the Paris Text of the Berne Convention' (Hébert 1996, 23).

Although Canada has not formally adhered to the Paris Text of the Berne Convention, it made several changes in its copyright legislation, including the following: a redefinition of what constitutes a 'publication' of a work for the purposes of the Act; revising the nationality criteria for copyright protection in Canada; prescribing copyright terms for works that previously lacked a specific term; and narrowing the scope of the 'gramophone' exemption (section 69), which would apply only to public performances in terms of 'radio receiving sets.'

Further trade-related changes occurred through the World Trade Agreement Implementation Act in 1994, which gave effect to commitments under the TRIPs agreement (Hébert 1996, 26). In particular, the changes sought to provide limited protection to performers against unauthorized broadcasts and sound recordings of their live performances. However, several exceptions were also introduced, such as making an unauthorized audiotape of the performance 'if the act constituted a "fair dealing" with the work for the purposes of private study, research, criticism, review or newspaper summary'; or making 'a temporary audiotape' of a public lecture if the audiotape was 'for the purposes of publishing a report of the lecture in a newspaper, unless the making of such a report was expressly prohibited at the place where the lecture was given' (section 28.02). As well, new sections were added that outline the course of action in cases of infringement (section 34 [1.01] et seq.) (Hébert 1996, 26–7).

Perhaps the most important institutional feature of this brief history is that for much of it there was very limited political will, compared to other governmental priorities, to advance the copyright file until it became increasingly a trade-related and trade-driven issue. Until 1993 the key departments involved were the Department of Communications (DOC) and the Department of Consumer and Corporate Affairs, but in neither location could sustained momentum be mounted. DOC did see itself as a cultural policy department, but its central political impulse was in other areas, including telecommunications and the cable and broadcasting industry. Consumer and Corporate Affairs was the government's main business and market-place framework-law department, but it was a politically less influential agency in the broader cabinet pecking order compared to other economic departments.

In 1993, as previous chapters have shown, the business framework areas, including aspects of copyright, went from the defunct consumer department to a much larger Industry Canada. The Department of Canadian Heritage 'replaced' the former DOC but, significantly, lost some of its telecommunications roles to Industry Canada. This may have had the effect of requiring the Heritage Minister to search for her remaining areas of influence in the cultural sector. This included now more prominently the creators of copyrighted property. While these internal changes affected the still twinned responsibilities for copyright matters, it was the trade agenda (and therefore also DFAIT) that was the larger engine of both change and sustainable political leverage.

Bill C-32: Key Provisions

Bill C-32, introduced in the House of Commons on 25 April 1996, was, in essence, the long-gestating 'second phase' of the copyright reform process. But even it would not begin to deal with the challenges of the Internet and related fast-changing technologies. As the Acting Minister of Canadian Heritage, Lucienne Robillard, noted when introducing the bill 'at the repeated request of Canada's cultural sector, we had to adapt the legislation to the realities of the marketplace and the major international conventions in effect, while responding to the most urgent concerns of the cultural sector' (Hansard, 4 June 1996, p.18). The Minister of Canadian Heritage, Sheila Copps, indicated that not only is copyright reform 'critical to maintaining Canadian identity and Canadian sovereignty at a time when globalization and the information revolution are erasing national borders,' but also with the cultural industry injecting $16 billion into the economy annually, the protection of this industry is key to encouraging job creation (quoted in Canadian Association of Broadcasters – Television Board 1996, 7–8).

Among the changes proposed, six were pivotal or contentious: (1) a levy on blank audio-recording media; (2) exemptions for non-profit educational institutions, libraries, archives, museums, and people with perceptual disabilities; (3) protection for exclusive book distributors; (4) statutory damages and wide injunction; (5) revisions to collectives regimes; and (6) the enactment of neighbouring rights. Also important for some writers was the elimination of perpetual protection for unpublished works. In addition, the law requires the Minister of Industry to undertake a study of the provisions and operation of the Act within five years of the bill's proclamation, and to refer the findings to committee. The committee would then undertake a similar study and report its findings to the House of Commons or both Houses of Parliament one year after the Minister tabled the report in Parliament.

Bill C-32 allowed sound recordings to be copied for private use in exchange for a levy imposed on the blank audio-recording material, such as blank audio cassettes (section 80 [1]). This provision is intended for the benefit of the rights owners of the works, performances, or sound recordings. The Copyright Board would set the levy (section 83), which would be imposed on the manufacturers and importers of the blank audio-recording media. The levy would be payable to the 'collecting body' created for this purpose, which would distribute the funds to the eligible authors, performers of musical works, and makers of sound recordings (section 84). In addition, the Minister of Industry has the authority to designate reciprocating countries for 'the purpose of entitling their nationals to a share of the levy imposed' (section 85) (Hébert 1997, 51).

Bill C-32 creates special defined exemptions for non-profit educational institutions, libraries, archives, museums, and people with perceptual disabilities. Generally, the bill allows educational institutions to reproduce, perform, or communicate by telecommunication 'works' or 'other subject-matter' (i.e., neighbouring rights works) for educational purposes under specified conditions. Libraries, archives, and museums can provide a patron with a copy of a published or unpublished work or other subject-matter under specified circumstances, or make a copy for the institution's collection under specified circumstances. The bill also allows the production of alternative-format materials for people with perceptual disabilities.

The bill protects exclusive book distributors in Canada by enabling them to block the entry of 'parallel book imports' into the country. New section 27.1 would implement new import restrictions on books, but only those books for which there was an exclusive distributor in Canada. This new section would make it an infringement of copyright for any person to import a book into Canada when copies of the book made in another country with the copyright owner's consent were imported into Canada without the consent of the Canadian copyright owner; and when the person knew or ought to have known that, if made in Canada by the importer, the book would have infringed copyright (section 27.1[1]). It would also be an infringement for anyone to deal with such copies in order to sell or rent them out (section 27.1[2]).

Used books, except textbooks for use within an educational institution, are exempted. In addition, individuals can import two copies of a book for personal use; federal and provincial government departments may import an unrestricted number of copies for their use; and libraries, archives, museums, and educational institutions may import a single copy for their use (new section 45).

Bill C-32 provides for a strengthened compliance regime, namely, through new 'statutory damages' which guarantee a minimum award of $200 (or maximum of $20,000) in case of infringement. The bill also enables the court to prevent the defendant from infringing the copyright in any other 'work' or 'other subject-matter' 'if the plaintiff was the copyright owner or had an interest in the copyright by licence and if the plaintiff satisfied the court that the defendant was likely to infringe the copyright in those other works or subject-matter, even works or other subject-matter that the plaintiff did not own the copyright or have an interest in by licence at the time the proceedings commenced, or to works or other subject-matter that did not exist at that time' (Hébert 1997, 40).

With regard to the self-regulatory aspects of the regime, the bill provided for three types of collectives currently regulated under the Act. The three types of collectives will now be called 'collective societies.' The term 'collective body' will refer to that entity which is established to collect the levy imposed on 'blank audio recording media.' The three regimes governing the collective societies are subject to several provisions. The first is that the Governor in Council is empowered to provide policy directions to the Copyright Board (clause 44; section 66.91). The second is that the Performing Rights Collectives (sections 67 and 68 of the Act) are broadened to include performances of performers and sound recordings (clause 45). In addition, various regulatory measures are imposed, such as the requirement to answer public requests for information about repertoires that the collective administered or those that are in current use. A third provision regarding collectives is that the statutory criteria for the approval of proposed tariffs (by the Copyright

Board) for musical performances and sound recordings are set out (section 68). In particular, 'wireless transmission systems' must pay an annual $100 royalty fee on the first $1.25 million of annual advertising revenues and pay incrementally for advertising revenues in excess of the $1.25 million threshold. 'Community systems' must pay a flat annual royalty fee of $100, and 'public transmission systems' are subject to an incremental rate (section 68.1).

Furthermore, the regulations governing collective societies for those other than the performing rights are laid out. These collectives have the option of filing a proposed tariff through the Copyright Board or entering into an agreement with the users for any acts or rights mentioned in current section 3 of the Act with respect to works; under new section 15 with respect to performers' performances; under new section 18 with respect to sound recordings; and under new section 21 with respect to communication signals (clause 46 of the bill; sections 70.1 to 70.2). The regime applicable to this type of collective would be similar to the regime for the performing rights collectives (i.e., SOCAN) (clause 46 of the bill; sections 70.1 to 70.191).

And finally new regulations governing collectives for specified compulsory licences are laid out. These collectives are empowered to issue licences that authorize the following acts, subject to prescribed royalties and other conditions: the reproduction and public performance of a news program, news commentary, or other program by an educational institution for educational purposes; and the re-transmission of distant signals (clause 46 of the bill; section 71). These collectives would be required to file a proposed tariff with the Copyright Board. The regime applicable to this type of collective would be similar to the regime for the performing rights collectives (i.e., SOCAN) (clause 46 of the bill; sections 70.1 to 70.191).

As mentioned in the brief historical section above, neighbouring rights were not recognized in earlier reform stages. Bill C-32 provides 'protection afforded to performances and sound recordings, notably by granting eligible recording artists and the makers of sound recordings the right to be paid royalties for the public performance and broadcasts of their works.' Prior to Bill C-32, only music composers and lyricists were entitled to payment when their music was played in public or broadcast (Hébert 1997, 6). By thus enacting neighbouring rights, Canada is able to adhere to the 1961 International Convention for the Protection of Performers, Producers of Phonograms and Broadcasting Organizations (the Rome Convention), adherence to which is mandated under section 91 of the Act. Prior to Bill C-32, Canada was a party to two copyright conventions only – the 1886 Convention for the Protection of Literary and Artistic Works (the Berne Convention) and the 1952 Universal Copyright Convention (the UCC) – neither of which is considered to apply to neighbouring rights.

Issues and Interests: Creator versus User Interests and Emerging Copyright Institutions

While this chapter does not provide an account of the actual dynamics of amending Bill C-32, it is clear that the views of creator versus user groups were in conflict and that the lobbying on ministers and on the Standing Committee on Heritage was intense. We need to profile these interests but also show how newer copyright institutions, such as collective bodies and the Copyright Board, strengthened by phase one of copyright reform, were now emerging as more prominent parts of the regime.

It is important to note from the outset that views varied as to what user versus creator groups thought the broad purpose of phase two of copyright reform was all about. For example, one assessment written from the point of view of an education user interest, the Canadian Association of University Teachers (CAUT), argued that 'since phase one of the bill had clearly favoured the interests of the creators of works subject to copyright, phase two was promised to facilitate a balance between the interests of creators and the needs of users' (Westaway 1997, 1). The implication of this view was that balance in phase two meant a tilt towards user interests. The CAUT writer saw the final bill as amended as a decisive victory for creator interests since the copyright law had been 'ambushed' by what was seen as the pro-creator biases of the Heritage Committee of the House of Commons.

However, the initial bill had been especially criticized by the creator interests. They saw the exemptions for educational institutions, libraries, archives, and museums as being too broad. Some groups argued that there should be no exemptions or, where there were exemptions, that they should not apply if it was possible to obtain authorization from a collective (Hébert 1997). Performers and record producers were critical of the proposed neighbouring rights, which they argued should grant them exclusive public performance and telecommunication rights in relation to their performances and sound recordings, rather than simply the 'right to equitable remuneration' for such uses. Moreover, performers were disappointed because the right to equitable remuneration would extend only to performances in terms of sound recordings, and not audio-visual media.

Broadcasters objected because the proposed telecommunication right, with respect to their communication signals, would apply only to re-broadcast by communication signals and not to other methods of re-transmission, such as cable and direct-to-home services. Furthermore, the proposed levy for private copying of sound recordings was criticized by the creator groups on the basis that it would apply to audio-recording media only and not to audio-visual recording media and recording equipment.

The book publishing industry was satisfied with the restrictions on the parallel importation of books, apart from the proposed used books exemption. Other creator groups – computer program, sound recording, and film creator groups – recommended that the parallel importation restrictions be extended to other works.

Creator groups generally supported the proposed new civil remedies of wide injunction and statutory damages, but some groups felt that the proposed maximum statutory damages award of $20,000 was too low. In addition, there was concern about the proposed statutory criteria that the Copyright Board would have to apply in setting various royalty rates. Performers and record producers were critical of the proposed exemption that would allow broadcasters to pay only $100, and not the full tariff, on their first $1.25 million of advertising revenues for the broadcasting of sound recordings and the performances of performers. They were also concerned that the tariff that would apply to advertising revenues over this threshold would be phased in.

As mentioned above, the pro-users lobby was in some respects led by educational institutions defined broadly. Thus, in general, such institutions, as well as libraries, archives, and museums, were satisfied with the bill, particularly with the exemptions. But they strongly questioned the proposed inclusion of educational institutions in the statutory damages provision. The proposed exemptions for persons with perceptual disabilities were also controversial in that user groups criticized the exclusion of persons with a hearing disability from the exemptions. User groups were also concerned that the royalties for making multiple copies for the perceptually disabled would be fixed in a tariff approved by the Board. Non-profit institutions, such as the Canadian National Institute for the Blind, would then have to make costly and time-consuming representations to the Board with respect to the tariff that should be approved.

User groups also criticized the proposed levy on blank audiotapes. Some argued that the imposition of a levy at the manufacturing/impor- tation level would lead to a 'grey market' in audiotapes, as in the European Union. Other groups contended that the levy should be applied at the retail level in order to keep costs down. Others argued that the levy was too broad and should exempt those engaged in such copying activity for legitimate purposes.

The proposed right of performers and record producers to be paid 'equitable remuneration' for the public performance/broadcast of their performances/sound recordings was also a point of controversy. Radio broadcasters condemned this measure, emphasizing the financial plight of their industry and the inability of many radio broadcasters to pay additional royalties for the broadcast of music. One of the members of Parliament who opposed key parts of the bill was a former radio station owner.

Both radio and television broadcasters were also concerned with the absence of 'time-shift' and 'transfer of format' exemptions. They ar- gued that without such exemptions broadcasters would be vulnerable to any and all kinds of infringement proceedings, particularly with the introduction in Bill C-32 of statutory damages.

One hundred and twenty-three amendments were made to Bill C-32 in committee, and fifteen at the reporting stage. Overall, creators did have a better-mobilized lobby. For example, well-known Canadian nov- elist Margaret Atwood appeared before the Heritage Committee and opposed exemptions for educational institutions. She spoke on behalf of the Writers' Union of Canada and the League of Canadian Poets and took up the case of poorer Canadian writers who survive on average incomes of $15,000 a year. She argued that 'writers should not be asked to subsidize libraries and schools' (*Ottawa Citizen*, 22 Nov. 1996, p. A6). When the final bill was pushed through just prior to the 1997 federal election, spokespersons for such groups as the Canadian Recording Industry Association and the Canadian Publishers Association were quick to praise the Minister of Heritage, Sheila Copps, for her tenacity in defending the interests of creator groups (*Globe and Mail*, 26 April 1997, p. C9).

The educational institutions, libraries, archives, and museums suf- fered the most from the amendments. For instance, wording changes

effectively removed exemptions from selected uses of protected material by educational institutions for 'distance education.' Educational
exemptions conditional on the commercial non-availability of the work
would now be subject to 'the further condition that authorization to use
the work must not be obtainable from a collective society.' In addition,
these institutions would now be required to obtain a reprographic
licence from a collective in order to shield them from liability for the
photocopying carried out by their patrons. Selected exemptions for
these institutions would also be subject to the overriding condition that
the exempted activities not be conducted for profit (Hébert 1997, 58).

With respect to broadcasters, their request for full exemption from
the payment of royalties under the proposed right of 'equitable remuneration' for performers/record producers was denied. They would
also be required to pay the applicable royalties sooner than envisaged –
the five-year phase-in period was reduced to a three-year period.
Also the statutory criteria that the Copyright Board would have had applied in fixing royalty rates, and which were considered favourable to
broadcasters, were eliminated from the bill. But broadcasters were
granted a 'transfer of format' exemption and an 'ephemeral recording'
exemption.

There were some amendments made that did satisfy users groups.
For instance, amendments were made to enable archives to supply
copies of archival material under specified circumstances. Exemptions
for those with perceptual disabilities were extended to include persons
with a hearing impairment. The initial proposed period of copyright
protection for unpublished works was shortened, while the current
fifty-year term of copyright protection for photographs was extended.
And the revised non-derogation clause (new section 90), which makes
clear that the advent of neighbouring rights for sound recordings /
performers' performances should not affect the amount of royalties
paid to the copyright owners of traditional 'works,' satisfied music
composers, lyricists, and other creators.

As mentioned above, attention must be drawn to the role of other
emerging institutions in the Canadian copyright regime which were
also interests in the Bill C-32 process. For example, among the pro-
creator groups to whom CAUT and others attributed great influence
was the Canadian Copyright Licensing Agency (CANCOPY). It warrants special mention in this chapter as well because it is a primary
example of the role of a collective society, as defined under Bill C-32
(CANCOPY 1996, 5). It was established in 1988 by Canadian creators

and publishers as a non-profit organization to license photocopying. Its membership comprises '30 national and provincial organizations representing writers, artists and publishers and affiliates.' The Union des Ecrivaines et Ecrivains Québécois (UNEQ) is the sister organization of CANCOPY. These organizations have 'a reciprocal agreement under which each includes in its repertoire the works in the repertoire of the other and so offers its licensees across Canada a comprehensive English and French langauge repertoire of Canadian works.' CANCOPY is also a member of the International Federation of Reproduction Rights Organizations (IFRRO), and 'through reciprocal agreements with similar licensing bodies or copyright collectives in other countries, CANCOPY has an international repertoire of over two million works' (CANCOPY 1996, 5).

CANCOPY generally supported Bill C-32, and the way that the bill acknowledged collective societies as the 'agents of choice for copyright owners' (CANCOPY 1996, 2). But it then lobbied hard to get the further amendments through that minimized the exceptions sought by the education lobby. For some, CANCOPY was cast as the licensing 'monopoly,' a term meant to convey its considerable influence (Westaway 1997, 1).

Another collective society is the Society of Composers, Authors, and Music Publishers of Canada (SOCAN). It is currently the only performing rights society in Canada. It was formed in 1990 with the merger of two former performing rights societies: the Composers, Authors, and Publishers Association of Canada (CAPAC) and the Performing Rights Organization of Canada (PROCAN) (SOCAN 1996, 2). SOCAN is a non-profit organization that is responsible for the collective administration of the performing rights of 'composers, lyricists, songwriters and publishers of musical works from Canada and around the world' (SOCAN 1996, 1). SOCAN licenses its members' music and collects and distributes performing royalties in accordance with tariff rates set by the Copyright Board; it represents music creators abroad with respect to their performing rights; and it promotes the performance of Canadian musical works in Canada and abroad (SOCAN 1996, 6).

And, finally, we need to take special note of the Canadian Copyright Board and how its mandate and role are affected by the legislation passed in 1997. The Copyright Board was established in 1989 under Bill C-60 as the successor to the Copyright Appeal Board, itself created in 1936. The Copyright Appeal Board functioned as an administrative body regulating the rates that collectives could charge for the use of the works included in their repertoires. While the new Copyright Board assumed this role, its mandate was expanded to comprise five key areas of jurisdiction, as outlined in the Copyright Act. They are the following: establishment of tariffs for the re-transmission of distant television and radio signals; establishment of tariffs for the public performance of music; adjudication of rate disputes between licensing bodies representing classes of copyright owners and users of their works; ruling on applications for non-exclusive licences to use published works of unlocatable copyright owners; and setting compensation, under certain circumstances, for formerly unprotected acts in countries that later join the Berne Convention, the Universal Convention, or the agreement establishing the World Trade Organization (Copyright Board 1996a, 5).

As a regulator, the Board is tiny, consisting of 'not more than five members, including a Chairman and a Vice-Chairman who is the Chief Executive Officer, appointed by the Governor in Council, for a maximum term of five years, renewable once only.' The Board has a staff of only six employees, among them the General Counsel, the Secretary, and the Researcher-Analyst (Copyright Board 1996b, 1). The royalties payable under the tariffs certified by the Copyright Board presently total about $135 million annually.

Under Bill C-32, the mandate of the Copyright Board has been broadened and augmented. Thus it now establishes tariffs with respect to neighbouring rights and takes on other specific responsibilities inherent in the summary of changes examined above. For example, with respect to educational institutions, the Board is empowered to adopt regulations prescribing the information to be kept in relation to the making, destruction, performance, and marking of copies, as well as the information to be sent to the collective societies involved. Partly because of fast changing events, the legislation also provided for the Governor in Council to issue policy directives to the Copyright Board with respect to the rights conferred by law (Copyright Board 1996b, 3–4; Hébert 1997, 44–55).

As the user and creator interests battled over Bill C-32, they knew full well that all of phase two was just a catch-up exercise. New disputes were already under way, many of them centred on the Internet and the protection-versus-dissemination issues that were almost endemic to the new medium. Space does not allow an examination of these here. Suffice it to say, that these debates about the copyright regime will broaden the set of interests and will be, indeed already are, an international and national debate and lobbying process.

Conclusions

Unlike in the patent process, the creator of copyrighted works does not have to formally register to have his or her creations approved. A copyright exists from the moment a work is created and is endowed, moreover, with a tradition of both moral and economic rights. The Canadian copyright regime follows the broad contours of world copyright regimes in this regard, and also involves a structure of institutions and interests that is by definition more pluralistic and dispersed. The patent and trademark realms have to deal with complex interests, but copyright has no dominant power centre to equal that supplied by an interest such as the pharmaceutical industry in the patent field.

The analysis makes clear that on both the creator and user sides of the copyright interest-group equation, there are diverse sets of interests. Creator interests are centred around collective associations of authors, performers, and musicians who need the state to help enforce their rights and collect and disburse royalties. User groups also exhibit great diversity, and range from broadcasters to universities and local community libraries.

The evolution of copyright policy shows a history in which, for a very long period, it was difficult to get copyright law changed. The situation altered in the mid-1980s, and then was energized by the emergence of trade policy players and interests in the copyright and IP policy process. Copyright also enjoyed an ascendancy because, for the Department of Canadian Heritage Canada, it was possible to cast it as a cultural policy which – unlike many cultural policies, which were seen as antithetical to market liberalism – could be presented as being entirely in keeping with pro-market framework rules. Cultural policymakers could no longer as easily protect Canadian culture using subsidies, and thus they turned, propelled again by international pressures, to the IP realm as the next available policy tool. As we have seen above, there were intensive disputes between creator and user interests, but, as the new Millennium begins, there is little doubt that creator interests are in the ascendancy in the copyright realm of IP.

7. IP Protection and Key Established Interests

Having examined the basic features of the patent, trademark, and copyright institutions and regulatory processes in chapters 5 and 6, we can now look more closely at the IP protection function as a whole. For such a closer look to be meaningful, it must include an analysis of the key established interests that support and give primary emphasis to the protection function in the core IP trade-off. These interests were given an introductory sketch in chapter 1, but we must probe further into the general nature of these interests. Chapter 8 will take this one step further by looking at the pharmaceutical industry as a special core interest within the larger cluster of interests.

The chapter is organized into five sections. First, we examine the nature of the protection function. Thereafter our focus is on key interests, with separate sections on big business and key industrial sectors the IP professions, trade departments and the protection role, and the special case of copyright protection interests. Conclusions follow.

The Centrality of the Protection Function

The protection role is central to the existence of the Canadian intellectual property institutions being examined. They exist to establish rights to intellectual property. In this section, we examine the protection role in patents through the prism of the following three issues or processes: (1) the quality and efficiency of pendency performance or of the central processes of granting patents and registering trademarks, particularly the patent examination process; (2) issues and debates regarding the length and quality of patent protection and IP protection, in general; (3) international enforcement and compliance issues, in which, though patents are important, our focus will be on copyright.

In terms of understanding essential institutional features of the protection role, there are several reasons for selecting the above three issues. The first issue centres on pendency rates or on the basic processes of examination and approval. Thus, in this case, we are assuming an *existing* set of laws and practices and how CIPO processes its 'case load,' so to speak, within these laws. This is an efficiency (time and cost) issue, but it also involves crucial aspects of the quality of regulation (time and technical validity and capacity) since the patent must have integrity and validity. These core processing aspects are also bound up in the agency's financial 'essence,' since it is on both initial and renewal fees for patents and trademarks that CIPO is totally dependent.

With respect to the second issue, discussion shifts to the length and quality of the protection afforded. This means that we must look at pressures to change the legal basis of the length of protection (the situation in recent years), but there are also various other aspects to this issue (Trebilcock and Howse 1995, ch. 10). For example, in some jurisdictions, but not to date in Canada, the issue of shorter-term and less rigorous utility models or petty patents has arisen. Differences also arise between developing and developed countries over the length and nature of protection (Rapp and Rozak 1990), and there can be sectoral differences within industry.

The third issue concerns enforcement and compliance. Once an intellectual property right has been acquired, the key longer-term question is whether it is enforced. We cannot fully examine this feature in this chapter in that it takes us into the role of the courts and into realms such as border measures and customs administration. However, we do need to examine enforcement in the sense that national and international IP institutions have been influenced greatly by concerns about whether nations have viable commitments to, and mechanisms for, enforcement. This has affected patents and trademarks, but it has been especially crucial in the copyright field, the IP area where there is, in most countries, no registration process. In the United States, registration is not required for a copyright to exist, but it is a prerequisite to a suit for infringement of U.S. works. Accordingly, it is enforcement and related dispute-settlement concerns that have primarily transformed relations between IP and trade institutions through the new WTO.

Pendency, Efficiency, and CIPO Revenues
CIPO, along with other national IP offices, has paid increasing attention to lowering or improving its pendency rate and to making it the central operational performance criterion. A pendency rate, for example, could

be expressed as the average time in months from filing to either issuance of a patent or abandonment of a patent application. A central focus in recent years has been to improve such performance features, in part, because they have been linked to the growing trend to finance national offices almost totally from the fees earned and to reduce government tax-based financing to zero. The logic here was unassailable. If businesses and inventors (but mainly big business) were paying the way, then they wanted improved performance. Faster – but effective and valid – patent approvals became the order of the day. Computerized and automated processes were also making it possible to handle large and complex kinds of information more efficiently.

There is considerable variation in the degree to which different national IP agencies were prepared to commit in detail to such basic performance criteria and to be bound by them. Moreover, there is often a reluctance to express them as a single pendency indicator. For example, the Australian Industrial Property Organization (AIPO) indicates in its 1995 to 1999 business plan that it seeks to increase the processing of patent filings from 40,615 in 1995–96 to 49,385 in 1997–8 and 54,365 in 1998–9. But these targets for each year are then broken down into subtasks such as 'provisionals, completes, designations, and petty patent applications' (Australian Industrial Property Organization 1995, 10–11).

CIPO became ever more aware of this central engine of its existence and its status as an SOA, and general pressure across the federal government to publish service standards concentrated this awareness. However, CIPO was also aware of the many factors which could affect performance. First, some of the newer technological areas such as computers and biotechnologies produce patent applications which, on average, take longer to process because the examinations are inherently more complex. Prior art searches are difficult and there is far less jurisprudence to guide examiners.

As soon as there are pressures in one country on such core pendency rates (and on the fee structures around them), the pressure on other national offices follows quickly, but in varied ways. The fact that the USPTO was pressured to improve its performance had an immediate impact in Canada, where CIPO was under pressure because both firms and the patent profession in Canada, who knew both systems, could point to the slower Canadian pendency performance. They protested to CIPO and have maintained the pressure in their regular meetings with CIPO officials.

The Length and Quality of Protection

The discussion above has been premised on an assumption that we were dealing with operations within a more or less *given* set of laws. However, the protection role of IP institutions writ large is also affected by pressures to change the basic length or quality of the protection stipulated in laws and treaties. The pace of such changes has increased greatly in recent years, and thus is itself an indicator of the degree to which IP is a growing concern in governmental and business strategies for growth in a knowledge-based information economy.

By far the most important development has been the achievement in the Uruguay Round of a harmonized patent of twenty years' duration (from filing date). The length of patent protection is an issue replete with both economic and political calculation and pressure. Such obvious questions as 'why twenty years?' or 'why one period for all industrial sectors or kinds of invention?' lead to complex answers that in fact show protections are often not that long or rigid.

Patents are intended to produce a temporary monopoly to reward intellectual effort and ingenuity. But, as suggested in chapter 1, simple economic logic suggests that these periods of protection ought to vary greatly by field or sector, depending on varying cost structures, investments, and payback periods. As we saw in chapter 1, this also suggests that countries would have different views about what kinds of protection across sectors would make the most sense, given their national state of development and strategies for development. Thus, the underlying economics of patent protection suggests the suitability of many periods of protection, and that these could also change over time.

The political and institutional logic proceeds somewhat differently. First, for key players, the basic logic is simply the longer the protection period the better. This view is driven by firms such as those in the national and global pharmaceutical industries who seek out maximum effective protection (see chapter 8). Their desire for maximum periods is driven by factors such as high upfront costs in R & D and in ever-lengthening drug approval processes by other government regulators in several countries. In the 1960s they saw their *effective* protection being reduced and sought change in national laws and trade regimes. The 'longer is better' logic was also the driving force behind the strategies of the United States, and later the European Union, in successive trade negotiations. U.S. power was crucial in this regard in that the Americans saw IP as increasingly vital for American economic devel-

opment and related it both to developing countries with weaker regimes on patents but also to fellow-developed countries such as Canada,
which it pressured to change its patent laws as well (Trebilcock and
Howse 1995). In Canada, this pressure focused on preferences given to
generic drug manufacturers and was brought to bear both before and
during successive FTA, NAFTA, and GATT negotiations (Doern and
Tomlin 1991).

The central political reality was that there were few if any effective
counter-pressures. Developing countries mounted some counter-pressure but were eventually worn down by more powerful forces. Consumers, in some overall sense, had a vested interest in less monopolistic
practices, but, at national and certainly at international levels, they
were a weak, diffused, and often voiceless interest. Perhaps the only
exception to this was in the health sector, where health ministries were
often a surrogate representative of consumer or patient interests.

In an overall sense, some of this political-economic logic could also
be justified because IP institutions knew that patents in many sectors
were not maintained over anything like twenty years. On average,
patents lapsed (that is, were not renewed or maintained through renewal fees) after about seven to ten years, depending on the country.

The issue of the length and quality of patents is also bound up in
policies and practices regarding utility models, petty patents, and short-
term patents, or what is often labelled more generally as 'second tier
protection.' Although Canada does not, many other countries do have
such forms of lesser protection, with the IP regime characterized broadly .
by a lower level of inventiveness, shorter terms of protection, and limits
on the scope of coverage of technologies and the number of claims.
Second tier protection regimes have been growing in recent years in
that some fifty countries have such systems today compared to only
eleven in 1978 (Advisory Council on Industrial Property 1995, 21).
Countries such as Germany and Japan have had utility model protection for decades, whereas the United Kingdom and Canada have not
adopted such a system.

A further issue relating to the length and quality of protection can be
seen as simultaneously a sectoral concern and/or a concern related to a
country's view of its 'state of economic development.' Among nations
(developed and developing / among developed / among developing)
there can and will be different judgments about which sectors of comparative advantage each possesses. These differences have affected
debates in a North-South context in the TRIPs negotiations and are

examined further below in our discussion of enforcement and the WTO. But meanwhile sectoral dynamics are themselves a variable in the protection equation.

CIPO has faced problems of adjustment as new families of technology/invention come on the scene. These difficulties show up in terms of the need to recruit examiners with the right technical expertise, but an expertise which is arguably more cross-disciplinary than in the past. Pharmaceuticals have been a source of such change, but in recent years it has been in areas such as biotechnology and computer and information sciences that adaptive problems have been greatest. Not only must the right people be acquired (in a fiercely competitive and high-salaried professional labour market), but also, because these sciences and their products are complex, applications and examinations can take longer, pendency performance can be slowed, and oppositions and litigation may increase.

There is also a wider array of institutions involved that may have a say in how these IP issues are resolved at a basic policy level or even on individual cases. For example, in recent years, the negotiations about intellectual property rights in the biotechnology area have been bounded as well by discussions with Environment Canada on matters such a biodiversity. Negotiations were occurring simultaneously in the mid-1990s in the WTO-TRIPs arena and in the Biodiversity Convention process (Purdue 1995). The American government, pressured heavily by the U.S. Biotechnology Association, the main American business lobby in the field, took steps to ensure that any biodiversity provisions were made subordinate to the intellectual property provisions of TRIPs (Purdue 1995, 102).

All of the above examples suggest that issues concerning the length and quality of protection will continue to be important. They will also likely become more contested and thus test the degree to which IP laws can be kept as framework laws, as opposed to a set of sectorally varied laws, institutions, and practices.

International Enforcement
Enforcement of intellectual property rights, in general, is obviously crucial for the protection function since if the rights are not credible and infringements occur there is no incentive to acquire them and hence to innovate (World Intellectual Property Organization 1995d; 1994b). The rights holder must be able to take action against infringers and there must be recourse to state authorities to deal with counterfeits. The

courts are accordingly a crucial feature, largely operating under civil law, but criminal law is also important. Equally, however, it is important to view IP enforcement as going well beyond litigation or the threat of litigation. The broader compliance underpinnings involve the right holder's own knowledge of competitor's practices; the opposition process provided for in the trademark registration process; and the use of negotiation, mediation, and alternative dispute settlement mechanisms. The value of these broader compliance approaches lies especially in the knowledge that litigation, especially in areas of patent litigation, can be extremely expensive, and have very uncertain outcomes.

In recent years, this aspect of the basic protection function has differed from the first two discussed above in one major respect. It has been driven by concerns about enforcement regimes at the international level regarding copyright issues. Hence it is about TRIPs and the WTO and deals with the emergence of the trade policy community and its values into IP realms, a topic we looked at briefly in chapter 4.

Big Business and the Protection Role

Many business firms – small, medium, and large – seek intellectual property rights, but it is big business and, in particular, large multinational firms that are most crucial in understanding the core protection role (Warshovsky 1994). Mention will be made of small and medium-sized enterprises, but they are more fully examined in chapter 9. It must be stressed that CIPO never suggests publicly that big business constitutes its primary clientele. If anything, as we have seen, its descriptions of its customers range across a broad array, which includes the individual as inventor – the ultimate populist vision of an enterprising and innovating economic culture.

It is not at all surprising, however, that big business should in many ways drive the Canadian IP agenda and the protection function. The large chemical and pharmaceutical firms have by far the biggest stake in an efficient, effective, and valid patent system and see the Canadian system as only one cog in the larger global IP system. They have been joined in recent years by firms in the biotechnology and computer industries, and now as well by the more amorphous and fast-changing telecommunications and information-service industries, the latter including the banks and financial institutions, who are among the fastest-growing users of the IP system (U.S. Information Infrastructure Task Force 1995). On the copyright side, big business includes the media, entertainment, and recording industries, which have vast lobbying resources, especially in the United States.

In stressing this influence, and its intensification under the pressures of globalization, one is not describing some simple version of conspiratorial power among CIPO, Industry Canada, and big business. The basis of the relationship is more multidimensional and subtle than that, and hence its roots must be understood in the context of the present chapter and the next. First, the relationship is a functional one inherent in capitalism itself. Governments depend on business as the major job creator and as the major source of innovation. Second, the influence of big businesses is based on superior lobbying resources, nationally and internationally, with a far greater capacity to mobilize than the more dispersed interests which we examine in chapter 9. Indeed, at the international level, their direct lobbying with the agencies is augmented by their own governments' membership in the international agencies, since each nation's national IP offices are most concerned either with their own large firms or with a desire to attract incoming investment. In considering the sources of large businesses' power, it is important to stress that their power does not come just from their national or international interest groups, but also from the firms themselves, working on their own in the councils of national governments at the bureaucratic and ministerial levels. This is why it is crucial to define IP institutions as going beyond the IP agencies themselves to include industry and trade ministries.

A third source of the influence of big business is that no other single interest, save that of the IP professions (see more below), has the organizational staying power to interact almost daily with CIPO and other IP agencies. As chapter 9 will show, small and medium-sized businesses and their interest groups have greater difficulty in being represented, especially in a way that focuses on IP as opposed to a host of other industrial policy concerns and innovation-related activities. Other interests, such as consumer or environmental interests, are usually too diffuse for sustained influence. New advisory bodies have been established around CIPO to ensure that a broader array of clients are advising it. These are discussed in chapter 9, where our focus in on CIPO's effort to become a more service-oriented agency. But our concern in this chapter is with big business's leverage as both an interest group and as the dominant customer.

One variation on this theme to note, however, is that of business interests in the trademark realm of IP. Trademarks are certainly a concern of big businesses and multinational firms, but, on average, the trademark area is more likely also to involve more medium and small firms. The business interests in this IP realm are also more likely to be seeking and thinking about trademarks only in national or Canadian terms.

A fourth source of the big business influence arises from the fact that so much of the IP debate is often cast as a technical debate. CIPO has seen itself, quite rightly in most respects, as a technically competent regulatory body performing an important operational function in a politically neutral manner. This sense of technical neutrality has been aided by the recent increased emphasis on the need for it, along with other Industry Canada agencies, to implement good *framework* market-place law that is sector-neutral.

Thus, in saying that big business has a privileged place in the IP agency–business relationship as a whole, the argument here is not that other segments of business receive no attention. But an institutional perspective does have to include a good sense of the basic relationships of power in any regulatory system.

The first part of this chapter and earlier chapters as well indicate other important instances where big business influence is in evidence. First, in the realm of pendency rates and the new fee-based financing of CIPO, there is little doubt that major firms, which see themselves as global competitors, are the main source of pressure to improve pendency rates. Indeed, it could be argued that the more that fees are the only source of agency income, the more that business, in general, and big businesses, in particular, will want to call the tune.

With respect to changes to the length of patents and with regard to copyright enforcement and trade-related measures, there is no doubt at all that the engine of change is large multinational firms which are focusing their lobbying around trade policy institutions in Canada and the United States, but quickly finding allies in the EU, as well. More than any other factor, it is these business interests that forced the changes examined in chapter 4 regarding the relationship between WIPO and the WTO.

Even the spread of petty patents or utility models can be linked to these basic roles of big business versus small business influence. In short, it may simply be that their spread is really an admission globally that 'first tier' protection is a big business, or largely big business, preserve, in essence, an IP game that increasingly only a few can play. Almost everyone else must seek out a lower form of protection, although in Canada this second-tier protection does not exist.

The IP Professions and the Protection Role

Our discussion of the place of the Canadian IP professions in the protection role must also be brief and illustrative. Again it is necessary to state that our linking the IP professions with the protection function is not intended to imply that there is no interest by the professions in the IP dissemination issues, which we discuss in chapter 9.

The first issue is obviously that of defining what the IP professions are in the 1990s, and how they are structured and related to CIPO and other agencies. As we saw in chapter 2, the IP professions of patent and trademark agents emerged as separate professions, distinct from the legal profession. However, there are now many practising professionals who are both members of the bar and of the IP professions.

Another key feature of the IP professions and of their close links with major IP business firms is the transformation of law firms and the contracting out of IP functions by many large IP firms to law firms. As we saw in chapter 2, during earlier periods in Canada the largest R & D–oriented firms had their own in-house stable of patent agents or lawyers. Some of the largest still do. But in general, there has been a tendency for such firms to hand over their patent and other IP functions to law firms which had developed IP or patent specialties. In recent years, developments in the legal profession, more generally, have also caused law firms to see IP as a growth area, and hence a business opportunity.

In most respects, the IP professions are relatively lucrative professions requiring extensive technical and legal knowledge. There are, however, some divisions within the professions or among their professional components. For example, the trademark profession is often seen as a secondary area both in terms of volume of business and level of technical and educational background. Nevertheless, the IP professions as a whole are also characterized by a quite justifiable sense of professional pride about what they see as their independent public-interest role, as an intermediary between the IP applicant and the state authorities.

The nature of the relationship of the IP professions to the core protection role of IP agencies is threefold in nature. First, the professions supply a realm of expertise and independent competence which, if the professions did not exist, CIPO would undoubtedly have to reinvent within the agency to ensure quality control of the application process. Second, for the inventor or IP applicant, the professions supply an objective and experienced person who can enhance the overall efficiency, quality, and validity of a patent or trademark. Third, and at the same time, the inventor or applicant, especially the smaller applicant/business, is in a basic trust relationship with the professional, dependent upon the latter's honesty, expertise, and judgment.

Because of these features of mutual dependence between the inventor or applicant and the IP professions, the Commissioner of Patents and Registrar of Trademarks has been given roles by statute in ensuring or certifying the basic qualifications of IP professionals. Thus, in varying ways, the Commissioner and Registrar regulates the IP professions. The professions live off the regulatory system in both a public-interest and private-interest sense, and the IP professions, especially in the context of large law firms, are themselves also businesses.

Accordingly, there is a broad symbiotic relationship between the IP professions and major IP-oriented business firms, both nationally and internationally. But the basis of their influence and interest is somewhat different. The IP professions are, in fact, a mélange of individual professionals practising their profession; their national association, which both lobbies for their interests and promotes professionalism; and a set of legal or IP firms aligned to IP businesses and clients. Accordingly, the IP professions, because of their own interest and because of their links to large IP firms, have also pushed hard for more efficient pendency rates. Like the business interests, the IP professions are more aware than others of the relative speed and quality of service that might be available in CIPO versus other national offices. At the same time, however, the Canadian IP professions are leery of measures or developments that might take away business from them or CIPO. In this regard, they face not only pressures directly associated with IP policy and regulation, but also pressures from changes in trade law which are beginning to encourage freer trade in services, including, of course, professional services.

The IP professions arguably have the most regular access to CIPO. But the professions are also troubled, or at least ambivalent, about the recent institutional changes at CIPO. The IP professions focus on the IP protection role because that is what they know best and that is how they make their living. But they increasingly see CIPO describing its role, as we have already seen, in terms of broader IP dissemination functions. The IP professions do not typically in principle oppose such roles, but they are not sure whether this is a role for them, and whether they will lose or gain economically from it. And there is uncertainty about what it might mean if these dissemination roles become the main focus for national offices as broader protection functions 'move up,' so to speak, to regional or world IP agencies.

The IP professions are also global professions. In other key jurisdictions, they are pushing for faster pendency processes, often by pressuring their national offices to hire more examiners and to advance the processes of computerization. Both Canada and Australia have launched studies or reviews concerning how the agencies ought to be linked to the IP professions in the new, more complex circumstances of the mid-to-late 1990s. For some time, and at several levels, the IP professions have been concerned about how their own members can be kept up to date, given the knowledge explosion and the new scientific and technical disciplines from which innovations are emerging.

Trade Departments and the Protection Role

It is crucial to emphasize that two powerful voices within the federal government largely emphasize the protection function, the Department of Foreign Affairs and International Trade (DFAIT) and Industry Canada. Both are 'trade' departments in that the former has basic legal and foreign policy jurisdiction, while the latter has sectoral industry expertise as well as responsibilities for investment and trade promotion and for market-place framework laws. To this core duo, one could easily add the Department of Finance, and thus a powerful trio of voices exists whose stances are far more on the protection side of the trade-off. There are several related reasons for this political-institutional reality.

First, since 1986, DFAIT and Industry Canada (and its predecessor departments) have been engaged in a process of virtually continuous trade negotiations, starting with the FTA, then NAFTA, and finally the GATT-WTO. This means that the core dynamic of decision-making has been that of trade negotiation and the establishment of framework-oriented rules. IP was a side-bar to the FTA negotiations but increasingly became more important in the NAFTA and GATT-WTO negotiations. The Canadian positions on IP became trade positions, where the 'real politique' was how to respond to the American insistence that patent and IP protection be strengthened.

Second, as we saw in chapter 3, Industry Canada had in 1993 acquired many of the market-place framework-law areas previously managed by the former Department of Consumer and Corporate Affairs (Doern and Tomlin 1996). The basic logic in its new home base in an industry department is that, as one of these framework laws, IP should be precisely that, 'framework' in nature, supplying rules of the game across all sectors of the economy and, once established, not subject to frequent change.

Third, an operational logic emerged out of trade-related and negotiation-centred decision-making. It will be recalled from our discussion above that the pressure from the core IP business community was for longer protection periods. But reinforcing this was the political and administrative logic of trade negotiations and their subsequent implementation. It was simply easier to agree on one longish period of protection for all sectors because it would be easier to implement. Moreover, it would preserve the notion that IP was indeed an area of real *framework* law which applied across the economies of member states and did not constitute a form of sector-specific 'industrial' policy, which it would be if many periods of protection were possible.

The Special Case of Copyright Protection Interests

Chapter 6 has already examined the key Canadian copyright institutions and processes, and includes a discussion of the recent Bill C-32, which brought together several long-needed amendments to Canada's basic copyright framework law. In the context of the present chapter on the protection function, it is crucial to draw attention to the special configuration of copyright protection interests. As chapter 6 showed, this configuration is different than that which exists in the world of Canadian patent protection in that the latter has a quite concentrated set of interests centred around the pharmaceutical industry, whereas the interests that support copyright protection are more diffuse.

As chapter 6 showed, the pro-protection interests in copyright include organizations and collectives (note again that even the language describing the groups is different) representing authors and performers. In the past, these groups have formed a copyright coalition. The essential reality for these groups is that they are composed of numerous small producers of intellectual property. This basic political fact helps explain why there has been slower progress in enshrining the full array of protection rights.

Lined up against this copyright coalition are user groups or groups interested in the dissemination of copyrighted material, which on average are larger and more cohesive, though none has the clout of the pharmaceutical lobby in the patent field. This coalition of users includes the broadcasting industry (including numerous small local radio stations), schools, libraries, museums, and the like. These groups fought to maintain or expand the exemptions from protection because they sought the free or unconstrained use of the creations of other producers.

The nature of the protection function in copyright matters is also different within the structure of federal departments. For example, Industry Canada has been more supportive of user industries, such as the broadcasting sector, whereas Heritage Canada took up the case for the primary cultural producers. In short, Industry Canada's ardour for true framework law shifts somewhat in this realm of IP.

A final point to note regarding the protection function in copyright is that the configuration of interests is likely to change markedly in the next round of copyright law reform in Canada. This is because it will have to deal frontally with the issue of the Internet and other matters related to the communications revolution. This will bring to the table some powerful business sectors, ranging from the telecommunications and software firms to the banks. On balance, these are likely to greatly strengthen the pro-protection side of the copyright IP political equation.

Conclusions

The protection role is without doubt the central driving force within CIPO, despite the recent effort to give more emphasis to broader IP dissemination functions. With respect to basic pendency performance and the efficiency and quality of the patent or trademark application process, this chapter shows that there has been an increased pressure, led by large IP firms and industrial interest groups, to improve and make more transparent the performance criteria of such examination and registration operations.

Recent years have seen, as well, pressures to change the length and quality of IP protection. The TRIPs negotiations saw the realization of a harmonized twenty-year rule, despite other analytical logic which suggests that time periods could vary by sector. At the same time, there have been increased pressures, largely from the small-business sector, but arising also from different national traditions, to expand the use of utility models and petty patents, which provide shorter, less expensive, and less rigorous forms of protection. Such lesser forms of protection have not been provided in Canada yet, but they well could be as IP becomes more thoroughly debated.

The nature of the protection function has also been significantly influenced by Canadian and international concerns about enforcement, especially in the copyright realms of IP, but in others as well. However, within Canada, the special case of the configuration of copyright protection interests has been emphasized. Compared to patents, it is a much more diffuse, and hence weaker, political coalition.

Finally, the chapter shows the tight links between big business interests and the IP professions in the reinforcement of the protection function. Their interests are not identical, but it is important to identify both the differences and the similarities in their positions as the dominant interests in the protection role. They bring to CIPO, especially under the conditions of globalization, a strong pressure to improve the efficiency of pendency, but also its quality. IP agencies themselves are increasingly seeking to broaden their own sense of their clientele beyond these two primary sets of interests, but, at the same time, they know that they are extremely dependent on each other.

8. The Core Politics of IP Innovation: Pharmaceuticals, Health, and Global Patent Change, 1987 to 2000

While the overall established interests that underpin the protection function have been examined, we need to return in greater detail to the special nature of the pharmaceutical industry and the core politics of IP in Canada. The historical roots of these issues were examined in chapter 2, including key changes made in the 1960s, at which time a central issue was compulsory licensing. In this chapter, we look more closely at the period from 1987 to 2000, when global patent regimes took hold, the elimination of compulsory licensing was achieved, and the federal government sought to foster an even broader biotechnology industry.

This period is also significant in that the tension established in the 1960s between health and industrial priorities was re-engaged. In the patent rationality of the 1960s, equal access to health care and industrial profits were constructed as opposing priorities, in that access was equated with lowering pharmaceutical costs through the increased availability of generic alternatives. The pharmaceutical patent debates in the 1960s, therefore, involved more than balancing innovation with dissemination; the 1960s debates also involved balancing the profits of industry against the health and welfare of society, and balancing the need for intrusive regulation of industry against industrial autonomy.

These themes were resurrected between 1987 and 2000, along with the theme of rationalizing domestic regulation with internationally mandated standards, making this period one of the most active in terms of pharmaceutical patent legislation. What emerged was a resolution of the health-industry dichotomy within a new international context, the innovative global economy. This chapter deals with these changes in two sections. First, the key legislative changes are profiled. The second part of the chapter then examines several overall aspects of this transformative period in IP policy and institutions.

The C-91 Process: Pharmaceutical Patents in a Global Economy

The Three Stages of Legislative Change

Between 1987 and 1997, three instances of legislative change occurred: Bill C-22 in 1987, Bill C-91 in 1993, and a review of Bill C-91 in 1997. Although each legislative event will be examined separately in this section, they form three stages of a larger process, in which the priorities of pharmaceutical patent regulation moved from encouraging equitable access to pharmaceutical health care (the legacy of the late 1960s) to incorporating Canada into a global, 'innovative' community of health provision.

Bill C-22, passed on 7 December 1987, was the first step in altering the provisions of the 1969 Patent Act. It emerged in a context defined by two key political phenomena: the Eastman Commission and the Free Trade Agreement. The Eastman Commission reported in 1985. Appointed by the Liberal government, it had been established out of governmental concern about the lack of investment in the pharmaceutical sector and out of a perceived political need to reach a new consensus on compulsory licensing. The primary recommendation of the Commission was that compulsory licensing be maintained (Eastman 1985).

Regardless of the Commission's recommendation, however, the crucial political reality about this first period of change was its concurrence with an evolving macro-regulatory environment, namely, the Canada-U.S. Free Trade Agreement (the FTA). Although not a part of the FTA, many opponents of Bill C-22 saw it as a de facto side-deal to the treaty (Doern and Tomlin 1991). There is little doubt that the pharmaceutical industry on both sides of the border used the tense climate of the FTA to press their case.

Bill C-22 made two key changes to the pharmaceutical patent regime. First, it increased the period of patent protection before the system of compulsory licensing could come into effect to ten years (seven if manufactured from Canadian fine chemicals). By 1987, the time taken up by safety and efficacy (and other) testing meant it ordinarily took seven years between the filing of a patent and the entry of the drug to market. With the additional seven to ten years of monopoly, this provided a patent holder with an effective fourteen to seventeen years of exclusivity. In response to criticisms levelled by generic producers (spearheaded by their representative voice, the Canadian Drug Manufacturers Association) and health providers (including some provincial health ministries) that this expanded patent term would unreasonably raise the cost of pharmaceuticals, the second major change made by Bill C-22 was the establishment of a review board to regulate drug prices, the Patent Medicines Prices Review Board (PMPRB).

Bill C-91, passed in February 1993, also had two major effects. It eliminated compulsory licensing altogether, and it extended effective patent protection up to twenty years. In doing so, it matched the international standards set by the Uruguay Round of GATT (initially proposed as the Dunkel Draft). C-91 also expanded the powers of the PMPRB.[1] A later addition to Bill C-91, dealing with Notice of Compliance[2] issues, was passed in March 1993. This amendment prevented the Minister of National Health and Welfare (now Health) from issuing a Notice of Compliance (NOC) to a generic manufacturer if the patent holder of the drug in question issued a challenge under patent regulations. Under certain conditions, these challenges could extend patent monopolies up to an additional thirty months.

NOC regulations also figured prominently in the promised Parliamentary review of C-91, which reported just before the 1997 election. Generic manufacturers used the review to challenge the NOC system, arguing that patent holders were abusing the challenge system, effectively extending their patents by issuing challenges and then drawing out the processes of legal adjudication (Canadian Drug Manufacturers Association 1997; 1994). These criticisms resulted in minor changes to the NOC regulations during the C-91 review. Six months were cut from the NOC dispute process, and patent forms were restricted to active products (i.e., patents could not be extended by introducing new versions of existing products; for example, introducing the same drug in gel-tab form rather than tablet did not entitle a new patent).

In addition to its re-evaluation of the NOC system, the C-91 review offered an preliminary assessment of the impact of C-91 (House of Commons 1997). Since the passage of C-91, there had been extensive global restructuring of the industry. Patented medicine sales had increased by 10 per cent in 1995 (some critics of C-91 had expected them to decrease). At the same time, the price of patented medicines had declined by 1.75 per cent. The Canadian generic drug industry appeared to be prospering and there were increased numbers of strategic

---

1 Chiefly in terms of its capacity to generate information about the industry, and its ability to enforce price regulation.
2 An NOC was issued to indicate the pharmaceutical in question had met safety and efficacy requirements. Drugs could not be marketed without a Notice.

alliances between pharmaceutical and biotech companies (which consequently blurred the differences between innovative and generic firms).
The foreign-owned firms represented by the Pharmaceutical Manufacturers Association of Canada (PMAC) had increased their R & D investments in Montreal, a commitment made in conjunction with the
C-91 debate. Although there were debates over the precise nature of
this R & D (with opponents of C-91 arguing it consisted of minor
technical activity rather than primary research), the overall level of new
R & D investment by PMAC firms was higher than its 1993 critics had
anticipated.

The C-91 review also revealed changes in the circumstances and
players; the political equation in 1997 was different than that of the
early 1990s. First, the importance of the industry and its ties to the
biotechnology industry (see more below) were now much more central
in the eyes of Canada's trade and industry policy-makers (Canada
1998a). Second, the provinces were much more actively involved in the
pharmaceutical patent debate, as health providers, than they had been
in the early 1990s. Although the provinces had been involved earlier,
chiefly because of their role as health insurers and their concern that
health authorities reduce health costs overall, many provinces had
made concrete rationing decisions which were already contributing to
the increased purchase of generic drugs. Third, the array of institutional concerns was now widening. For example, the multinational
firms were now concerned about effective protection, a concept which
embraced not just patent law but also how efficient and effective related
drug-approval processes were in agencies such as the Therapeutic Products Program of the Health Protection Branch in Health Canada (Doern
2000).

Fourth, these new developments took place in an environment characterized by a near-universal embrace of the language of international
competition and global health. Even the Canadian Drug Manufacturers
Association (which represented Canadian generic manufacturers), one
of the most virulent opponents of C-91, began to use this language in its
policy discourse, a significant departure from the identification with
lower costs and a Canadian context for health care which had characterized its position in the C-91 debate.

Although it retained the notion that the pharmaceutical industry was
a mainstay of the health-care system, the focus of the CDMA's discussion had shifted to the industry's role in the wider, that is, global,
environment of competitive R & D. Unlike such early advocates of Bill

C-91 as the PMAC, however, the CDMA argued that it was the generic producers, not the multinationals, who were best suited to capitalizing on the global economy for Canada.

In 1995, in response to a document co-commissioned by the Montreal and Toronto boards of trade, which solicited further patent protection for the brand-name companies, Brenda Drinkwalter (then the CDMA president) wrote that over the past twenty-five years, 'Canada's generic drug industry has grown into a sophisticated, technologically-advanced, knowledge-based industry with a global outlook. Generic drug manufacturers ... export made-in-Canada pharmaceuticals to countries all over the world, and the largest are among the top R & D spenders in Canada,' (*In Response by the CDMA to ...*: 1996, p.i). This characterization, drawing as it does on concepts of high technology, global orientation, and competitive R & D product exporting, is eerily reminiscent of the self-description of PMAC, which characterizes itself as the 'national association of Canada's research-based pharmaceutical industry ... Comprised of companies of all sizes, the PMAC membership is part of the global pharmaceutical industry whose members are responsible for developing in excess of 90% of the medicines that are available today.' (PMAC 1997a, 52). This similarity is repeated in the CDMA's submission to the 1997 Parliamentary review committee, in which it suggests that 'Canada should adopt a viable and sustainable public policy environment to support the state of development of its domestic industry. Building an industry in the complex, science oriented, highly competitive and costly pharmaceutical industry requires a long term commitment to supporting Canadian based companies' (CDMA 1997, 11).

By the time of the review, although the CDMA retained the claim that it represented the Canadian pharmaceutical industry (in opposition to the foreign multinationals), it had almost completely adopted the discourse and characterization of the pharmaceutical industry advanced by PMAC as early as 1986. At the same time, however, CDMA's instrumental prescriptions remained unchanged. It still advocated the elimination of NOC regulations, and still sought to shorten the effective monopoly life of patents via the return of compulsory licensing. However, the rationale for doing so had almost entirely changed. Rather than implementing these regulations to secure the Canadian healthcare system, CDMA argued these alternative institutional prescriptions would foster precisely the sort of industry that, according to the Mulroney government and PMAC, Bill C-91 was intended to foster. The

only difference was that the generics insisted that they, not multinational subsidiaries, were the appropriate site for the growth of Canadian pharmaceutical R & D.

The appropriation of 'competitive innovation' discourse by the CDMA
indicates that the C-91 process did more than alter pharmaceutical
patent regulations. Taken as a coherent process of three stages, the 'C-91
process' also embedded the assumptions and rationality of the 'global
innovative economy' in the pharmaceutical patent debate. At the beginning of the process, the changes embodied by Bill C-22 were associated
with the politically charged issues of the FTA (such as economic sovereignty), and the threat these issues posed to the maintenance of the
health-provision infrastructure in Canada. By the end of the process,
however, the debates surrounding the C-91 review generally accepted
the assumptions underlying the FTA and other institutions of global
competition, and were more concerned with the technical details of
managing the Canadian component of a global pharmaceutical industry. Although the cost of medications was still an issue to participants
such as the provincial health insurers, the innovative aspects of the
pharmaceutical industry had assumed a new ascendancy, with both
governmental and non-governmental participants seeking a stake (institutional or otherwise) in evolving industries such as biotechnology.

C-91 as Transformation: Becoming an Innovative Global Economy
One of the most distinctive features of the period after 1987 was the
range and complexity of issues uncovered in the nature of patent rationality. It was dominated by many of the same debates which occurred during earlier periods, such as reconciliation with international
regimes and the impact of pharmaceutical regulation on equitable access to health care. Debate was further complicated, however, by new
issues, such as the impact of the global economy and globalization.
These new issues demanded a re-examination of not just how to regulate, but also of what, precisely, was being regulated. What distinguished the C-91 process was the context it ascribed to the innovation/
dissemination balance. Although this balance was still maintained by
the state, it was understood (at least in the case of pharmaceutical
patents) to operate in a global economy which intrinsically encouraged
innovation through competition. Innovation was guaranteed by the
competitive pressures of this global economy, and the dissemination of
innovation was implicitly ensured by developing the institutions equated
with participation in the innovative economy.

One of the dominant explanatory refrains throughout the 'C-91 debate' was the assertion that the changes mandated in Bills C-22 and C-91 were required by international treaty, a claim which echoes Secretary of State Rinfret's assertions in the1920s. This 'need' for legislation was affirmed both by the government and the bills' industry supporter, the Pharmaceutical Manufacturers Association of Canada. The PMAC went so far as to view the effects of C-91 as having removed a blight on Canada's international reputation, eliminating a practice which had removed Canada from the 'modern' society of states (PMAC 1992, 1).[3] Bills C-22 and C-91 were characterized as necessary steps to return Canada towards parity, towards meeting Canadian responsibilities towards our major trading partners (PMAC 1993, 35).[4]

Although the government was not so explicit in its condemnation of former practices, it did respond to the pressure which surrounded it, acknowledging an obligation to 'reform' its patent practices. During the review of Bill C-91, the Minister of Industry, John Manley, noted that 'our ability to change our patent law is defined by these obligations. We must give all patentees, pharmaceutical or otherwise, a minimum 20 year patent term. It is not possible to return to our pre-1993 compulsory licensing regime and remain in conformity with our international obligations. Any recommendations should be looked at in the context of these international obligations' (Manley 1998, 9). The departure of this interpretation from that advanced by the government in the 1960s is obvious. Although the Mulroney government had acknowledged the role pharmaceuticals played in the Canadian health-care system, it maintained that its capacity to regulate was limited by international treaty. In other words, the government appeared to side with international industrial interests, rather than domestic health interests, in its execution of pharmaceutical patent change.

---

3 The blight, of course, being the practice of compulsory licensing. Although some 'developing' countries, such as India, do have large generic pharmaceutical industries, in Europe and the United States, where most of the multinational patent holders are based, compulsory licensing was relatively unknown.

4 The PMAC was quite explicit in its condemnation of compulsory licensing, describing it as an irresponsible, immature practice, characteristic of the 'Third World.' This attitude was visible in a public statement by then PMAC Chairman, Nelson Sims, made in preparation for the review of C-91 scheduled in 1997. Sims suggested that alterations to the structure established by C-91 would have disastrous consequences for Canada's international status. He argued that '... either we seize the opportunity to preserve and enhance our country's position on the issue of intellectual property rights or we face the consequences of being relegated to the status of a third world country, relying on the innovation and initiative of scientists in other parts of the world, to the eventual detriment of healthcare in Canada' (Sims 1996, 1).

It should be noted, however, that fear of a punitive response was not the only factor prompting the drafting of Bills C-22 and C-91. The two bills also can be seen as an attempt by the government to capture the forces of globalization, to take advantage of a visible market trend, and steer the development of Canadian industry in such a way that it took advantage of the supposed growth potential and innovative capacity of global industry. This is confirmed in a 1991 Industry, Science and Technology Canada profile of the Canadian pharmaceutical industry, which reviewed the industry after the impact of C-22. The profile argued that an increase in domestic R & D had occurred as a result of Bill C-22, and suggested that securing more international R & D and manufacturing would boost industry competitiveness (Industry, Science and Technology Canada 1991, 7). Acquiring such new investment would result from further immersion and participation in the global innovative economy, an economy defined in large part by trade agreements such as the NAFTA or the WTO.[5]

Given this emphasis on participation in a wider community of regulation, and the innovative opportunities to be derived from that participation, it seems clear that Bill C-22 and Bill C-91 were to provide access to a particular form of global market. Specifically, they incorporated Canada into a homogenized system of pharmaceutical patent regulation supported by inter-reinforcing, multi-lateral agreements. Regulation, in the context of C-91, overlapped the territorial powers which regulated. Patent regulation extended beyond the state border, insofar as limits on production affected both exports and domestic production. A global economy was a globally regulated economy. Moreover, it was an efficiently regulated economy, in that regulation did not need to be imposed in every country, only those capable of production.[6]

---

5 One of the key provisions of such treaties in reference to pharmaceuticals was the capacity of patents to be cross-filed, a practice which C-91 made possible. If a patent is cross-filed, it means that it is illegal for Canadian companies to manufacture drugs in Canada for export to countries where patents have expired or do not exist, provided that the drug in question is under patent somewhere among the signatory countries. Competition was not limited just within the Canadian market, but within the multi-laterally regulated market, as well.

6 It was also intended to be a static regime. In its testimony before the review committee, the PMAC suggested that 'for the past ten years, Canada has undergone regular reviews of its intellectual property protection policies. Future parliamentary reviews should be conducted only in order to ensure that Canada's patent laws remain competitive with international standards' ('Summary of Testimony,' p. 29).

Much of the debate around C-91 was rooted in different responses to Canada's inclusion in this system of global regulation. As such, the C-91 debates echoed the tensions noted in chapter 2 regarding the 1928 set of patent changes: the tension resulting from the need to mediate between international and domestic priorities. Unlike the debates in the 1920s, however, the C-91 debate incorporated the connection between pharmaceutical patents and health provision advanced in the 1960s debates around Bill C-190. In the 1960s, health provision was associated with the disseminative function. Institutions of dissemination such as compulsory licensing were intended to reduce costs and increase access to therapeutic drugs. Although the C-91 debates incorporated this association of pharmaceutical patents and health provision, the patent rationality of the C-91 period did not privilege the role of the dissemination function in health provision. Rather than approaching the extension of patent duration, and incorporation into a global regulatory regime, as a course of action opposed to the priorities of technological dissemination and domestic health, the patent rationality implied by C-91 equated participation in the global regulatory regime with both the innovation and dissemination functions, as well as health provision.

Ultimately, the patent rationality of Bill C-22 and Bill C-91 implied that the health of Canadians was dependent on a long-term view; that health was dependent on research and the development of new drugs, rather than relatively inexpensive access to drugs currently available. Second, it was understood that health provision was only possible if Canada participated in the 'global' multilateral regulatory regime which created the competitive conditions of innovation. Taken together, these implied a larger context for ensuring the health of Canadians, a community of health assurance related to global markets. It was not so much a question of guaranteeing the health of Canadians, as it was a question of guaranteeing Canada's access to a community of health, a community that could better serve Canadians than Canada itself (Sharaput 1998). To be global was to belong to an innovative community of health, and efforts to oppose or undermine Canada's inclusion in this community, attacking as they did the ultimate foundations of health for Canadians, were seen at best to be parsimonious and short-sighted.

The significance of Bill C-22 and Bill C-91 lies in the fact that they represented a conceptual transformation in the subject of regulation, that is, a reconception of the pharmaceutical industry in Canada. Rather than being viewed as a branch of domestic industry subject to international treaty, as in the 1920s, or as a component of the domestic health infrastructure, as in the 1960s, in the late 1980s and early 1990s, the pharmaceutical industry came to be viewed as a component of an innovative global economy. Bills C-22 and C-91 did more than change pharmaceutical regulation in Canada, insofar as the bills constituted more than a legislative change in regulation. By changing the implicit notion of what was under discussion, the adoption of Bill C-91 changed how it was possible to talk about the regulation of pharmaceuticals in Canada.[7] For the first time since 1928, the Canadian government did not have to mediate between the priorities of industry and health, because it occupied (at least in its public discourse) a space for thought in which the priority of domestic health care for Canadians could only be met by meeting the demands of global industry. It was only by adopting an innovative policy, which is to say, a policy which seemed attractive to innovative companies, such as that provided by C-91, that one could develop the industrial infrastructure which would ensure the health of Canadians.

This link between industry, innovation, and health was confirmed with the emergence of broader biotechnology strategies and conceptions of Canada's having 'health industries' on which it could build competitive advantage and health innovation. In purely institutional terms, this was illustrated by Industry Canada's establishing in 1993 new industrial sector branches for 'health industries' and 'bio-industries' (Industry Canada 1997a; 1997b). These have since become one branch for health and biotechnology industries. These institutional changes confirmed Canada's health system as a health industry, one which included not only drug companies but also 'telehealth,' hospitals, medical researchers, and others who might contribute to both IP development and health innovation (Industry Canada 1997c). At a government-wide level, involving eight ministers, the federal government also announced a renewed Canadian Biotechnology Strategy (Canada 1998c; Doern and Sheehy 1999). In addition, pharmaceuticals and biotechnology have become showpieces in the federal govern-

---

7 It also changed who could talk about regulation of the industry and in what context. For example, with the conception of the industry implicit in C-91, it became legitimate for the PMAC, as a representative of producers of global health, to discuss health care in Canada – they were part of Canada's global health community. In some ways, it was the PMAC, or at least, the group it represented, which made that community possible.

ment's competitive strategy. The sectors feature prominently as targets for growth in both the Agenda: Jobs and Growth initiative and Science and Technology Strategy policy initiatives (Industry Canada 1994a; 1997). Pharmaceutical patents are understood to retain a role in health provision, but ensuring this role has become dependent on the successful formation of pharmaceutical production as a competitive industry in the innovative global economy.

Pharmaceutical patent change in Canada has become increasingly complex over time. The issues surrounding pharmaceutical patent change, by the 1990s, had taken on a sedimentary quality. Some of the earliest themes, such as opposition between the perceived interests of the domestic and international contexts, were still present. They had been joined however, by the complexities prompted by the inclusion of health concerns into patent policy, as well as by the difficulties and debates which emerged when the line between domestic and international blurred, as in the case of globalization and the global economy. At this point, it seems clear that under C-91, what patents were supposed to do had changed, and that these changes related, at least in part, to the responses generated by earlier periods of change.

Innovation, Health, and Pharmaceutical Patents

Patents exert an institutional influence over the industry they govern by determining, in part, the conditions of profitability. The balance struck between innovation and dissemination is determined by the extent to which innovative practices are rewarding. This is the case for pharmaceutical patents as with others. Pharmaceutical patents, however, have been given distinctive treatment in the broader IP field since the 1960s because they are not governed exclusively by the usual intellectual property tensions, but are also associated with health issues. As a result, pharmaceutical patent change not only constitutes a shift in the balance between monopolistic reward and the dissemination of innovation, but also concerns the issue to what extent industrial priorities can be reconciled with those of health. This reconciliation is not constant, insofar as it is based on what the perceived industrial and health priorities are for innovation at any given time.

Since the 1960s, pharmaceutical patents have consisted of an attempt to mediate and resolve health debates via an industrial regulatory institution, and to understand health policy through industrial filters rather than through the larger health politics of spending money and investing in hospitals and services. Thus, the last section of this chapter examines key dimensions of this 'industrialization of health' in an attempt to illustrate the contingent and interdependent relationship between the mediation and health provision functions of pharmaceutical patents.

The Structural Influence of the Patent Institution
Patents are effective as a mechanism of change for the pharmaceutical industry because they define some of the key structural elements of pharmaceutical production, insofar as they determine who can produce what drugs when. Controlling the length of patents, and the existence (or lack thereof) of mechanisms for diluting or subverting patents, establishes the conditions of profitability for pharmaceutical development, influencing both the degree of 'pure' versus 'marketable' research, and the scale of research (the maximum length of time, for example, which researchers can devote to developing a particular drug). The influence patents exert at a structural level means that their manipulation can affect a broad range of policy issues, over a long period of time. Although these issues can be addressed via other means, these other means are often limited, either by the scope of their influence, by the lack of government money in a high deficit era, or by being subject to regulation themselves. While patent change may be relatively indirect, it is often easier to accomplish, longer-lasting, more comprehensive, and less regulated than other means of enacting change.

Although patents can be used to exert a comprehensive or systemic influence over an industry, their influence is indirect; historically, this has exposed them to criticism. Whether in the 1960s or 1990s, other instruments were available to governments, instruments which would generate precisely the same sort of change which Bill C-190 and Bill C-22 or C-91 were enacted to achieve, but via far more direct means. In the 1960s, for example, some of the opposition MPs questioned why, if the goal of Bill C-190 had been to lower the cost of medications, the government had not simply used existing mechanisms, such as the anti-combines or competition legislation, to address the problem. In the 1990s, similar criticism was levelled against the government's decision to enact patent change in an effort to stimulate research and development, rather than using more direct methods, such as establishing research quotas for private industry or establishing a publicly directed research fund.

In the 1960s debates surrounding Bill C-190, one of the MPs opposing the bill questioned why the government had chosen to manipulate patents, rather than use existing mechanisms (such as anti-trust legislation), in its efforts to increase competition. Specifically, he argued that the government should use existing mechanisms if the pricing practices of drug producers were improper. He argued that 'if there is wrongful price maintenance or restraint of trade or any other abuse capable of correction by the combines investigation branch, let [the government] use that machinery instead of this shotgun approach, in the hope that the legislation will have beneficial side effects by lowering drug prices to consumers' (Hansard, 14 Feb. 1968, p. 6742). This criticism can be interpreted in two different ways. One possibility is that it consisted of a simple inquiry, based on curiosity, into the government's methods, questioning their apparent awkwardness. A second possibility, however, is that by noting that methods existed for correcting price abuses, and the failure of the government to employ these methods, there was a suggestion that pharmaceutical prices were not abusive, and that the government's employment of patent re-regulation to lower prices was an attempt to avoid the need to justify its actions before the combines investigation branch.

One could argue that patent change was used as a mechanism to increase competition and lower price because the government could not sustain the burden of proof necessary to succeed in a combines investigation. Although Canadian competition in the late 1960s was not robust (Doern 1995), John Turner (then Minister of Consumer and Corporate Affairs) was quite careful to note that he was not alleging any 'sinister behaviour by the industry' (Hansard, 12 Feb. 1968, p. 6622). In choosing to alter the industry's regulatory structure, via altering the patent regime, the government avoided the need to prove that pharmaceutical prices were abusive, patent legislation requiring a far lower 'burden of proof.' One could also argue, however, that patent change offered a broader and longer-lasting means of change than that offered by an anti-trust investigation. Because patent change operated at the structural level, in effect, changing the conditions for profitable operation, it influenced all companies which researched, manufactured, or marketed drugs. It thereby achieved a goal which may have required several different investigations, had the government attempted to achieve lower pharmaceutical prices by other means.

In the 1990s, Bills C-22 and C-91 were subject to critiques reminiscent of those levelled at Bill C-190. In this era of patent re-regulation, the goal of the two bills was ostensibly to encourage the growth of R & D and innovation in the Canadian pharmaceutical industry. Opponents of the bills, such as the Canadian Health Coalition (an adjunct of the Canadian Labour Congress), questioned the utility of patent regulation in stimulating research and innovation, arguing that more direct means were available. In a CHC media release, Dr Joel Lexchin suggested that setting mandatory private sector research targets would do more to stimulate R & D investment in Canada than increasing manufacturers' products (via extended patent monopolies) in the hopes that money would trickle down to basic research in Canada (Canadian Health Coalition 1997a). The CHC noted that between 1991 and 1995, only 8 per cent of 'new' medicines constituted actual therapeutic break-throughs. The remainder consisted of line extensions (drugs packaged in different delivery systems) and drugs offering equivalent efficacy. The CHC advocated, in fact, a publicly administered research fund, which would inject the target sums into R & D, but would retain control of how and where such funds were distributed (Canadian Health Coalition 1997b).

To some extent, then, the critiques of the 1990s echo those of the 1960s; opponents of legislative change suggested that patents were a clumsier mechanism than the alternatives. Unlike the 1960s debates, however, it is difficult to argue that patent change was enacted in the 1990s because it was a less-demanding, less-regulated mechanism of change. Given the degree of controversy surrounding Bills C-22 and C-91 (which were widely criticized by both the press and the public), it cannot be said that patent legislation was the easier option for change.

In addition, rather than adding to the flexibility of policy alternatives (by opening up new uses for patent legislation), Bills C-22 and C-91 seem to have restricted the range of uses to which patents could be put. It would be understandable to conclude that the elimination of compulsory licensing and the extension of patent terms, by re-emphasizing the industrial and innovative aspects of the pharmaceutical industry, constituted a contraction of the structural influence of patents in pharmaceutical manufacturing. This apparent contraction, however, can also be interpreted as symptomatic of an expansion in the context of regulation. The purpose of the two bills was not so much the use of patents to subvert existing policy, but the subversion of the context for patent policy formation.

We have noted that one of the dominant features of the 1990s era of patent change was an attempt to incorporate pharmaceutical patents into a broader regulatory scheme. John Manley's comments to the effect that the government was limited in its capacity to regulate by its commitment to the GATT/WTO have two dimensions: the government was limited in terms of its capacity to differentiate patent terms between pharmaceuticals and other commodities; but it was also limited in terms of its capacity to isolate patent regulation from other regulatory processes. The Dunkel draft of the GATT was developed through a long process of multilateral negotiation, incorporating benefits and liabilities to all who participated in its formation. Participants in such shared regulatory-guidance structures must generally abide by the treaty as a whole.[8] While previously, pharmaceutical patent regulation, and patent regulation generally, could be considered a discrete form of industrial policy (taking into account the complication of the field which health issues bring to pharmaceutical patent regulation), for those who participated in GATT, patent regulation became a policy component of a larger, consensual regulatory system. As a result, the apparent restriction in use-options for patent policy in the case of pharmaceutical patents can be seen as a consequence of their incorporation into a larger consensual regulatory framework.

When taken in light of the criticisms levelled by the Canadian Health Coalition, the implication of this larger regulatory context becomes clear. The strategies advocated by the CHC (direct grants, federally administered research program, etc.) were appropriate to a national or domestic context, in which the Canadian government was the sole arbiter. This was a conceptual context (a space for thought) in which both the initiation of policy and its effects were framed by the limits of the state (both physical and conceptual). As such, research and innovation, if they were to be stimulated within Canada, must be stimulated by Canada, resulting in a Canadian community of innovation. In contrast, the regulatory environment established by Bills C-22 and C-91 envisaged a regulatory community in which the Canadian government was a participant. In this conceptual context, innovation was viewed as a resource of the community, and policy, as the result of joint, consensual negotiation. Given that a particular form of structural regulation was viewed as the condition of participation in the global community, stimulating innovation required re-regulation, via the structural ma-

---

8 Although, admittedly, one can advance a number of arguments to the effect that some participants benefit from the treaty more than others, and cases exist where states have been able to pick and choose.

nipulation patent change brings about, to coordinate domestic standards of regulation with 'global' norms.

Bills C-22 and C-91 were not just about creating research or adjusting the balance between innovation and dissemination; if so, these goals could have been realized by the sort of policy options advocated by the Canadian Health Coalition. What the government sought to achieve with Bills C-22 and C-91 was a structural change in the operation of the pharmaceutical industry, a structural change prompted, in turn, by a change in the conceptual context for understanding the industry. Pharmaceutical patent regulation in the 1990s was structurally subversive; rather than subverting existing national policy, it acted to expand (or perhaps displace) the context and location for the conceptualization of policy.

Analysing the choice to enact change through altering patent regulations in the 1960s and 1990s offers some insight into the use of pharmaceutical patents as a regulatory instrument. As should be clear at this point in our discussion, the regulation of pharmaceutical manufacturing through patents has been pervasive since the 1960s. This association of pharmaceutical manufacturing and patent regulation has existed through periods in which other policy instruments and options (taxation, public-service dissemination, or public ownership, for example) have held general popularity. In recent years, regulation has become more popular as a policy instrument (with governments) because it offers governments a degree of control and influence, while shunting most of the cost and liability onto the private sector or onto provincial health-care providers (Doern, Hill, Prince, and Schultz 1999). Governments establish and enforce regulation, but it is private industry which must respond to regulation and bear its costs, because it is industry which is ultimately liable to the government for adhering to regulation.

What has made patent regulation the recurring mechanism for change in the pharmaceutical industry, however, is not the currently popular capacity of regulation to lower costs for government. Rather, it is the capacity of patents to exert a structural influence by controlling the permissible costs of operation. The structural influence of patents stems from their ability to control who manufactures what drugs, when (and, to a certain extent, where). Pharmaceutical research is high-cost and high-risk, and the ability of manufacturers to recoup their expenses and make a profit is dependent on the degree of patent protection available (and the monopoly such protection brings). Patents set the conditions of profit for the manufacturers of pharmaceuticals,[9] and it is this which allows patents to be used to exert a structural influence over the industry.

The Pharmaceutical Industry as a Provider of Health

Pharmaceutical patents exert the same structural influence as other patents. The impact of this influence is not limited, however, to the balance between the innovation and dissemination functions. The structural influence of pharmaceutical patents has extended to health provision since the association of that issue with patents in the 1960s. Pharmaceutical patents define, in part, both the nature of the 'health' being provided and how that health is provided to the public. As the patent institution changed, so did the historical role it fulfilled (or was intended to fulfil) in health provision.

In the 1960s, the association of pharmaceutical patents with the Canadian system of health provision was pivotal to both sides: it was the rationale behind the legislative goal of encouraging price competition (to promote accessibility of pharmaceutical health products), and it was the justification for those who opposed Bill C-190 on the grounds of safety (that the health of Canadians would be at risk from imported chemicals produced in unregulated, 'foreign' environments). In the 1990s, the rationale behind Bill C-22 and Bill C-91 implied that the new pharmaceutical patent regime would give Canada access to a larger, innovative, and global community of health provision. In contrast, opponents of the bills argued that health provision was a domestic concern, and the two bills' impact on drug prices would cripple the existing health system.

During the 1960s, much of the opposition to Bill C-190 was based in arguments that the new regulatory structure the bill established would interfere with the role the pharmaceutical industry played in providing

---

9 Or, perhaps, it is more accurate to say that patents set the conditions for profitable operation. In the 1960s, for example, the changes to the compulsory licensing structure were not intended to make the production of pharmaceuticals less profitable per se, but rather to make the current industry practices (such as advertising-based competition) unprofitable. Facing potential competition from lower-priced imports, it was hoped, manufacturers would recognize that inflated advertising budgets were no longer practicable. The drop in prices Bill C-190 was intended to produce would stem, not from manufacturers' profits, but from a reduction in the advertising budget. Bill C-190, by manipulating patent regulations, did not so much make pharmaceutical manufacturing unprofitable, as it made carrying a large advertising budget unprofitable for pharmaceutical manufacturers.

health. This criticism centred on the argument that the flow of imported drugs, the drugs which would supposedly lower the overall cost of pharmaceuticals through price competition, would be 'foreign'-made, and would not be subject to the same quality controls as domestically produced drugs. There was an explicit undertone to this argument, as if the government was being accused of irresponsibility or recklessly exposing Canadians to dangerous substances. Opponents claimed that alterations to the patent and trademark regulations would permit the importation of products manufactured outside Canada under the name they had borne while still manufactured in this country. They questioned what risks would emerge when drugs were imported from countries where Canada did not have the right of inspection, noting that many countries did not even have the sanitary standards of Canadian manufacturers (Hansard, 12–13 Feb. 1968, pp. 6633, 6698).

What is most interesting about these accusations was the way the government of the time responded: by acknowledging the health implications of its policy. It was quick to draw on the expertise of the head of the federal drug regulatory body, who stated on the public record that no significant difference existed between generic and brand-name drugs, and that both imported and domestically produced drugs were of the same general quality (Hansard, 13 Feb. 1968, p. 6682). The government actually turned the opposition's arguments around, drawing on the existence and results of the Hall Royal Commission as proof of its commitment to health priorities. It challenged the notion that a link existed between patents and safety, or patents and quality, and claimed that the body of evidence generated by the Hall Commission and the later special committee indicated that no such link existed (Hansard, 12 Feb. 1968, p. 6658). In effect, the government was implying that it had taken into account the pharmaceutical industry's role in health provision, and would not have proceeded with the legislation in question if the changes to patent regulation had put that role at risk.

The debates around Bill C-190 confirmed the institutional entrenchment of the health-provision function of pharmaceutical patents. Both sides of the debate acknowledged that a connection existed between the pharmaceutical patent regime and health provision, and that government must take into account the influence pharmaceutical patents had on health issues. More important, they acknowledged that the aspects of health-provision related to pharmaceuticals depended on the form of the patent regime. The pharmaceutical health provision priorities acknowledged by the regulatory structure embodied in Bill C-190 were safety and cost-based accessibility. C-190 shaped health provision by ensuring access to high-quality, low-cost therapeutic products.

The arguments of those who opposed Bills C-22 and C-91 echoed the accusation of those who opposed Bill C-190: they suggested that the government had failed to recognize (or had deliberately ignored) the health impact of re-regulating the pharmaceutical industry. More specifically, they argued that re-regulating the industry to incorporate it into a global economy, and to court investment into a research and development infrastructure, would have disastrous effects on the domestic health infrastructure by raising the price of pharmaceuticals beyond the point at which the public health infrastructure could be sustained. In other words, by the time of the C-91 debate, the health-provision function of C-190 had assumed institutional status; the health infrastructure in Canada was composed, in part, of the pharmaceutical patent regime provided for in C-190. The opponents of C-91 based their critique of the bill on the assumption that undermining the patent institution would undermine the health-provision institution it defined.

As we have already noted, what lay at the heart of the health debate surrounding Bills C-22 and C-91 was the question of 'in what community?' health provision was to occur. The government's position in both cases was that the long-term success of the industry, and therefore, the long-term success of the health-care system, lay in incorporating the industry into an innovative global economy.[10] This long-term necessity, it seemed to argue, took precedence over any short-term difficulties which would evolve from increased cost. As in the 1960s, the government made the claim that it had acted with conscious knowledge of the health-provision role of the pharmaceutical patents, and

---

10 It should be noted that the process of establishing this argument was spread over the two bills. As Campbell and Pal have noted (1994, 28–9), much of the debate around C-22 was rhetorical (associated, as it was, with the Free Trade Agreement), and centred on establishing the validity of the concept of the global economy. The debate around C-91 had more to do with cost-benefit analysis, and attempted to determine whether or not Canada would benefit from joining the global economy. Whereas the C-22 debates were characterized by accusations of 'selling out' to the Americans, the C-91 debates were characterized by a duel of numbers, with each side trying to establish that C-91 was, or was not, a good piece of 'global economy' policy.

had taken this role into account when designing its pharmaceutical patent regulations.

Bills C-22 and C-91 purported to move the community of health provision to a global level, and shifted the implication of what health provision entailed. Rather than focusing on immediate access to inexpensive drugs, the bills gave higher priority to the potential for long-term access to new drugs (which presumably would offer greater therapeutic benefit). By matching the domestic regulation of pharmaceuticals to international 'norms' (or, at least, the norms which prevailed in the United States and Europe), Bills C-22 and C-91 incorporated the 'Canadian' drug industry into a global community of pharmaceutical innovation. Although the government did claim that this would boost R & D in Canada, it is perhaps more accurate to argue that it gave Canada access to R & D. 'Health' (i.e., new and improved drugs) was to be provided by participating in a broader context of innovation and dissemination. Whereas in the 1960s, the government used the patent institution to establish a context where health provision occurred in Canada, Bills C-22 and C-91 sought to include Canada in an emerging global context where innovation and dissemination supposedly occurred.

By the 1960s, pharmaceutical patents had become associated with the Canadian structure of health provision. It was recognized that changes to the patent regime governing pharmaceuticals would impact on how health (in the form of pharmaceutical therapy) could be provided, recognized, that is, to the extent that legislators anticipated, and prepared for, health-based criticism to pharmaceutical patent legislation. Between this period and the third round of patent change in the late 1980s and 1990s, however, the context of this association changed. Whereas in the 1960s, health provision was a domestic concern, by the 1990s those who formulated pharmaceutical patent policy had to take into account the emergence of the global economy or, at least, the perception that such an economy had emerged. Bill C-190 and Bill C-91 were both limited in their effect to Canada, but they incorporated radically different conceptions of what health was to be provided, and in what context. C-190 constructed a regulatory regime which provided access to therapeutic products by lowering their cost within Canada. C-91 was intended to give access to a space of innovative health through regulation. This shift in context is most visible in the balance between innovation and dissemination implied by Bills C-22 and C-91, a balance only capable of rationalization in the context of global community of innovative health provision.[11] It is this subject, how the balance between innovation and dissemination (and what those terms mean) has varied over time, that draws our attention next.

The New Innovation and Dissemination Balance
Under more conventional circumstances, patent regulation can be boiled down to finding a balance, a point at which innovators view the patent system as a more rewarding means of protecting their intellectual property than the means available from their own resources. The cost to society of making the system appealing to innovators must be balanced against the value eventually to be derived from innovation when it is released into the public domain. When the patents in question are pharmaceutical patents, however, and thus incorporate both industrial and health-provision dimensions, the situation becomes more complex. It is difficult to determine what entails 'just reward' when the product produced is interpreted as a provider of health. Although the industry is quick to conjure images such as that of Banting and Best's discovery of insulin, and attempts to characterize its members as selfless researchers of human well-being, such claims do not survive extended scrutiny. A recurring theme in the Canadian debates around pharmapatents has been the distinctly high rate of profit in the pharmaceutical industry, often several times the average industrial rate.[12]

---

11 Those who did not operate in the conceptual space (the space for thought) of Bill C-91 tended to interpret Bill C-91 as either a sell-out by the government (selling out the interests of Canadians in favour of those of multinational producers) or, at best, a subjugation of the government's power and the interests of Canadians to the power and interests of the multinationals. It was only for those who saw the global economy as an appropriate place for the mechanisms of regulation and the dissemination of technology that the implied innovation/dissemination balance of Bill C-91 held legitimacy. As we have seen, the entrenchment of the concept of the innovative global economy in C-91 discourse forced many opponents (such as the CDMA) to recast their arguments in new terms by the time of the review.

12 To give some idea of these profit levels, between 1958 and 1963, profit rates in the pharmaceutical industry averaged 19.71 per cent, against an average of 10.40 per cent for all manufacturing (Hansard, 13 Feb. 1968, p. 6686). Between 1979 and 1987, the after-tax profits of the pharmaceutical industry averaged 8.3 per cent annually, compared to an average of 3.7 per cent for all manufacturing (Industry, Science and Technology Canada 1991, 3). It must also be pointed out, however, that drug research is a high-cost, high-risk process. The PMAC estimates that it takes more than $500 million to produce a new drug and have it meet safety and efficacy requirements, with the whole process taking in excess of fourteen years (PMAC 1997a, 1).

The relation between pharmaceutical patents and health provision complicates the question of what constitutes an appropriate innovation/dissemination balance, insofar as it introduces debates over what, precisely, is being disseminated and innovated. Is society to encourage the development of any and all new drugs, or only those which extend or improve our means of combatting particular diseases?[13] Can patent regulation be tailored to only encourage the development of certain drugs? The association of health issues with pharmaceuticals changes as well the ethical calculation of dissemination issues: is it ethical, under any circumstances, to limit the accessibility of new methods of treatment, even if this impinges on the traditional rights of new innovators, thereby risking the development of further therapeutic options? Changes in the answers to these questions or, more accurately, changes in how various groups have answered these questions, have prompted the recurring periods of pharmaceutical patent debate and re-regulation in the last century.

We have noted that in both the 1960s era and the 1980s/1990s era of pharmaceutical patent change, the role pharmaceuticals played in health provision was acknowledged. Consequently, by the 1990s, there was an entrenched understanding that alterations to the regulatory scheme structuring the industry would impact the larger system of health provision. What the impact of these alterations would be, however, was hotly debated. At the core of these debates was a conflict over what dissemination entailed in the context of pharmaceutical patents. What health provision meant in the context of pharmaceuticals depended on how one interpreted the appropriate method of disseminating pharmaceutical technology. Debates over pharmaceutical patent regulation were, at their core, debates over how pharmaceutical innovation would be incorporated into a larger strategy of health provision.

When mediating the tension between motivating and disseminating innovation, it is this larger strategy, this larger conceptual context, which is key. When context is taken into account, the tension between motivation and dissemination is not polar in nature, except in the most absolute of senses, because what motivation and dissemination imply

---

13 Is society to encourage the development of drugs such as Viagra or Rogain, which treat impotence and hair loss, to the same degree as it encourages the development of drugs such as AZT or 3TC, which treat AIDS, especially given that the large market available for the former makes them more profitable, and therefore more attractive products to research and produce?

changes. In the 1920s, for example, the development of the compulsory licence seems to have been an attempt to balance the desire for international standards of intellectual property governance against the need to provide the negotiators of these standards with a mechanism to protect their national interest. If, in the eyes of patent regulators, the patent system was being abused (i.e., a state extended the protection of the patent system, but did not see adequate compensation, either in the form of dissemination of innovation or in industrial development), they could take steps to rectify the situation. It was not necessarily the case that states would invoke the mechanism of the compulsory licence, but that drug manufacturers understood that the potential existed and would modify their behaviour accordingly (the potential for 'correction' thus sustaining an appropriate balance between innovation and dissemination). Levels of 'encouragement' for innovation were agreed upon at an international level, but mechanisms existed so that dissemination could be regulated at the national level.

In the 1960s, the explicit intrusion of the 'health provenance' aspect of pharmaceuticals skewed this arrangement in Canada, prompting a manipulation of pharmaceutical patent regulation which would accommodate this new role. Specifically, this meant finding a way to lower costs (and raise accessibility) by introducing price competition into an industry chiefly characterized by patent monopolies – or, at least, by introducing patterns of behaviour consistent with price competition. As John Turner's remarks quoted in chapter 2 indicate, the goal of Bill C-190 was not necessarily to expose domestic production to a high level of actual competition from imports, but rather to introduce the threat of competition from lower-priced imports, which would in turn modify the behaviour of domestic producers in a positive manner (i.e., they would effectively maintain their monopolies, but curtail their monopolistic pricing behaviour). This would retain the incentive to innovate (by retaining the overall structure of the patent system), while meeting the new need for dissemination implied by the role pharmaceuticals played in health provision (by lowering the cost, and therefore increasing the accessibility, of drugs).

In the 1990s the issues considered in determining the appropriate balance between innovation and dissemination in formulating patent regulation took on almost sedimentary characteristics. The issues addressed in earlier patent changes, such as the tension between international standards and domestic control, the need to account for the role pharmaceuticals played in health provision, etc., were present in the

C-22 and C-91 debates. In addition, the changes called for by Bills C-22 and C-91 had to come to terms with balancing the demand for motivation and dissemination of innovation in a changed context, that of the global economy.[14] The resolution of this layering of issues was the strategy of incorporating Canada into the innovative community of health noted above. Opponents of the C-22 and C-91 patent regime argued that it appeared to favour the interests of multinational drug producers, by significantly extending the duration of pharmapatents (thus extending patent monopolies and the amount of time in which an innovating company could profit from its innovation), while simultaneously removing mechanisms, such as the compulsory licence, which interfered with the maximization of monopoly profits. As we have noted, however, these criticisms depend on a perspective in which industrial priorities are intrinsically opposed to those of domestic health. In such a context, the removal of mechanisms such as the compulsory licence might be interpreted as favouring innovation over dissemination in patent mediation, but this is only the case if understood in a context where the balance between innovation and dissemination is maintained within the national policy space. In contrast, those who favoured participation in the global innovative economy argued that the effect of the bills would be to ensure that Canada's structure of health provision would have access to innovation. The C-22/C-91 regime did not so much sacrifice dissemination in favour of innovation, as it purported to ensure dissemination by giving access to a community of innovation. It seems clear that the context for interpretation plays as much a role in establishing and understanding the balance between innovation and dissemination as does the role the industry plays as a provider of health. Equally, we can argue that changes in the balance between innovation and dissemination have implications for the role of the industry in health provision, and the context in which this role operates. Finally, we have seen that a given role for the pharmaceutical industry in providing health demands, in turn, both a particular balance between innovation and dissemination and a particular context of understanding.

---

14 Or, as we have noted, a context which was perceived to have changed. The existence and nature of the global economy is obviously a question whose scope exceeds this chapter. That the actors involved in formulating and debating the pharmapatent changes implied by Bill C-91 spoke as if they apprehended such an economy, is, however, clear.

When pharmapatents change, it seems clear that three interdependent factors are reassessed: the context for regulation, the perceived health-provision role of the pharmaceutical industry in that context, and consequently, what is understood as the appropriate balance between motivating and disseminating innovation. The politics of pharmaceutical patent change in Canada have centred on how those in power interpret the interaction of these factors, and how those with different interpretations respond.

Conclusions

This chapter has focused on the core politics of Canadian IP, which in the post-1987 period, as in earlier eras, centred on the pharmaceutical industry. The three main legislative changes and events have been examined in an era of unambiguous global pressure but also as a manifestation of changing views of what constitutes protection, innovation, and dissemination.

We see again that patents, ultimately, are incentives given to industry or other inventors in return for the eventual dissemination of innovation and new technology. The incentive lies in that it is the government (the public, the public sphere, etc.) which bears some of the costs of securing the innovation through granting its period of monopoly. In this sense, patents operate as a public subsidy to the profits of innovators, ensuring that there exists a structural incentive to innovate. For the public (or government), patents are viewed as a mediation, a process of balancing. Patents are worthwhile as long as the benefit eventually to be derived from innovation outweighs the cost of sustaining that innovation through its period of monopoly.

From this closer exploration of pharmaceutical patents, two further conclusions emerge. The first is that patents can exert tremendous influence as regulatory instruments and mechanisms of change in industries which depend on patents for profit. In such industries, where patents establish the conditions for profitability, they can be used to exert an influence over how the industry is structured and operates. Second, we have seen that such industries can be subject to regulatory change as the public estimation of 'worthwhile cost' or 'legitimate profit' changes. As these industries are dependent on the public's willingness to protect profit, such profits are subject to public review.

In the case of pharmaceuticals, the estimation of legitimate profit has been influenced by more than the usual industrial cost-benefit analysis.

This is, of course, because pharmaceuticals and pharmaceutical patents have been assiciated, since at least the 1960s, with the cost, accessibility, and quality of health care. The inclusion (or intrusion) of health policy issues into pharmapatents has made the balance between innovation and dissemination in such patents unusually volatile. Changes in how the pharmaceutical industry's role as a health provider is interpreted, and changes in the context for understanding health provision, have implied changes in both public and governmental impressions of what an appropriate balance between innovation and dissemination implies for pharmaceutical patents. This volatility, combined with the fundamental influence patents exert over the industry, has meant that pharmaceutical patents have been subject to recurring periods of change throughout this century.

As we saw in chapter 7, many of the recent changes in intellectual property have contributed towards the creation of an IP policy framework. This emerging IP framework operates at two levels: it implies consistency both across national boundaries and across sectors within nations. Our discussion of the recent changes in pharmapatent legislation reveals a similar trend within the pharmaceutical sector. Much of the argument which supported Bills C-22 and C-91 suggested that the changes in regulation were mandated by international trade obligations. A major consequence of enacting these changes was the equation of pharmaceuticals with the product of other 'innovative' sectors. Thus, not only did Bill C-91 and Bill C-22 contribute to the incorporation of Canada into a global IP framework, they also served to incorporate pharmaceuticals into the emerging IP framework of Canada.

What is ironic about this process, however, is that this incorporation of pharmaceuticals into framework universality was justified in terms of sector-specific issues. Like most other ironies associated with the pharmaceutical industry in Canada, this can be traced to the historical association of the pharmaceutical industry with health provision. Thus, although some note was made of Canada's trade and regulatory 'obligations,' what dominated the arguments of those who supported the legislative changes was that the framework approach to IP would tie the pharmaceutical sector into a network of innovation and thus, that the incorporation of pharmaceutical patent regulation into the IP framework would secure health. Cross-sector, cross-national universality was justified in terms of the issues and priorities of a specific sector. More important, it was justified in terms of priorities which predated (and inhibited) the new 'innovative' framework. One of the key lessons to be drawn, then, from pharmapatent change in the 1980s and 1990s is that while the overall trend in IP is towards the construction of an 'innovative' IP framework, this universality of structure and form is not incommensurate with 'inhibitive' political interpretation specific to nations and sectors. Although we may be moving towards a consistent balance, in form, between protection and dissemination, the significance of this balance can and is interpreted within a smaller, inherited, context of political meaning.

9. IP Dissemination and Dispersed Interests: Small Business, Universities, and Innovation

We now turn our attention to the dissemination half of the core IP trade-off and to the more dispersed and in many ways, more emerging IP interests. Many of these interests – small business, universities, and others – were briefly introduced in chapter 1, and also received some attention in chapter 6 in the discussion of copyright institutions and in chapter 8 in the context of pharmaceuticals and health. But we now need a more detailed account, albeit with a focus on the patent aspects of IP. Such an account must be based on two continuing cautionary points about this part of Canada's IP world. The first is that the dissemination role is more difficult to map than the IP protection function and its structure of interests. The second is that there is a tendency to initially portray the interests discussed in this chapter as being weaker politically and as being dispersed and more numerous precisely because they relate more to the dissemination function. This is indeed an important feature, but it must be immediately said that some of these weaker and/or dispersed interests are also producers of IP, or potential seekers after IP protection, and are not always playing from a weak political hand, even though they are small compared to such interests as the big pharmaceutical firms.

The IP dissemination role as a whole is both an old and new role for an IP institution such as CIPO, and the structure of this chapter indicates the plurality of dissemination roles it has assumed. We begin by examining the three roles of IP dissemination and the emerging context of innovation policy in which they are now situated. First, we look at the oldest IP dissemination role, namely, that of making available to IP users in the Canadian economy the current information held in the stock of patents, nationally and globally. Second, the chapter examines briefly a more recent variation on this role, in which CIPO and Industry Canada see opportunities, through computer information technologies, to make available to business new value-added kinds of commercially useful information from IP information held by the government. The third section of the chapter deals with IP dissemination in the form of efforts to expand awareness of IP among those parts of Canada's economy, and society, in general, which have not yet sought IP rights, so that more firms will use the IP systems and contribute to a more innovative economy. In some instances, such efforts can be seen as campaigns to produce an IP culture in Canada. Woven into this discussion is a look at the nature of interests and clients involved in these functions, including small and medium-sized businesses, and fast-forming knowledge networks and consulting firms.

The chapter concludes with an examination of the university sector, where there are complex pressures and relationships that are forcing these institutions to develop policies about IP. Some of these pressures are also linked to a broader set of university-business science and technology 'partnership' relations. In this section, the focus on IP dissemination must be altered because, clearly in matters of copyright and patents, universities are both users and producers of IP. As is the case with the small-business relationship to IP, the evolving IP debate in universities, and between business and universities, is tied to contending views of how innovation is best promoted as a complex learning process.

None of the account in this chapter is intended to suggest that big business and the IP professions have no stake in dissemination roles. They are also major users of IP information. There are also crucial international interests that see the dissemination aspects in a global context, increasingly tied to the emergence and growth of international IP protection and of the Internet. For example, in WIPO, in particular, the dissemination function is linked closely to a larger education and development role in developing countries. WIPO has also been involved in complex discussions over issues such as the links between Internet domain names and trademarks, where emerging interests see the Internet as an enabling institution that promotes a free exchange of information rather than just a new arena of IP protection (WIPO 1997; Drake 1995).

A final cautionary point to emphasize is that dissemination can be seen in ways other than those examined in this chapter. We have already seen this in previous chapters, where dissemination refers to the social use of the actual patented product or process, rather than just the stock of knowledge embodied in the patent. This is where compulsory licensing has historically come to the forefront in Canada and elsewhere, especially when linked to drug products and health.

IP Dissemination I: Informing about the Current Stock of IP Information

IP Dissemination I is the oldest dissemination role and flows from the heart of the basic IP policy and public interest trade-off. In exchange for the patent or other IP protection provided by the state, the IP information must be made public. Others can use it through commercial arrangements with the patent holders, such as licensing agreements, and they can search and study patents and accompanying information with a view to using them as a base for yet further invention. Hence, aspects of a socially and economically useful innovation chain emerge, nationally and globally (Knight 1995).

One way of distinguishing IP Dissemination I from IP Dissemination II is that, as traditionally seen, the first of these roles has been practised by CIPO (and other IP agencies) in a fairly passive public goods–oriented manner. That is, the information is not so much marketed as 'made available,' as a public library makes information available. We leave to the next section the issue of just how different a new, more aggressive value-added IP dissemination role is, but, in the meantime, the nature of this basic role and which interests it serves needs to be sketched out.

The first aspect of this role is that IP information is seen as but one part of a larger stock of information involved in the transfer of technology within nations and among them. In the overall realm of technology transfer, there are an immense number and variety of sources and forms of information. However, one of the advantages of IP information, as part of which one million patent documents alone are published worldwide each year, is that 'it is not only accessible to any country in the world but selected information is a reflection of current development of technology in a concise and uniform presentation' (World Intellectual Property Office 1995e, 100).

The second pattern for CIPO and other national IP agencies is that the basic stock of IP information is used by industry, research and development institutions, universities, and governments. Industry is by far the biggest user, with larger firms being the most frequent users within the industrial-user category. The other three categories are lesser users, but they are important clients of CIPO. Governments use IP information in different policy and operational situations in departments as varied as industry and health. Research and development institutions and universities are frequent users, although all of the agencies encounter what they regard as a misperception about patents in this sector. This misconception is that professors and students engaged in research have somehow formed the view that patents always deal with major breakthroughs and therefore do not relate directly to their narrower research tasks, and accordingly patent information is often not utilized. Some offices are therefore striving to ensure that universities both have access to and make better use of the basic IP information available.

A third feature of the basic dissemination function is the undoubted influence of computerization and the use of new information technologies for storage of, and access to, IP information. The latter include the use of CD-ROM and other technologies. CIPO, in common with virtually every public and corporate institution, has been transforming itself from a largely paper world to a computerized one. This has improved access to data and has reduced costs on an overall basis, but CIPO has also struggled with exactly what kinds of systems to adopt in a vortex of new technologies. Thus, along with the gains, have come complaints from users about adjustment problems, as well as the occasional horror story of how new systems went badly wrong or simply did not live up to oversold expectations. More will be said below about the effect of computerization and the Internet on the Dissemination II role, but, in relation to the basic role being examined here, there is no doubt that it has produced positive benefits.

One other user group of the basic IP information needs to be emphasized. These are the patent and trademark examiners within CIPO itself. They are primary users, along with Canadian and foreign patent and trademark agents and lawyers. For examiners, however, the information and data are crucial to their work at the core of the IP trade-off between protection and dissemination. This fact is also tied to the issue of the critical mass needed to enable a patent office to function properly. The conventional wisdom is that any such full-service IP office needs a critical mass of about one hundred patent examiners to cover the main areas of knowledge and expertise.

IP Dissemination II: A More Aggressive
Value-Added IP Dissemination Role

As mentioned above, there are some grounds for discussing, albeit briefly, a second IP dissemination role. It is not a role promoted or advocated by all national IP agencies, but it has implications that are worth noting because CIPO and Industry Canada have been interested in this concept. This role suggests that CIPO ind Industry Canada should husband and distribute, much more aggressively, value-added IP information. In some instances, the desire to move in this direction is accompanied undoubtedly by a concern that an IP agency or industry department might not survive, or would lose influence unless it can take on such a new and aggressive service-oriented role. But these suggestions are always almost immediately accompanied by caveats and counter-pressures regarding just how 'entrepreneurial' such agencies/departments could be, should be, or would be allowed to be.

An example of this line of thinking came from Canadian developments within both the Department of Industry and CIPO but it has been discussed in other jurisdictions, as well, such as Australia and the United Kingdom. Industry Canada, as we have seen in chapters 1 and 3, has clearly been shifting its philosophy and mandate, in line with developing ideas about industrial and innovation policies, towards playing a knowledge role rather than a spending and subsidizing one (Doern 1995c). In addition, there has been a strong desire to begin to look at its business-framework regulatory areas, not just as protective rules, but also as a source of new information and set of services for business. Thus, data on bankruptcy trends, patterns of new incorporation of firms, and patents and other intellectual property information could be supplied to business, it is felt, in new and useful ways. These and other related service aspects were also seen as being a logical outgrowth of thinking in the Canadian Intellectual Property Office as well as in the Canadian government's overall initiative on service delivery. The more embellished versions of the need for reinvented and more entrepreneurial government, including finding new sources of revenue, were also present in this climate of thinking. Computer and information-system enthusiasts also added grist to this mill because of the ability of such systems to manipulate data in new, fast, interesting, and inexpensive ways. In Industry Canada, these enthusiasms were also further linked to developments to produce one-stop shopping for government information about business and for business. These developments have been spearheaded by Strategis, Industry Canada's web-based information dissemination initiative, which not only offers a proliferating number of framework profiles and effective business strategies, but also information on regulatory practices and processes relevant to Canadian business.

But both CIPO and Industry Canada were immediately aware of what the counter-arguments and pressures would be. First there was the frequently expressed opposition within government to federal agencies attempting to be entrepreneurial in any way that would compete with business. Another counter-pressure came from key IP protection interests, which simply said that any spare resources should go towards supporting the basic IP protection function and to improving pendency performance. This pressure came, and continues to come, from big business IP interests, Canadian patent and trademark agents, and from CIPO's own examiner cadre.

A further kind of opposing argument was that CIPO and Industry Canada, if allowed, would simply not be very good at such implied entrepreneurship. An agency such as CIPO that was geared to a culture of technical control and the protection function would not be good at entrepreneurial or innovative activity. Besides, the proffered IP and other business framework information has many legal and other constraints around its collection that totally or partially prohibit its unfettered or repackaged dissemination.

The final line of argument and pressure was simply that if value-added IP information could be supplied, it was the private sector itself that would discover these possibilities. Moreover, it would be far more nimble and inventive in identifying and profiting from such business opportunities. In brief, CIPO and Industry Canada should not be allowed to play such value-added roles, an argument made by the aggressive small-business lobby, including the fast-growing consulting and information industries.

Because of these immediate counter-pressures, CIPO's descriptions of such a role stress that, if feasible, it would be carried out only as a limited facilitating activity. Thus, for example, CIPO might develop new potential information products and then make them known to business, which would then market them. The ultimate reason for keeping this kind of aggressive role on the institutional analytical agenda, however, is that IP interests, as a whole, including the IP professions, might already be witnessing the presence of what might be called rogue traders in IP-related information. The IP professions have always been concerned about unqualified people practising in their name and have asked CIPO to police these activities.

One of the key features of new information technologies, however, is that they almost immediately have the potential to break down definitions of who carries out what lines of business. If the business is seen simply as providing information or as helping out in brokering innovation, then the presence of new value-added (including incompetent) IP information is quite possible and all the more likely. The United States has seen these developments emerge more than anywhere else, in part, because it has a more entrepreneurial economy to start with.

Thus the pressure for a more value-added IP dissemination activity is likely to come from the private sector, including small business. But the potential should not be ruled out of it coming from IP agencies themselves, especially if national offices become concerned about their own survival or if the general trend develops that many national offices need to specialize in dissemination roles and to provide information to small and medium-sized businesses. The need for national offices to rely on fees rather than tax dollars may also exert pressure over the long run to charge for basic information and to find new sources of information that can be charged for. This is happening in many countries in respect of other government agencies which have similar information roles (e.g., statistical agencies, geological survey agencies).

IP Dissemination III: New Users, Small Business, and the Fostering of an IP Culture

The IP Dissemination III role refers not necessarily to the stock of IP information but rather to getting information out about the IP regime as a whole to firms and inventors which do not yet use it. In one sense, this also is a role which CIPO has been informally carrying out for some time, but the difference now is that it is frequently linked to a more explicit goal of fostering a greater IP culture, or an innovation culture, in the national (and global) economy. Perhaps the best way to locate the issues involved in this third area of IP dissemination is to examine the main features of a Statistics Canada–Industry Canada study of innovation and IP in Canada. Its findings illustrate the complexity of devising policies for expanded IP use by firms not currently using IP (Baldwin 1997). The study examined the use made of IP by firms in Canada's manufacturing sector, as well as by a subset of firms that had just introduced major new products or processes. The forms of IP surveyed were patents, copyrights, trademarks, industrial designs, and trade secrets.

The study found that less that 25 per cent of all firms made use of at least one of these forms of IP, with only 7 per cent using patents but that these firms account for 50 per cent of employment (Baldwin 1997, 9). When data from large and small firms were separated out, it was found that over 62 per cent of large firms (those with more than 500 employees) used IP, compared to less than 30 per cent of small firms (those with less than 100 employees). When those firms which had innovated recently were looked at, the percentages for large and small firms were not much different than for the overall population of firms, 62 per cent of large firms and less than 30 per cent of small firms. (Baldwin 1997, 9). Patents were found to be the IP protection most used by the recently innovating firms.

Interesting, as well, were the reasons given by the innovating firms for not making use of IP protection. The Baldwin study notes that the most frequently cited reason was that the innovation was not deemed to be sufficiently novel to be patentable. Indeed, 'only 15 per cent of innovations in large firms are world-first and only some 30 per cent are firsts for Canada' (Baldwin 1997, 9). A second prominent reason for not using IP was that many innovations are simply not suitable for patent protection. This is especially the case for process innovations, for which secrecy is the preferred mode of protection.

In addition to the direct information about usage and non-usage of IP, the Baldwin study also provided insights into the broader dynamics of business views about, and approaches to, innovation. Reinforcing other U.S. studies, the Baldwin study concludes that 'innate forms of protection, like being first in the market, or having complex product design, are seen by almost every subgroup – large, foreign-owned, innovative firms – as being equally if not more effective in preventing an innovation from being copied' (Baldwin 1997, 10). Perhaps even more importantly, the study concludes that this is broadly true for small firms and that 'small firms do not feel that protection for intellectual assets that they might develop during innovation is lacking,' but rather that they 'feel that innate strategies such as being first in the market, are effective while patents are not' (Baldwin 1997, 10).

Finally, the study also concludes that foreign-owned firms are more likely to make use of IP and to value it more highly and that there are differences among sectors of manufacturing. The obvious sectoral finding is that IP, especially patents, is found to be used and valued to a far greater extent in industries such as the chemical, pharmaceutical, petro-leum industries, as well as by manufacturers of machinery and electri-cal products (Baldwin 1997, 10).

The findings of this study show that it is likely to be difficult to devise policies that target IP-centred dissemination and innovation strategies for small business in some overall sense. This is because small business is not itself a homogeneous category; moreover, small firms perceive themselves in different ways relative to the menu of innovation needs that public policy or public information services might or might not fill. This latter dilemma can perhaps be shown even more starkly through reference to a 1994 study by the European Patent Office (EPO 1994). The EPO study examined the utilization of patent protection in Europe. The context for the study and for the EPO's concerns was centred on Eu-rope's declining patent usage as compared to that of the United States and Japan. For example, the study showed that between 1987 and 1993 first filings in the United States had risen by 47 per cent, from 68,000 to 100,000 (EPO 1994, xi). In Japan, where strict comparison is more difficult, first filings had increased from 310,000 to 332,000 in the same period, despite a policy in Japan to encourage the filing of *fewer* patents (EPO 1994, xi). This latter, seemingly curious, policy was launched because of the tendency of Japanese industry to patent almost anything, often tactically at prematurely early stages of thought and invention.

In contrast, patent usage in Europe had stayed constant at about 89,000 for several years after a period of growth in the early to mid-1980s. As a further indicator of IP usage, the study noted that if data on first filings per million inhabitants were compared, Japan stood at 2,665, the United States at 388, and Europe at 245 (EPO 1994, xii). The study also showed that European patents were mainly in traditional technologies with stagnating markets and were not growing in the such newer areas as biotechnology and computers and information sciences.

The EPO study sought on this basis to obtain information about actual and potential patent applicants among the production industries of Europe. The EPO agenda was also strongly motivated by the desire to seize the potential of small and medium-sized enterprises (SMEs) since they were seen as a crucial link in the overall innovation chain or set of dynamics.

The EPO study concluded that 'the target group for patent activities in Europe is relatively small,' perhaps only 3 per cent of 13 million companies (EPO 1994, 17). Only 16 per cent of these approximately

360,000 companies had already filed patents at the national, European, or international levels. The study also found wide variations in patent usage and potential among European states, strongly correlated with their overall level of economic development. Among the other main conclusions drawn in the EPO study were the following:

- The large group of non-applicants ... has (so far) banked mainly on secrecy for securing their competitive advantage and thus would have to be convinced of the advantages of protection.
- As non-applicants in particular put a higher premium on quality and service aspects than on patents as a competitive tool, SMEs ... must first be made aware of this essential means of protecting innovation.
- In comparison with Japan ... SMEs (in Europe) are more cautious in assessing the inventive value of their developments and are more reticent when it comes to filing patents. This leads us to conclude that access to patents should be made easier, especially for SMEs, so that the length of the procedure or its cost cease to be the determining factors in any decision whether or not to file.
- The fact that the commercial utilization of patented inventions is relatively high among (European) SMEs ... shows that – unlike in Japan – fewer patents are filed for purely strategic reasons (e.g. in order to control a product market). As markets become increasingly global European SMEs will certainly have to place greater emphasis on integrating strategic aspects more closely into their innovation and patent policy.
- There is generally a serious lack of awareness of patent protection procedures among non-applicants, so companies (especially small and medium-sized ones) in the relevant sectors need to be approached directly ...
- As a source of information on technical developments non-applicants in particular rate patent documentation well behind talks with customers, specialized literature, trade fairs and technical research ... (EPO 1994, 17)

Both the Canadian and European studies show that there is certainly room for improvement in increasing the number of firms that are aware of, and that use, IP. But they also suggest, not surprisingly, that the innovation system at the level of the firm is varied and complex, and that varied needs must be met or supplied to *firms*, not just to small-business lobbies as undifferentiated interest groups. In short, it is difficult for CIPO and Industry Canada to reach out to these firms and identify their needs, and then to deliver appropriate services.

Despite these difficulties, small business is clearly a key client group for the expansion of IP awareness and for innovation. Small-business lobby groups in Canada, such as the Canadian Federation of Independent Business (CFIB) or the Canadian Advanced Technology Association (CATA), vary in their political interest and their success in these innovation issues. In the United States, the small-business lobby long ago secured a fee structure that offers lower patent fees for small firms compared to big business (U.S. Patent and Trademark Office 1995). Canada also has special lower charges for small business. Small-business policy agendas, however, are far broader than IP, and, indeed, these firms see innovation as a seamless web of many related activities.

The most evident formal vehicles through which CIPO and other national IP offices are striving to relate to these more dispersed and diverse interests is through advisory bodies and through a greater and more regular use of surveys of user needs and assessments by users of the quality of the services provided. CIPO's Management Advisory Board is composed of individuals knowledgeable about key aspects of these wider dissemination aspects and about parts of the CIPO clientele who might be future users of IP protection. The Management Advisory Board does not include persons from the IP professions or from dominant IP interest groups such as the pharmaceutical industry.

A final point about the various kinds of IP dissemination roles is that they must be linked institutionally and politically to the question of who ought to pay for these activities. Should current IP users who have patents or trademarks and who pay for the protection function through their fees to CIPO also pay for other users, including future users. Or, alternatively, should these costs be paid from some other source? If it is a general taxpayer source, then the government must maintain a strong say, perhaps more than is recognized by the move to give CIPO special operating agency status and the use of mechanisms of fee-based financial flexibility. Inevitably, such issues also raise questions about the division of labour among CIPO, Industry Canada, and other entities seeking to promote an innovation economy. Thus, if dissemination roles are intricately tied to other aspects of innovation in the modern knowledge economy, then might such roles not be better carried out by other combined parts of Industry Canada or indeed provincial industry departments?

CIPO retains the dominant role in IP administration, but it does so in a ministerial context increasingly governed by these larger concerns over innovation and competition. Over the last five years, Industry Canada has embarked, in fact, on a large-scale project to redefine its role in encouraging innovation in Canada. This redefinition of the government's role involves leading and facilitating the growth of productivity and innovation, in partnership with the private sector, and has encompassed a number of initiatives. One was the attempt to foster the growth of innovative workplaces, that is, to make innovation part of the everyday practice of doing business. The key goal was to ensure that business and labour were able to share and disseminate innovative information. To this end, the Ministry of Human Resources Development Canada (HRDC) was to take on the role, of dissemination, acting as a 'clearing house' for innovative practices (Industry Canada 1994a, 34). In addition, HRDC was to initiate a series of sectoral initiatives, in conjunction with the private sector, to improve workplace training, and to identify and rectify skill deficiencies. HRDC began a youth internship project to provide opportunities for work-specific training for those entering the workforce. The government also initiated a review of the Labour Code to ensure that workplace relations could more flexibly adapt to the needs of the innovative global economy.

Another component of the attempt to encourage innovation was the creation of an infrastructure which would support the burgeoning innovative economy, and major goal of this infrastructural project has been the integration of existing communications networks. Although the government recognized the high quality of existing cable, telecommunications, and computer networks, it argued that their integration into an 'information highway' was critical to the development of the Canadian economy. In part, the urgency of this integration stemmed from projects already under way in the United States, Europe, and Japan. An integrated communications net has become the new standard of competition, and the Canadian government argued that it was compelled to respond (Industry Canada 1994a, 53).

The government also took other steps to develop Canada's innovative infrastructure, both expanding it and making it more generally accessible. A CRTC-led regulatory reform of telecommunications sought to increase the level of competition in the sector. The government also encouraged the expansion of wireless communication, making it more accessible both in terms of price and presence; it initiated the CANARIE project, an attempt to encourage research in, and the establishment of, high-speed communications networks; and it sought to expand the percentage of Canadian society integrated into the emerging communications network through such programs as SchoolNet, which would provide schools and educational institutions with access to the Internet. The goal of the latter project was to both ensure that education included training in emerging technology, and to expand Internet integration outside the urban cores (by providing Internet access to rural and remote communities).

Although the expansion of the technological infrastructure was a key initiative of the government's role in encouraging innovation, it is important to note that most, if not all, of its new policy regarding competitiveness has been phrased in such terms. There is a recognition on the part of government that the ability to compete in the global economy necessitates innovation and innovative practices. As such, the bulk of its microeconomic policy is concerned with creating an environment in which firms themselves can innovate (Industry Canada 1994a, 59). The role of the government in creating an innovative economy is as a facilitator and supporter of actions taken by the private sector.

Finally, the new innovative orientation of Industry Canada has been specifically directed towards small business. Most regulatory and service-delivery reform has centred on making government more accessible to new, smaller businesses, which lack the traditional connections to government. A prime motivator of this new 'small is beautiful' orientation is job creation; 87 per cent of new jobs in the 1980s were created by small business (Industry Canada 1994a, 19). Small business is important to the innovative economy to the extent that it is able to capitalize on innovative microeconomic niches (especially within the global innovative economy). The capacity of small business to capitalize on these global micro-niches depends, to a large part, on information flows and organizational flexibility. Thus, the importance of the government's facilitating the development of an enabling infrastructure, without directly interfering in the pursuit of innovation by small-scale private industry.

Increasingly, the IP sector is situated in a larger ministerial context which reflects many of the key issues characteristic of IP debates: how innovation is to be stimulated and disseminated; what the role of government should be in this process; how best to expand the innovative community; and so on. What is important to bear in mind is that the evolving connections between the IP community and its larger context represent an expansion of IP issues well beyond the context of IP itself. Innovation is no longer viewed strictly as a commodity to be husbanded;

rather, it has become a larger social process. Consequently, the protection (and dissemination) of intellectual property has become one component of a larger debate on the role, development, and disbursement of innovation in Canada and the global economy.

University Interests as Users and Producers of IP

Universities and educational institutions and interests are a major example of one of the sets of dispersed interests that cluster around the dissemination function. However, they are also IP players which, though they have traditionally seen themselves as mainly users of IP, are now increasingly having to deal with their role as producers of IP. We have already glimpsed something of this in our analysis of copyright institutions in chapter 6, but the ways in which IP issues are emerging in the university-education sector are quite multifaceted, a fact which is making it difficult for universities to devise their own policies about IP.

At their broadest level, universities have been strongly committed to the support of basic and non-commercial research that is freely exchanged via a peer-review system through numerous national and international journals. In this sense, the very concept of intellectual property and ownership would seem to be almost the opposite of the university ideal (Etzkowitz 1996; Etzkowitz and Leydesdorff 1998). Obviously, however, there have been other ways in which universities have been supportive of intellectual property. Their faculty members, as authors of published books and articles, have their works protected by copyright. There are provisions regarding graduate student research, both to ensure that the student's own work receives proper attribution and recognition by supervising faculty members, and that students also properly attribute the work of others (including professors as authors) in essay and research writing. However, universities, their libraries, and their faculty had for a long time used photocopies from journals and books as course materials, without payment to the authors, and thus had become used to viewing such copying as a free user's right. By the late 1990s, these freedoms were being changed by copyright law, which imposed quite stringent liabilities on universities if they violated copyright. Thus, from this brief summary, three interests can be seen to be present in even a simple university-IP equation: the university as a corporate (usually state-financed) entity; faculty and other employee interests; and students.

In recent years, universities have been influenced by numerous external and internal pressures that further complicate the range of IP choices (Bower 1992; Science Council of Canada 1987). At a broad level, university finances are increasingly centred on the need to obtain partnership funding, especially with business, with the latter insisting on some reasonable commercial relevance (Slaughter and Rhoades 1996). Canadian universities in 1980 obtained about 18 per cent of their basic research funding from private sources, but by the early 1990s, they had become 30 per cent dependent on such funding. Universities have been increasingly seen in industrial policy thinking to be central to how nations, regions, and cities can be made to be more competitive and innovative. Whether cast in terms such as 'Silicon Valley' or as clusters of institutions that promote bottom-up 'network'-centred industrial policy, universities are seen as multi-purpose sources of linkage to local firms and communities (Etzkowitz and Leydesdorff 1998; Roy 1995; Wegloop 1996). These developments produce many different pressures on university research, especially in terms of its purposes and funding. Such pressures affect university policies concerning patenting products and processes, and concerning how profits that might accrue are to be managed and shared.

As is the case with IP and the small-business sector, it is difficult to separate out IP from other aspects of the overall university-industry (U-I) relationship in science and technology. Historical analysis has shown that in Canada's early development there were intricate links among scientists and engineers, their inventions, and university involvement, often tied to natural resource development in mining and agriculture (Langford, Langford, and Burch 1997). A 1995 Industry Canada study by Doutriaux and Barker surveyed an eclectic set of sources and reached several overall conclusions. These were that

- University R & D and U-I linkages generate a high social rate of return;
- Basic research should continue to be adequately supported at universities ... (because research excellence was central to technology transfer);
- Because Canadian universities perform a high share of domestic R & D, and Canadian firms are not, on the whole, highly innovative, the efficient transfer of technology to the domestic market is important;
- University and College Industry Liaison Offices (ILOs), when professionally staffed and allocated sufficient resources, are an important asset for U-I links and technology transfer. A well-run office appears to have a significant impact on the commercial activity generated by a given university;

– Other intermediary organizations, such as networks, consortia and regional economic development organizations, also have critical roles to play in local U-I linkages and technology transfer or diffusion, and they tend to be more approachable to small and medium-sized enterprises (SMEs);
– Industrial sponsorship of university-based R & D is on the rise in Canada. (Industry Canada 1995, 107–8)

It is important to keep these broader observations in mind when considering the study's more specific, but quite limited, conclusions regarding IP and universities, especially regarding patents. In this respect, the study concludes that

> intellectual property rules are mixed, with inventions entirely owned by the university in some cases, or entirely by the professor in others, but typically, arrangements are such that the net result is a 50–50 split. Five of the universities surveyed are affiliated with a research park. Linkages with the local business community are considered important: in most cases the director of the ILO or a representative sits on the boards of the regional economic development organization and participates actively in the activities of other regional or local development groups and networks. (Industry Canada 1995, 92)

Another study that explored university-industry R & D collaboration offered alternative insights and solutions (Conference Board of Canada and NSERC 1995). For example, it suggested that university technology transfer offices (ILOs in the terminology above) 'should be abolished since they tend to bureaucratize the partnership process and inhibit creative solutions'; and that 'universities should not own patents ... rather they should focus on their traditional role of creating knowledge, leaving the role of wealth creation to industry' (Conference Board of Canada and NSERC 1995, 6–7). The quid pro quo, then, is that business should generously support university-based research.

Thus, within Canadian universities, there seem to be two models of IP-related institutional policy or strategy. One might be seen as the Stanford model and be exemplified in Canada by universities such as the University of Waterloo. Though actual policies and practice are rarely this pure, the Stanford model would lean towards encouraging faculty and students to invent and commercialize with little or no IP ownership by the university itself. The pay-off to the university is that it would become known as a dynamic place where researchers, students, and innovators would want to come. The polar opposite model, which some see in policies such as those of the University of Toronto, would be to take the position that all inventions are the university's IP and then, on that basis, negotiate sharing a return.

In 1998 a further review paper was published in a joint endeavour by Industry Canada and the Association of Universities and Colleges of Canada (ARA Consulting Group and Brochu 1998). Part of a symposium titled 'Capturing the Benefits' and clearly an effort to encourage IP in Canadian universities, the paper focuses on major issues surrounding IP management in Canadian universities, including the following: paying for IP management; dealing with conflicts of interest; disclosure practices; spin-off companies versus licensing; and human resource challenges. Also in 1998, Statistics Canada released its data on IP commercialization in higher education, a report which, among other findings, showed that universities in the mid-1990s had established 312 spin-off entities (Statistics Canada 1998).

Although these various mid- to late-1990s studies and reviews indicate an ever-growing interest in IP and universities, they are still quite limited studies which only begin to deal with the issues concerning innovation and its impact on the national economy and on the local-regional economies which universities might serve and draw on.

More specific examples also reveal the trend towards IP and university research funding. One example is the University of Toronto's announcement in 1997 of what the university called the 'largest university intellectual property agreement signed in Canada' (*Montreal Gazette*, 28 Jan. 1997, p. A6). Linked to previous research on Alzheimer's disease, the IP agreement is between the university and Schering Canada, the subsidiary of an American pharmaceutical firm. According to the agreement, the company will provide the university and the Toronto Hospital for Sick Children with up to $34.5 million for further research. It also provided that any drugs or therapies that emerge will be owned by Schering, with the university and hospital promised a share of the royalties, but with the university also owning the 'rights to any diagnostic products that emerge' (*Montreal Gazette*, 28 Jan. 1997, p. A6).

A second example also centred on the Hospital for Sick Children. A dispute arose between one of its doctors and the pharmaceutical company Apotex over clinical trials. The researcher signed a confidentiality agreement with the company but later went public with her scientific concerns about the drug. She was threatened with legal action by the company, and, among many problems that emerged, the hospital was unwilling to support her in her legal problems with Apotex. An inquiry resulted within the hospital, and the episode became a major media story, which raised issues about conflict of interest, ethics, and university and hospital dependence on corporations for financing research (*Ottawa Citizen*, 11 Sept. 1998, p. A22).

And finally, to show the growing range of issues, one can also note IP issues regarding teaching and course content material. Although textbooks always involved copyrighted material, older teaching methods using blackboards and professorial lecture notes did not. In an era of the Internet, multimedia content material, and even lecture note transparencies, IP has a wider relevance as universities see their courses taught in distance learning and, indeed, in global course delivery.

Conclusions

The dissemination function in the IP trade-off is a key part of what a national IP agency such as CIPO must manage, but it is still its secondary rather than its primary impulse. IP dissemination is also crucial to views about innovation policy, national systems of innovation, and innovating institutions as flexible learning agencies. The analysis shows that CIPO has been seeking to enhance its dissemination functions, a task which invariably means broadening its view of, and contacts with, a quite diffuse set of interests. The ethos of reinvented government has also influenced both CIPO and Industry Canada, more generally, to seek out and service its full range of customers and clients.

This chapter suggests that the IP dissemination function needs to be characterized in a threefold manner. It embraces a traditional role in the use of the existing stock of IP information. It also involves a role in which CIPO and/or Industry Canada seek more aggressively to provide a value-added IP service to business and other users. And, last but not least, it involves activities to foster the greater use of IP by businesses and other institutions which are not yet users of IP.

In the analysis of both small business and universities as more dispersed IP dissemination interests, the chapter shows that much diversity exists at the level of individual firm or institution as to how IP is viewed and as to where in the menu of innovation-promoting activities and policies IP is seen. It is also evident from the analysis that the more one probes the interests themselves as simple aggregates (small business, universities), the more it is necessary to recognize that they themselves are composed of sub-interests who have benefits and costs that accrue on both the protection and dissemination sides of the IP coin.

Universities, in particular, are undergoing a transformation regarding their own sense of where the IP trade-off should be made. Propelled partly by a greater reliance on business funding for research, universities in Canada are only beginning to deal with their own IP strategies. As they become more aggressive advocates of IP protection and as their faculty and students become more entrepreneurial, the image of universities as objective sources of knowledge for society will undoubtedly change. Universities are also under intense pressure, both from within and from advocates of national and local/regional systems of innovation, to become a central part of local/regional networks of invention and innovation in ways that were not expected during the earlier era of industrial policy.

10. Conclusions

Intellectual property policy and institutions in Canada and elsewhere are centred on a crucial trade-off between protecting IP and disseminating IP. But the nature and point of that trade-off has been changing over the last twenty years in ways that require us to understand innovating institutions from a number of different vantage points. Accordingly, this book has been about innovating institutions in three senses. Its focus has been on Canadian intellectual property institutions, including their relations with key interests, whose very purpose is to encourage invention and innovation through laws, policies, and decisions that both protect IP and disseminate it. It has dealt with IP institutions which are themselves being compelled to innovate in the global economy and in the face of pressures to change the nature of governance in many policy fields, in part through the concepts of reinvented government and the New Public Management. And it has dealt with IP institutions and policies that are embedded in a larger transformation of policy, from an era of industrial policy to one centred on innovation policy and to an era of changing conceptions of national versus international innovation and access by Canadians to an international community of innovation.

This book has provided the first comprehensive account of Canada's IP institutions. Other important policy fields typically have more of this groundwork already done by scholars, but this has not been the case for IP. IP institutions and interests have long needed a more focused scrutiny. Both the protection and dissemination aspects of the core IP trade-off are embedded in increasingly complex and changing conceptions and perceptions of innovation; the various national and global systems and communities have different notions of what innovation is, and how it operates. As we have seen, the state is itself simultaneously a creator, grantor, enforcer, and user of intellectual property. In matters of IP, as in other policy domains, the state is not a neutral player. Its interdepartmental and institutional politics help define IP policies and implementation, and are in turn influenced by changing interest-group coalitions.

The analysis has shown that recent changes and redefined IP trade-offs are not the product of some set of immutable laws of economics. Though clearly influenced by economics and changing technologies, they are also the product of pressure by interests, the articulation of new ideas about what policy reality is, and the preferences and inertial forces within IP institutions. Our intent has been to supply a clearer analytical portrait for those interested in how IP institutions function as political and governmental bodies and sets of competing and cooperating interests. Above all, we have sought to examine the diverse and complex interplay among IP ideas, institutions, and interests, not only in Canada but internationally, as well.

While the book has provided a more integrated middle-level look at Canada's IP institutions and core politics than any available at present, we have been careful to point out the limitations of the analysis, as well. First, among the four realms of IP policy and operations, the focus has been primarily on patents, and secondarily on copyright and trademarks. Industrial designs have not been covered. Second, we have by no means examined all Canadian IP, or IP-related, institutions in that this would have included a macro-level approach to overall systems of law and other ministries and elements of the federal government, including the courts and related enforcement processes. Third, although we have referred to many policy issues inherent in the functioning of Canada's IP institutions, this has not been a book on all aspects of Canadian IP policy as such.

We now proceed with some concluding observations on the five main arguments advanced about Canada's IP institutions and interests in the Introduction, and discussed in several different ways throughout the analysis. We also highlight some other policy and institutional issues still left unresolved as new pressures mount which may further change the nature of the central IP trade-off.

Explaining IP Policy's Slow Rise to Prominence

Our first overall historical argument has been that, despite over seventy years of history and linkage to international IP treaties and rules, IP in

Canada has only very recently emerged from political obscurity in national economic and political debate. IP policies and issues have remained in the backwaters of political and economic debate, in part, because the keys to Canadian prosperity and the preferred policies and policy levers were seen historically to reside in other realms, be they a reliance on natural resource–driven growth, Keynesian macroeconomic policy, tariffs, subsidies, and R & D spending, or any number of particular policy initiatives. In the 1990s, IP has ridden the conceptual coattails of innovation policy to greater political-economic prominence, but innovation policy, as we have seen, is hardly a beacon of clarity as the new Millennium begins.

The legal and policy history in chapter 2 has shown a long lineage of basic laws since Confederation, but also a distinct pattern of IP issues being episodic, with long periods between major changes in the law. The policy reviews of the Ilsley Commission and the Economic Council of Canada showed gradual post–Second World War changes in thinking through to the end of the 1960s. They confirmed that most patents in Canada were filed by foreigners, and they documented the change among Canadian patent holders from largely independent persons to corporations. Gradual shifts in thinking were evident in these policy reviews about what the right balances were for Canada between protection and dissemination, and just how much protection is needed to be an effective incentive to innovate.

The role of compulsory licensing was always a component of this discussion but there were mixed views about the value of this provision for Canada's IP trade-offs as a whole. The Economic Council's 1971 report was remarkably ahead of its time in its discussion of IP as a central feature of innovation and even of an information economy. But not much resulted from these reviews, largely because IP was still seen as peripheral to the economic priorities of government. Even the policy history of the 1970s and 1980s, outlined in chapter 3, showed again the almost total lack of salience of IP in the context of traditional industrial policy that characterized this period. In brief, IP simply was still not a high priority for key industrial policy-makers in the federal government.

Thus, relative to its long-term history, it is not hard to show an IP ascendancy in the 1990s, but it has been a painfully slow rise out of obscurity. Even now it is important to stress that though IP has a greater salience than it had during earlier decades, it is still not at the very highest levels of policy consciousness. Its relatively elevated status is nonetheless a result of overall global pressures and ideas which have caused governments to look more widely, and with perhaps more subtlety, for the many kinds of answers that might be needed in a knowledge economy to ensure economic prosperity and to foster innovation on a continuous basis. The analysis has shown that IP's rise to prominence has also come about because older policy levers are simply not available in the ways they once were. The tariff and the use of subsidies, in particular, were greatly reduced as policy tools, either because new trade regime rules reign in on their use or because governments have run out of money. But if IP policy is being paid more attention, it still does not arrive on the new innovation policy agenda unaccompanied. It remains clustered in a broad set of market-place framework policies, and, of course, it coexists with some remaining policies from the old tool kit of traditional industrial policy.

Canada as an IP Policy-'Taker'

The second argument to emerge from an institutional and political focus is that the main impetus for change in Canada has come ultimately from U.S. corporate and political forces seeking to strengthen IP protection at the expense of IP dissemination. The analysis has shown that Canada initially resisted such pressures but then ultimately adopted them as being in the national interest in the new innovation age. In an overall sense, Canada has become more of a policy-taker than a policy-maker on matters of IP.

The IP protection function, especially for patents and copyright, is undoubtedly being driven mainly by U.S. industry lobbies with IP protection interests, backed by an American government which sees such industries as areas where U.S. economic advantage can be maximized, as well as by U.S. political power in international trade and economic relations. Chapter 4 has shown that at their broadest level, global changes emanate from the changed role and importance of bodies such as WIPO and GATT-WTO, and the formation of regional IP bodies such as the EPO. But the analysis overall has shown that the crucial engine of change has come from the United States, reflecting changes not only in the interest-group politics of trade and intellectual property policy in the United States but also leadership changes in the USPTO, which became more copyright-centred.

Somewhat in between these broad and more concerted causal forces of change have been parallel and reinforcing changes in the nature and structure of IP agencies in other key countries. All have become more fee-dependent, conscious of comparative pendency efficiency rates and performance, and seeking to become more service- and dissemination-oriented IP bodies. These developments, in turn, put national offices in a situation of both conflict and cooperation with regional and international bodies.

But it has also been shown that this does not mean that the Canadian government always opposes such a global and U.S. emphasis on IP protection. Domestic pressure and the government's own changing views of the microeconomy may have been sufficient to move policy in the direction it has moved in the last decade in any event, though probably not as far. Thus, as was described in chapter 6, copyright enjoyed an ascendancy in the 1990s because it was possible for Canadian policy-makers to cast it as a cultural policy which, unlike many other subsidy-based cultural policies which were seen as antithetical to market liberalism, could be presented as being entirely in keeping with such pro-market framework rules. This did not mean that there were not intense disputes between creator and user interests in copyright, but there is little doubt that creator interests have been in the ascendancy during the last several years because of the federal government's encouragement of global forces.

The analysis of pharmapatents, especially in chapter 8, also has shown that by the late 1990s the federal government, in response to pressure and arguments from its industry and trade departments, was gradually adopting the view that the global agenda was in Canada's interests. The three legislative events examined in chapter 8 showed first a reluctant acceptance of global forces, then mild support for them, and finally a sense of almost enthusiastic endorsement, in part, because the appeal of the global innovation agenda was congealing in the inner economic soul of the federal government.

More Concentrated Institutional Power amid Greater Institutional Complexity

The third argument advanced is that, within the federal government, IP policy has increasingly been taken over by trade policy agencies, whose power has been consolidated despite the fact that IP policy as a whole has become institutionally more complex, involving more agency and departmental players. IP policy influence is concentrated in Industry Canada and the Department of Foreign Affairs and International Trade

(DFAIT), where IP protection norms are all-pervasive. They – along with CIPO at an operational level – have become ever more dominant over departments such as Health Canada and Canadian Heritage and their ministers.

The analysis has shown that the central institutions of IP policy are spread across at least four departments of the federal government and involve at least six identifiable agencies. This is especially the case when one thinks of these departments and agencies as being at the core of the protection function in IP. When one adds the dissemination function, the IP regime widens, as we have seen, into a secondary set of departments and agencies which extend into provincial government domains and into an array of educational institutions.

In one sense, it is possible to conclude that this IP policy and institutional regime within the federal government as a whole does have a more integrative sense of itself as an *intellectual property* field per se than it did a decade ago, but in other respects it still functions as different subsets of issues, ideas, and players. Any broad policy field has this characteristic to some extent. For example, the federal government department National Resources Canada sees itself as a maker of policies about 'natural resources,' but in practice it still works with policies that deal separately with oil and gas, nuclear power, mining, and forestry.

In the case of the components of IP, the separate realms of patents, trademarks, and copyright have lives of their own, in part, because there are crucial technical bases for doing so and, in part, because the structure of interests insists on it, with historical inertia helping preserve the separate realms. On the technical side, we have seen in chapters 4 and 5 the separate processes needed to handle patents, in which a scientific-technical judgment must be made about a very particular invention. The situation regarding trademarks is quite different in that the judgments required are much closer to an art than a science-based decision. Meanwhile, copyrights involve a 'process' in which there is no mandatory registration (in Canada); rather, an immediate moral and economic claim is established.

The interest-group pressures that keep the realms partly separate have also been evident in the course of the discussion. The structure of political interests in and around the three areas of IP are different, and they have themselves helped design the sub-elements of the institutions to meet their economic needs and political values. Trademark institutions have been shaped by big business, but have also been forged by smaller Canadian firms functioning in national markets. And copyright policy has separate institutions partly because the interests seeking protection are smaller dispersed players organized into collective associations. Patent institutions and processes are increasingly dominated by big business and the IP profession, both functioning in a global economy. But, more significantly, big business, in essence, is creating the global economy (or, at least, the conditions for a global economy). What gives Canada access to the global innovative economy is a regulatory regime consistent with the perceptions/ideals of that economy, a regulatory regime mandated by international treaty, which in turn is supported by big business.

IP as Sectoral Policy in the Guise of Framework Policy

Our fourth argument is that despite the claim that IP is becoming one integrated policy field with beneficial 'framework'-oriented non-discriminatory features, institutional evidence suggests that it is still overwhelmingly driven in crucial ways by sectoral politics, centred especially in the pharmaceutical and biotechnology industries. Indeed, it must be said that even patent policy on its own is not easily elevated to a high degree of political consciousness if it is seen as a genuine framework issue. It is only in specific sectors, where IP either is inherently of key interest or is associated with sector-specific issues such as health, that it is brought to light. In other words, establishing IP as a framework hides it as a point of contention, unless it piggy-backs on another contentious issue. Since these issues are driven by sectoral political interest groups and key firms, patent policy, though rationalized increasingly as a framework 'one size fits all' policy, is still significantly and crucially sectoral policy.

The economics of IP does not support the view that one length of patent protection fits all circumstances of invention and economic returns on investment. Nor does it support the view that all countries should have one defined regime of protection length, when different invention versus imitation strategies are quite justifiable on economic grounds. It is largely the sectoral politics-cum-global politics of the pharmaceutical and biotechnology industries that explains the preference for twenty years of protection. Chapter 7 showed that industry and trade departments (in Canada and elsewhere) are reluctant to admit that *framework* really does not mean *framework* because if they did, it would mean admitting that different sectoral IP policies are possible and justifiable. If so, IP would simply look like another form of industrial policy, with IP being a functional substitute for the tariff or for earlier subsidies. However, as we have seen, IP is in other respects not just a substitute policy instrument in that it is inherently linked to invention and knowledge creation in a way that traditional tariffs and subsidies were not.

Nor do the potential clashes of framework versus sectoral arguments or of interest groups end with those examined in this book. As suggested in chapter 3 and elsewhere, various configurations of such conflicts are likely to arise in areas such as IP and biodiversity, the patenting of life forms and biotechnology, IP and the Internet, and IP and competition policy. Biodiversity is just one of many trade and environment tensions, but there are direct IP issues which Canada must deal with both in its own biodiversity and IP laws and in its negotiation and implementation of international agreements with the developed and developing world. IP-linked policy controversy centres on the patenting of higher life forms and the broader economic and ethical issues inherent in regulating biotechnology. At present, the situation in Canada is that Canadian law does not allow higher life forms to be patented, whereas U.S. IP law does. There is no strong domestic industry yet pushing for changes in the law, but Canada will have to face these issues since they are on the WTO negotiating agenda.

Another crucial area where IP issues arise is in the area of digital technology and the Internet or 'information highway.' As has been indicated, debates have evoked a range of views about just where the IP trade-offs should be made. Some argue that copyright protection should be reduced or that, de facto, national sovereignty IP rules simply cannot be effectively applied in the global realm of cyberspace. In addition, the new technologies blur some distinctions between when a creation is a good or product, and thus perhaps patentable, as opposed to when it is authored information and involves copyright protection. Last, but far from least, the Internet is itself seen as an enabling technology for competitive innovation activity, and thus it is not seen just as a new site for IP debate and conflict.

Competition policy and implementation is also likely to be an arena for interesting potential clashes with IP. Competition policy is not the same as policy aimed at competitive innovation in that the former deals with particular anti-competitive acts within definable markets. Thus there is a potential clash between IP, which grants monopolies, and competition policy, which seeks to reduce predatory and other anti-competitive behaviour. National IP institutions believe broadly that their realms have a kind of precedence over competition law, and that it is competition law and policy that are 'fenced out' and deemed not in general to apply to situations where intellectual property rights per se apply. Second, competition laws themselves vary across countries as to whether their main purpose is competition as defined above or is linked to related economic concepts such as consumer surplus, economic efficiency, economic integration, or broader public interest or even industrial policy objectives. They also vary in their enforcement mechanisms, including whether private actions are possible. It would seem highly likely that producer or consumer interests will increasingly launch cases nationally and globally to test IP laws that are viewed as too protectionist and anti-competitive. In this context, one nominal framework policy will do battle with another nominal framework policy, but mainly in regulatory bodies and in the courts.

Emerging IP Interests and the Changed Nature of IP Dissemination and Innovation

Finally, we have argued that the dominance of the protection function in IP institutional politics and interest-group relations seriously underplays the importance of other emerging interests for whom IP dissemination is crucial, but who have not yet found their voice in the IP policy process. In part, this lack of voice for emerging interests is a result of their inherent political weaknesses as dispersed smaller IP users, but it is also the result of the complex nature of how IP and innovation are viewed in practical terms.

With regard to the dissemination function and its structure of interests, the overall picture that emerges is a paradoxical one. In the IP policy process as such, it is undoubtedly the case that protection interests are in the ascendancy. However, CIPO, while still supporting this emphasis, is trying to expand its IP dissemination activities to reach the weaker more diffuse user interests. Chapter 9 has shown that the search by CIPO for a broader sense of this part of its clientele is likely to be a long uphill battle, unless such interests themselves secure more influence and representation.

We have argued that the IP dissemination function needs to be characterized in a threefold manner. It embraces a traditional role in the use of the existing stock of IP information. It also involves a role in which

CIPO and/or Industry Canada seek more aggressively to provide a value-added IP service to business and other users. And, last but not least, it involves activities to foster the greater use of IP by businesses and other institutions which are not yet users of IP. In the analysis of both small business and universities as more dispersed IP dissemination interests, it has been shown that there are quite diverse views at the level of the individual firm or institution as to how IP is viewed and as to where in the menu of innovation-promoting activities and policies such entities see IP. It is also evident from the analysis that the more one probes the interests themselves as simple aggregates (small business, universities), the more it is necessary to recognize that they themselves are composed of sub-interests who have benefits and costs to trade off on both the protection and dissemination sides of the IP coin.

We have shown that there is certainly a desire among federal IP and industrial policy-makers to promote a greater awareness of IP rights, technology transfer, and innovation in an overall sense. It has also been shown, however, that small businesses, in particular, rightly see the innovation process in varied ways, and therefore seek a menu of policy and industry services that may or may not centre on, or include, intellectual property. Universities are also only beginning to come to grips with their role as both creators and users of IP. A strong case exists for expanding IP awareness and education throughout the economy, but it will have to be done with a sophisticated sense of the different perceptions of the diverse players in the knowledge economy, and in a way that preserves the independence of universities.

In a final overall sense, the five main arguments show that an understanding of innovating institutions is a complex task, demanding analysis at several levels. IP is central to the innovation process, but its core trade-off is being continuously renegotiated as innovation is redefined and as IP institutions and interests test out the limits of their political power both in Canada and globally. Our account of the changing nature of the pharmapatent debate shows that basic conceptions of the meaning of innovation within IP and outside it have changed. In earlier stages, innovation meant not only the encouragement of new drug products but also, through compulsory licensing, a socially enforced obligation to make them available for use. During other periods, innovation linked invention incentives with provisions to ensure reasonable prices. And more recently, innovation has been deemed to be tied to IP policies that guarantee long-term, twenty-year protection, on the grounds that this will attract innovative firms to Canada and will gain access for

Canadians to a world stock of health-care innovation and, indeed, to world systems of innovation.

But pharmaceutical industries or even biotechnology industries and other future knowledge industries are not, and will not be, the only creators of intellectual property in its various forms. The chances are high that Canadian IP institutions and policies will involve a far wider set of players than has been the case during the period covered by this book. However, it is not clear what kind of Canadian players will emerge – whether they will be those able to operate in the global market, or global players in the Canadian market, or players who are capable of doing both. A far greater searchlight of scrutiny will have to be brought to bear now that IP has become a preferred weapon of choice in the global and national knowledge-based economy and in the transformation of innovating institutions writ large.

References

Abbott, Frederick M. 1989. 'Protecting First World Assets in the Third World: Intellectual Property Negotiations in the GATT Multilateral Framework.' *Vanderbilt Journal of Transnational Law* 22(4): 689–746.

Acharya, R. 1992. 'Patenting of Biotechnology: GATT and the Erosion of the World's Biodiversity.' *Journal of World Trade* 25(6): 71–87.

Advisory Council on Industrial Property. 1995. *Review of the Petty Patent System*. Canberra: Australian Industrial Property Organization.

Albert, Michel. 1993. *Capitalism against Capitalism*. London: Whurr Publishers.

American Intellectual Property Law Association. 1995. *Statement to the Subcommittee on Courts and Intellectual Property, Committee on the Judiciary, House of Representatives*. Statement on Bills to Incorporate the Patent and Trademark Office. Washington, 14 September.

Anderman, Steve. 1998. *EC Competition Law and Intellectual Property Rights*. Oxford: Oxford University Press.

Appleyard, Bryan. 1999. *Brave New Worlds*. London: Harper Collins.

ARA Consulting Group and Mireille Brochu. 1998. 'Approaches of Canadian Universities to the Management and Commercialization of Intellectual Property.' Paper prepared for the Symposium on Intellectual Property, 26 November, Association of Universities and Colleges in Canada, Ottawa.

Arrow, Kenneth. 1962. 'Economic Welfare and the Allocation of Resources for Invention.' In *The Rate and Direction of Inventive Activity*, ed. National Bureau of Economic Research. Princeton: Princeton University Press. 22–41.

Ashford, Tony. 1996. 'Regulating Agricultural Biotechnology: Reflexive Modernization and the European Union.' *Policy and Politics* 24(2): 125–36.

Association of Universities and Colleges of Canada (AUCC). 1996. Submission to the House of Commons Standing Committee on Canadian Heritage regarding Bill C-32 An Act to Amend the Copyright Act. 1 September.

Aucoin, Peter. 1997. *The New Public Management: Canada in Comparative Perspective*. Montreal: McGill-Queen's University Press.

Australian Industrial Property Organization. 1995. *Strategic Directions 1995–99*. Canberra: AIPO.

Bainbridge, David I. 1994. *Intellectual Property*. 2nd ed. London: Pitman.

Baldwin, John. 1997. *Innovation and Intellectual Property*. Ottawa: Statistics Canada and Industry Canada.

Bellamy, Christine, and John A. Taylor. 1998. *Governing in the Information Age*. Buckingham: Open University Press.

Benko, Robert. 1987. *Protecting Intellectual Property Rights*. Washington: American Enterprise Institute for Policy Research.

Berkowitz, M., and Y. Kotowitz. 1982. 'Patent Policy in an Open Economy.' *Canadian Journal of Economics* 15(1): 1–19.

Best, Michael. 1990. *The New Competition: Institutions of Industrial Restructuring*. Cambridge: Polity Press.

Bhagwati, J., and H.T. Patrick, eds. 1990. *Aggressive Unilateralism*. Ann Arbor: Michigan University Press.

Bhat, Mahadev G. 1996. 'Trade-Related Intellectual Property Rights to Biological Resources: Socio-Economic Implications for Developing Countries.' *Ecological Economics* 19: 205–17.

Bogsch, Arpad. 1992. *Brief History of the First Twenty-five Years of the World Intellectual Property Organization*. Geneva: World Intellectual Property Organization.

Bower, J. 1992. *Company and Campus Partnerships Supporting Technology Transfer*. London: Routledge.

Bradley, Jane. 1987. 'Intellectual Property Rights, Investment, and Trade in Services in the Uruguay Round: Laying the Foundations.' *Stanford Journal of International Law* 32: 57–98.

Braga, Carlos Prima. 1995. 'Trade Related Intellectual Property Issues: The Uruguay Round Agreement and Its Economic Implications.' In *The Uruguay Round and the Developing Countries*, ed. Will Martin and Alan Winters, pp. 52–71. Washington: World Bank.

Brander, J.A., and B.J. Spencer. 1983. 'International R & D Strategy and Industrial Rivalry.' *Review of Economic Studies* 50: 707–22.

Brown, J.J. 1967a. *Ideas in Exile: A History of Canadian Invention*. Toronto: McClelland and Stewart.

– 1967b. *The Inventors: Great Ideas in Canadian Enterprise*. Toronto: McClelland and Stewart.

Brown, Kenneth. 1988. *Inventors at Work*. Washington: Tempus Books.

Brunet, C. 1994. *Copyright and the Information Highway*. Draft Final Report of the Copyright Subcommittee. September.

Campbell, Colin. 1996. 'Does Reinvented Government Need Reinvention?' *Governance* 8(7): 479–504.

Campbell, Robert M., and Leslie A. Pal. 1994. *The Real Worlds of Canadian Politics*. 3rd ed. Peterborough, ON: Broadview Press.

Canada. 1960. Royal Commission on Patents, Copyright, Trade Marks and Industrial Designs (Ilsley Commission). *Report*. Ottawa: Queen's Printer.

– 1984. *From Gutenberg to Telidon: A White Paper on Copyright*. Ottawa: Minister of Supply and Services.

– 1985. *Report of the Royal Commission on the Economic Union and Development Prospects for Canada*. Vol. 1. Ottawa: Supply and Services Canada.

– 1997. *Review of the Patent Act Amendment Act 1992*. Ottawa: Industry Canada.

– 1998a. 'Federal Government Releases New Biotechnology Strategy.' News release. Ottawa: Industry Canada. 6 August.

– 1998b. *Health Sector Consultation Document: Renewal of the Canadian Biotechnology Strategy*. Ottawa: Industry Canada.

– 1998c. *The 1998 Canadian Biotechnology Strategy: An Ongoing Renewal Process*. Ottawa: Industry Canada.

– 1998d. *Renewal of the Canadian Biotechnology Strategy: Related Resource Documents*. Ottawa: Industry Canada.

– 1998e. *Renewal of the Canadian Biotechnology Strategy: Roundtable Consultation Document*. Ottawa: Industry Canada.

Canadian Association of Broadcasters – Television Board. 1996. Submission to the House of Commons Standing Committee on Canadian Heritage respecting Bill C-32, An Act to Amend the Copyright Act. 3 September.

Canadian Association of Broadcasters – Radio Board. 1996. Submission to the House of Commons Standing Committee on Canadian Heritage respecting Bill C-32, An Act to Amend the Copyright Act. 3 September.

Canadian Association of Research Libraries / Association des bibliothèques de recherche du Canada (CARL/ABRC). 1996a. Brief to the Standing Committee on Canadian Heritage concerning Bill C-32 (An Act to Amend the Copyright Act). 15 August.

– 1996b. Position Statement on Copyright. January.

Canadian Association of University Teachers / Association canadienne des professeures et professeurs d'université (CAUT/ACPPU). 1996. Brief by the Canadian Association of University Teachers to the Standing Committee on Canadian Heritage on Bill C-32 (An Act to Amend the Copyright Act). August.

Canadian Copyright Licensing Agency (CANCOPY). 1996. Submission of the Canadian Copyright Licensing Agency to the Standing Committee on Canadian Heritage regarding Bill C-32, An Act to Amend the Copyright Act. 29 August.

Canadian Drug Manufacturers Association (CDMA). 1994. *The Impact of Bill C-91 on Canada's Health Care System: A Brief Overview.* Toronto: CDMA.

– 1996. *Response by the Canadian Drug Manufacturers Association to 'A Prescription for Success.'* Toronto: Canadian Drug Manufacturers Association.

– 1997. *Pharmaceutical Patents and the Review of Bill C-91: The View from Canada's Generic Industry.* Toronto: CDMA.

Canada Health Coalition. 1997a. *Media Release: Bill C-91 Review.* Ottawa: Canadian Health Coalition.

– 1997b. *Need, Not Greed: A Brief to the House of Commons Standing Committee on Industry Review of Bill C-91.* Ottawa: Canadian Health Coalition.

Canadian Intellectual Property Office (CIPO). 1993. *Business Plan 1993–94 to 1995–96.* Ottawa: Canadian Intellectual Property Office.

– 1994a. *A Guide to Trade Marks.* Ottawa: Industry Canada.

– 1994b. *CIPO Regional Intermediary Conferences: Final Report.* Ottawa: CIPO.

– 1994c. *1992–1993 Annual Report.* Ottawa: Industry Canada.

– 1995. *On the Canadian Patent Office Decision of the Commissioner of Patents (Re: Patent Application No. 484,723.* Ottawa: CIPO.

– 1996. *1994–95 Annual Report.* Ottawa: Industry Canada.

Canadian Publishers' Council. 1996. Submission of the Canadian Publishers' Council to the Standing Committee on Canadian Heritage regarding Bill C-32. August.

Canadian Recording Industry Association. 1996. Presentation of Canadian Recording Industry Association to the Standing Committee on Canadian Heritage. 22 October.

Carpenter, Thomas. 1990. *Inventors: Profiles in Canadian Genius.* Camden East, ON: Camden House.

Centre for Medicines Research International. 1997. *1997 Annual Report.* Carshalton, Surrey: Centre for Medicines Research International.

Chartrand, H.H. 1996. 'Intellectual Property Rights in the Postmodern World.' *Journal of Arts, Management, Law and Society* 25(4): 306–19.

Cohen, D., and K. Webb. 1999. *The Use of Voluntary Codes in Government.* Ottawa: Government of Canada.

Conference Board of Canada and Natural Sciences and Engineering Research Council of Canada. 1995. *University-Industry Synergy: Report of the Symposium on University-Industry R & D Collaboration.* Ottawa: Conference Board of Canada and NSERC.

Consumer and Corporate Affairs Canada. 1990. *Intellectual Property and Canada's Commercial Interests.* Ottawa: Minister of Supply and Services.

– 1991. *Intellectual Property: Litigation, Legislation and Education, A Study of the Canadian Intellectual Property and Litigation System.* Ottawa: Minister of Supply and Services.

Consumers' Association of Canada. 1996. 'Taxing Tape: "Who's Zoomin' Who?"' Submission to the House of Commons Standing Committee on Canadian Heritage on Bill C-32, An Act to Amend the Copyright Act. September.

Cook, T., C. Doyle, and D. Jabbari. 1991. *Pharmaceuticals, Biotechnology and the Law*. London: Macmillan.

Copyright Board Canada. 1991. Internal Document. Presentation made by Vice President on functions of the Copyright Board. December.

– 1996a. *Annual Report 1995–1996*. Ottawa.

– 1996b. Submission of the Copyright Board on Bill C-32, An Act to Amend the Copyright Act, to the Standing Committee on Canadian Heritage. 3 September.

Curtis, John. 1990. 'Intellectual Property and International Trade.' *Institute of Development Studies Bulletin* [University of Sussex] (January).

Davis, G. 1994. *Copyright and the Public Interest*. IIC Studies, vol. 14. Weinheim: VCH Verlagsgesellschaft mbh.

de la Mothe, John. 1994. 'Canada and National Innovation systems.' In *Science and Technology Resource Handbook*, ed. J.A.D. Holbrook. Ottawa: Government of Canada.

– 2000. 'Government Science and the Public Interest.' In *Risky Business: Canada's Changing Science-Based Policy and Regulatory Regime*, ed. Bruce Doern and Ted Reed, chapter 2. Toronto: University of Toronto Press.

de la Mothe, John, and Paul Dufour. 1995. 'Techno-Globalism and the Challenge to Science and Technology Policy.' *Daedalus* 124(3): 22–33.

de la Mothe, John, and Gilles Paquet. 1996. *Evolutionary Economics and the New International Political Economy*. London: Pinter.

– eds. 1998. *Local and Regional Systems of Innovation*. Boston: Kluwer.

Department of Industry, Science and Technology. 1995. *Australian Industrial Property Organization: Activities Report 1994–95*. Canberra: Commonwealth of Australia.

Department of Justice, Industry Canada, and Canadian Heritage. 1995. *Symposium on Digital Technology and Copyright*. Ottawa: Minister of Public Works and Government Services Canada.

Department of the Secretary of State. 1985. *Intellectual Property Rights*. Ottawa: Supply and Services Canada.

Dewees, Donald N., ed. 1983. *The Regulation of Quality*. Toronto: Butterworths.

Diebold, John. 1990. *The Innovators*. New York: Truman Talley Books.

Dillon, J. 1997. *On Feeding Sharks: Patent Protection, Compulsory Licensing and International Trade Law*. Ottawa: Canadian Health Coalition.

Doern, G. Bruce. 1972. *Science and Politics in Canada*. Montreal: McGill-Queen's University Press.

– 1987. *Modernizing Economic Framework Legislation: A Discussion Paper*. Ottawa: Consumer and Corporate Affairs Canada.

– 1990. 'The Department of Industry, Science and Technology: Is There Industrial Policy after Free Trade?' In *How Ottawa Spends 1990–91*, ed. Katherine Graham. pp. 49–72. Ottawa: Carleton University Press.

– 1994. *The Road to Better Public Services: Progress and Constraints in Five Federal Agencies*. Montreal: C.D. Howe Institute.

– 1995a. 'A Political-Institutional Framework for the Analysis of Competition Policy Institutions.' *Governance*, April 1995, pp. 195–217.

– 1995b. *Fairer Play: Canadian Competition Policy Institutions in a Global Market*. Toronto: C.D. Howe Institute.

– 1995c. 'The Formation of Industry Canada: Second Beginnings for a Department of the Micro-Economy.' Paper presented to the Workshop on the 1993 Federal Reorganization, Canadian Centre for Management Development.

– 1995d. *The Regulation of Patent and Trade-Mark Agent Qualifications: Institutional Issues and Options*. Ottawa: Canadian Intellectual Property Office.

– 1999. *Global Change and Intellectual Property Agencies*. London: Pinter.

– 2000. 'The Therapeutics Products Program: From Science-Based Regulator to Risk-Benefit Manager?' In *Risky Business: Canada's Changing Science-Based Policy and Regulatory Regime*, ed. Bruce Doern and Ted Reed, chapter 8. Toronto: University of Toronto Press.

Doern, G. Bruce, Margaret Hill, Michael Prince, and Richard Schultz, eds. 1999. *Changing the Rules: Canada's Changing Regulatory Regimes and Institutions*. Toronto: University of Toronto Press.

Doern, G. Bruce, Leslie Pal, and Brian Tomlin, eds. 1996. *Border Crossings: The Internationalization of Canadian Public Policy*. Toronto: Oxford University Press.

Doern, G. Bruce, and Richard W. Phidd. 1992. *Canadian Public Policy: Ideas, Structure, Process*. 2nd ed. Toronto: Nelson Canada.

Doern, G. Bruce, and Ted Reed, eds. 2000. *Risky Business: Canada's Changing Science-Based Policy and Regulatory Regime*. Toronto: University of Toronto Press.

Doern, G. Bruce, and Heather Sheehy. 1999. 'The Federal Biotechnology Regulatory System: A Commentary on an Institutional Work in Progress.' In *Biotechnology and the Consumer*, ed. Knoppers and Mathios. Dordrecht: Kluwer.

Doern, G. Bruce, and Brian Tomlin. 1991. *Faith and Fear: The Free Trade Story*. Toronto: Stoddart.

– 1996. 'Trade-Industrial Policy.' In *Border Crossings: The Internationalization of Canadian Public Policy*, ed. G. Bruce Doern, Leslie Pal, and Brian Tomlin, chapter 6. Toronto: Oxford University Press.

Doern, G. Bruce, and Stephen Wilks, eds. 1996. *National Competition Policy Institutions in a Global Market*. Oxford: Oxford University Press.

Drahos, 1996. 'Global Law Reform and Rent-Seeking: The Case of Intellectual Property.' *Australian Journal of Corporate Law* 7: 45–61.

Drake, W.J. 1994. 'Asymmetric Deregulation and the Transformation of the International Telecommunications Regime.' In *Asymmetric Deregulation: The Dynamics of Telecommunications Policy in Europe and the United States*, ed. E. Noam and G. Pogorel, pp. 88–101. Norwood, NJ: Ablex Publishing.

– ed. 1995. *The New Information Infrastructure: Strategies for U.S. Policy*. New York: Twentieth Century Fund Press.

Dufour, Paul R., and John de la Mothe. 1993. 'The Historical Conditioning of Science and Technology.' In *Science and Technology in Canada*, ed. Paul R. Dufour, and John de la Mothe. London: Longman.

Eastman, Harry. 1985. *Report of the Commission of Inquiry on the Pharmaceutical Industry*. Ottawa: Supply and Services Canada.

Eber, Dorothy. 1982. *Genius at Work: Images of Alexander Graham Bell*. Toronto: McClelland and Stewart.

Economic Council of Canada. 1971. *Report on Intellectual and Industrial Property*. Ottawa: Information Canada.

Eden, Lorraine, and Maureen Molot. 1993. 'Canada's National Policies: Reflections on 125 Years.' *Canadian Public Policy* 19(3): 232–60.

Edquist, Charles, ed. 1997. *Systems of Innovation: Technologies, Institutions and Organizations*. London: Pinter.

Ely Lilly Corp. 1996. *Honouring Innovation: The Case for Globally Competitive Intellectual Property Protection in Canada's Pharmaceutical Industry*. Toronto: Ely Lilly Corporation.

Etzkowitz, Henry. 1996. 'Conflicts of Interest and Commitment in Academic Science in the United States.' *Minerva* 34: 259–77.

Etzkowitz, Henry, and Loet Leydesdorff, eds. 1998. *Universities and the Global Knowledge Economy*. London: Pinter.

European Patent Office (EPO). 1994. *Utilization of Patent Protection in Europe*. Published as volume 3 of *EPOScript*. Munich: European Patent Office.

– 1995. *European Patent Office: Annual Report 1994*. Munich: European Patent Office.

Fédération Internationale des Conseils en Propriété Industrielle (FICPI). 1992. Congrès mondial, 1988. In *Revue et Bulletin*, pp. 82–120. London: FICPI.

– 1993. 'The Worldwide Association of Intellectual Property.' Brochure.

Feketekuty, Geza. 1991. 'Intellectual Property – the Major Shifts That Are Taking Place in the World Economy.' In *Global Rivalry and Intellectual Property*, ed. Murray G. Smith, p. 60–7. Montreal: Institute for Research on Public Policy.

Ferlie, Ewan, Lynn Ashburner, Louise Fitzgerald, and Andrew Pettigrew. 1996. *The New Public Management in Action*. Oxford: Oxford University Press.

Flatow, Ira. 1992. *They All Laughed ... From Light Bulbs to Lasers*. New York: Harper Collins.

Flood, J., and E. Skordaki. 1995. 'The Rise of the Corporate Advisor: Accountants and Solicitors.' Paper presented to the Conference on Regulating the Professions, University of Strathclyde, 20–1 April.

Fox, Harold G. 1969. *The Canadian Law and Practice Relating to Letters Patent for Inventions*. 4th ed. Toronto: Carswell.

Freeman, Chris, and Luc Soete. 1997. *The Economics of Industrial Innovation*. 3rd ed. London: Pinter.

Frischtak, Claudio R. 1995. 'Harmonization versus Differentiation in International Property Rights Regimes.' *International Journal of Technology Management* 10(2/3): 200–13.

Gallini, Nancy T., and Michael Trebilcock. 1996. 'Intellectual Property Rights and Competition Policy: An Overview of Legal and Economic Issues.' Paper presented to the Symposium on Competition Policy, Intellectual Property Rights and International Economic Integration. Ottawa, 12–13 May.

Gera, Surenda, and Kurt Mang. 1998. 'The Knowledge-Based Economy: Shifts in Industrial Output.' *Canadian Public Policy* 24: 149–84.

Goode, William J. 1969. 'The Theoretical Limits of Professionalism.' In *The Semi-Professions and Their Organization*, ed. A. Etzioni, pp. 77–94. New York: Free Press.

Grace, Eric. 1997. *Biotechnology Unzipped*. Washington: National Academy Press.

Gross, Neil. 1995. 'A U.S. Patent Corporation?' *Business Week*, 30 Oct. pp. 76B-E–76D-E.

Gualtieri, Roberto. 1994. 'Science Policy and Basic Research in Canada.' In *How Ottawa Spends 1994–95*, ed. Susan Phillips, pp. 301–38. Ottawa: Carleton University Press.

Harris, Lesley Ellen. 1995. *Canadian Copyright Law*. 2nd ed. Toronto: McGraw-Hill Ryerson.

Harris, Richard. 1993. *Trade, Money and Wealth in the Canadian Economy*. Toronto: C.D. Howe Institute.

Hart, Michael. 1994. *Decision at Midnight: Inside the Canada-US Free-Trade Negotiations*. Vancouver: UBC Press.

Hattenbach, Ben. 1995. 'GATT TRIPs and the Small American Inventor: An Evaluation of the Effort to Preserve Domestic Technological Innovation.' *Intellectual Property Journal* 10(1): 61–98.

Hébert, Monique. 1996. Background Paper: Copyright Reform. Ottawa: Library of Parliament.

– 1997. *Legislative Summary Bill C-32: An Act to Amend the Copyright Act*. Ottawa: Library of Parliament.

Hindley, B.V. 1971. *The Economic Theory of Patents, Copyrights and Registered Industrial Designs*. Background study. Ottawa: Economic Council of Canada.

Hoekman, Bernard, and M. Kostecki. 1995. *The Political Economy of the World Trading System: From GATT to WTO*. Oxford: Oxford University Press.

Hogwood, Brian W. 1984. 'The Rise and Fall of the Department of Industry.' Paper presented to the Conference of the Structure and Organization of Government Group, International Political Science Association, Manchester, November.

House of Commons. 1994. *rbST in Canada*. Report of the Standing Committee on Agriculture and Agri-Food. Issue no. 13. 24 March.

– 1997. *Review of Section 14 of the Patent Act Amendment 1992*. Fifth Report of the Standing Committee on Industry. Ottawa, April.

Howitt, Peter. 1996. 'On Some Problems of Measuring Knowledge-Based Growth.' In *The Implications of Knowledge-Based Growth for Micro-Economic Policies*, ed. Peter Howitt, pp. 9–29. Calgary: University of Calgary Press.

Hutter, Bridget M. 1989. 'Variations in Regulatory Enforcement Styles.' *Law and Policy* 11(2): 153–74.

Industrial R & D Advisory Committee of the European Commission. 1996. Report. Brussels.

Industry Canada. 1994a. *Building a More Innovative Economy*. Ottawa: Minister of Supply and Services.

– 1994b. *Growing Small Businesses*. Ottawa: Minister of Supply and Services.

– 1995. *The University-Industry Relationship in Science and Technology*. Occasional paper no. 11, by Jerome Doutriaux and Margaret Barker. Ottawa: Industry Canada.

– 1996. 'Biotechnology: What Is It All About?' *Consumer Quarterly* 1(3): 1–4.

– 1997a. *Sector Competitiveness Frameworks: Bio-Industries*. Ottawa: Industry Canada.

– 1997b. *Sector Competitiveness Frameworks: Pharmaceutical Industry*. Ottawa: Industry Canada.

– 1997c. *Sector Competitiveness Frameworks: Telehealth Industry*. Ottawa: Industry Canada.

Industry, Science and Technology Canada. 1991. *Industrial Profile: Pharmaceuticals*. Ottawa: Industry, Science and Technology Canada.

Jacob, Robin, and Daniel Alexander. 1993. *A Guidebook to Intellectual Property*. 4th ed. London: Sweet and Maxwell.

Jacobson, Harold K. 1984. *Networks of Interdependence: International Organizations and the Global Political System*. 2nd ed. London: McGraw Hill.

Jasanoff, Sheila. 1998. *Comparative Science and Technology Policy*. London: Elgar.

Jorde, Thomas M., and David J. Teece. 1992. Rule of Reason Analysis of Horizontal Arrangements: Agreements Designed to Advance Innovation and Commercialize Technology. *Antitrust Law Journal* 61(2): 579–620.

Jussawalla, Meheroo. 1992. *The Economics of Intellectual Property in a World without Frontiers: A Study of Computer Software*. New York: Greenwood.

Keplinger, Michael S. 1995. 'An American View on TRIPs: The Copyright Aspects of the U.S. Implementation Act.' Paper presented to the 10th Annual Seminar of the Dutch Foundation for Copyright Protection, Amsterdam, 10 November.

Keyes, A.A., and C. Brunet. 1977. *Copyright in Canada: Proposals for a Revision of the Law*. Ottawa: Consumer and Corporate Affairs Canada.

Knight, Jackson. 1995. *Patent Strategy for Researchers and Research Managers*. London: John Wiley and Sons.

Kratochwil, F., and E. Mansfield, eds. 1994. *International Organization*. New York: Harper Collins.

Krugman, Paul. 1994. 'Competitiveness: A Dangerous Obsession.' *Foreign Affairs* (March/April): 28–44.

– ed. 1986. *Strategic Trade Policy and the New International Economics*. Cambridge: MIT Press.

Langford, Cooper H., Martha Langford, and R.D. Burch. 1997. 'The Well-Stirred Reactor: Evolution of Industry-Government-University Relations in Canada.' *Science and Public Policy* 24(1): 21–7.

Leadbeater, Charles. 1999. *Living on Thin Air: The New Economy*. London: Viking.

Lee, Yong S. 1996. 'Technology Transfer and the Research University: A Search for the Boundaries of University-Industry Collaboration.' *Research Policy* 25: 843–63.

Lexchin, Joel. 1992. *Pharmaceuticals, Patents and Politics: Canada and Bill C-22*. Ottawa: Canadian Centre for Policy Alternatives.

Leydesdorff, L., and Henry Etzkowitz. 1998. 'Triple Helix of Innovation: Introduction.' *Science and Public Policy* 25(6): 358–64.

Lowndes, Vivien. 1996. 'Varieties of New Institutionalism: A Critical Appraisal.' *Public Administration* 74: 181–97.

Lucas, 1997. 'Innovation and Intellectual Property Protection: Ensuring Innovation for Current and Future Generations.' In *Medicines and the New Millennium: PMAC Annual Review 1997–98*, pp. 11–14. Ottawa: PMAC.

Lundvall, B.A., ed. 1992. *National Innovation Systems*. London: Pinter.

MacDonald, Mark. 2000. 'Socio-economic versus Science-Based Regulation: Informal Influences on the Formal Regulation of rbST in Canada.' In *Risky Business: Canada's Changing Science-Based Policy and Regulatory Regime*, ed. G. Bruce Doern and Ted Reed, chapter 7. Toronto: University of Toronto Press.

Manley, J. 1998. 'Statement: Speaking Notes ... 2/17.97.' (http://info.ic.gc.ca, 1/19/98)

Mansfield, Edwin. 1986. 'Patents and Innovation: An Empirical Study.' *Management Science* 30: 173–81.

March, J.G. 1996. 'Institutional Perspectives on Political Institutions.' *Governance* 9(3): 247–64.

Marlin Bennett, R. 1995. 'International Intellectual Property Rights in a Web of Social Relations.' *Science Communication* 17(2): 119–36.

Maskus, Keith E. 1991. 'Economic Analysis of Intellectual Property Rights: Domestic and International Dimensions.' In *Global Rivalry and Intellectual Property*, ed. Murray G. Smith. p. 120. Montreal: Institute for Research on Public Policy.

– 1995. 'Intellectual Property Rights in the Global Information Economy.' Paper presented to Conference on Policy Frameworks for a Knowledge Economy. John Deutsch Institute, Queen's University, Kingston, ON, 16–17 November.

Maybee, Gareth E., and Robert E. Mitchell. 1985. *History of the Patent and Trademark Profession in Canada*. Toronto: Patent and Trademark Institute of Canada.

McDonald, Bruce C. 1972. *Copyright in Context: The Challenge of Change*. Background Study. Ottawa: Economic Council of Canada.

McFetridge, Donald G. 1996. 'Intellectual Property, Technology Diffusion and Growth.' Paper prepared for Symposium on Competition Policy, Intellectual Property Rights and International Economic Integration. Ottawa, 12–13 May.

McRae, J. 1984. 'Compulsory Licensing of Drug Patents: Three Comments.' *Canadian Public Policy* 10(1): 10–22.

Merges, Robert. 1990. 'Battle of the Lateralisms: Intellectual Property and Trade.' *Boston University International Law Journal* (Fall): 239–46.

Mironesco, Christine. 1998. 'Parliamentary Technology Assessment of Biotech-
   nologies: A Review of Major TA Reports in the European Union and the
   USA.' *Science and Public Policy* 24(5): 327–42.
Nelson, Richard R. ed. 1993. *National Innovation Systems: A Comparative Analy-
   sis.* Oxford: Oxford University Press.
Niosi, Jorge. 1995. *Flexible Innovation: Technological Alliances in Canadian Indus-
   try.* Montreal: McGill-Queen's University Press.
– 1999. *Canada's National System of Innovation.* Toronto: Oxford University
   Press.
North, D.C. 1990. *Institutions, Institutional Change and Economic Performance.*
   Cambridge: Cambridge University Press.
Office for Harmonization in the Internal Market. 1995. *Trade Marks and De-
   signs.* Luxembourg: Office of Official Publications of the European Commu-
   nities.
Office of Fair Trading. 1986. *Review of Restrictions on the Patent Agents Profes-
   sion.* London: Office of Fair Trading.
Ogus, Anthony I. 1994. *Regulation: Legal Form and Economic Theory.* Oxford:
   Clarendon.
Okimoto, D. 1989. *Between MITI and the Market.* Stanford: Stanford University
   Press.
Organization for Economic Cooperation and Development. 1989. *Competition
   Policy and Intellectual Property Rights.* Paris: OECD.
– 1996. *The Knowledge-Based Economy.* Paris: OECD.
Ostrom, E. 1990. 'Rational Choice Theory and Institutional Analysis: Toward
   Complementarity.' *American Political Science Review* 85: 237–43.
Ostry, Sylvia. 1990. *Governments and Corporations in a Shrinking World: Trade
   and Innovation Policies in the United States, Europe and Japan.* New York:
   Council on Foreign Relations.
– 1991. 'The Place of Intellectual Property Rights in the Evolution of Innova-
   tion Policy.' In *Global Rivalry and Intellectual Property,* ed. Murray G. Smith,
   p. 56. Montreal: Institute for Research on Public Policy.
– 1993. 'Globalization, Domestic Policies and the Need for Harmonization.'
   Paper presented to Workshop on Competition Policy in a Global Economy,
   University of California, 8–9 January.
Paquet, Gilles, and Jeff Roy. 1995. 'Prosperity through Networks: The Bottom-
   up Strategy That Might Have Been.' In *How Ottawa Spends: 1995–96,* ed.
   S. Phillips, pp. 137–58. Ottawa: Carleton University Press.
Patent and Trademark Institute of Canada. 1991. *Information on the PTIC.*
   Toronto: PTIC.
Patented Medicine Prices Review Board. 1995. *Seventh Annual Report.* Ottawa:
   Patented Medicine Prices Review Board.

Pazderka, Bohumir. 1999. 'Patent Protection and Pharmaceutical R & D Spending in Canada.' *Canadian Public Policy* 25(1): 29–46.

Peters, Guy. 1999. *Neo-Institutional Theory*. London: Pinter.

Petrosky, Henry. 1993. *The Evolution of Useful Things*. New York: Knopf.

Pharmaceutical Manufacturer's Association of Canada (PMAC). 1992. *Patent Act Changes Will Benefit All Canadians Coast to Coast*. Ottawa: PMAC.

– 1993. *Towards Canadian Pharmaceutical Patent Law Reform*. Ottawa: PMAC.

– 1996. *Closing the Intellectual Property Gap in Canada: A Position Paper on Intellectual Property Protection for Pharmaceuticals*. Ottawa: PMAC.

– 1997a. 'Drug Development and Regulatory Approval: From the Research Laboratory to the Patient.' In *Medicines and the New Millennium: PMAC 1997–1998 Annual Review*. Ottawa: PMAC.

– 1997b. *Drug Development and Regulatory Approval: From the Research Laboratory to the Patient*. Ottawa: PMAC.

Phidd, Richard, and G. Bruce Doern. 1978. *The Politics and Management of Canadian Economic Policy*. Toronto: Macmillan.

Phillips, Jeremy, and Alison Firth. 1995. *Introduction to Intellectual Property Law*. 3rd ed. London: Butterworths.

Porter, Michael. 1990. *The Competitive Advantage of Nations*. New York: Free Pree.

Precious, Carole. 1984. *Bombardier*. Markham, ON: Fitzhenry and Whiteside.

Prime Minister's Science and Engineering Council. 1994. *The Role of Intellectual Property in Innovation*. Canberra: Commonwealth of Australia.

Purdue, Derrick. 1995. 'Hegemonic Trips: World Trade, Intellectual Property and Biodiversity.' *Environmental Politics* 4(1): 88–107.

Rapp, R., and R. Rozak. 1990. 'Benefits and Costs of Intellectual Property Protection in Developing Countries.' *Journal of World Trade* 24: 75–102.

Reichman, J.H. 1989. 'Intellectual Property in International Trade: Opportunities and Risks of a GATT Connection.' *Vanderbilt Journal of Transnational Law* 22(4): 747–892.

Renko, Robert 1987. *Protecting Intellectual Property Rights: Issues and Controversies*. Washington: University Press of America.

Richardson, David J. 1989. 'Empirical Research on Trade Liberalization with Imperfect Competition: A Survey.' *OECD Economic Studies* 12: 141–64.

Rosenberg, Nathan. 1990. 'Emergent Issues in Science Policy.' *Science and Public Policy* (June/July).

Rosenberg, Nathan, and Richard Nelson. 1994. 'American Universities and Technical Advance in Industry.' *Research Policy*, vol. 23.

Roy, J. 1995. 'Understanding Governance in High-Technology Regions: Towards a New Paradigm of High Technology and Local Development in Canada.' School of Public Administration, Carleton University, Ottawa.

Safarian, A.E. 1993. 'Foreign Direct Investment and International Cooperative Agreements: Trends and Issues.' Paper presented at Workshop on Competition Policy in a Global Economy, University of California, 8–9 January.

Savoie, Donald. 1986. *Regional Economic Development: Canada's Search for Solutions*. Toronto: University of Toronto Press.

Science Council of Canada. 1987. *R & D Links between Firms and Universities: Six Case Studies*. Ottawa: Science Council of Canada.

Searing, D.D. 1991. 'Roles, Rules and Rationality in the New Institutionalism.' *American Political Science Review* 85: 1239–60.

Sell, Susan K. 1998. *Power and Ideas: North-South Politics of Intellectual Property and Antitrust*. New York: State University of New York Press.

Sharaput, Markus. 1998. 'Bill C-91 as a Symbolic Moment: An Inquiry into Political Conceptions of the Pharmaceutical Industry in Canada, 1987 to 1998.' Unpublished research essay, Institute of Political Economy, Carleton University, Ottawa.

Sheehy, Heather. 1995. *Consumers and Biotechnology*. Ottawa: Office of Consumer Affairs, Industry Canada.

Sherman, Brad. 1995. 'Remembering and Forgetting: The Birth of Modern Copyright Law.' *Intellectual Property Journal* 10(1): 1–34.

Sherwood, Robert. 1990. *Intellectual Property and Economic Developent*. Boulder CO: Westview Press.

Siebeck, Wolfgang. 1990. *Strengthening Protection of Intellectual Property in Developing Countries*. Washington: World Bank.

Sims, N. 1996. *Pharmaceutical Patent Protection: Decision Time for Canada*. Ottawa: Pharmaceutical Manufacturers Association of Canada.

Slaughter, Sheila, and Gary Rhoades. 1996. 'The Emergence of a Competitiveness Research and Development Policy Coalition and the Commercialization of Academic Science and Technology.' *Science, Technology and Human Values* 21(3): 303–39.

Smith, Douglas A. 1988. 'Recent Proposals for Copyright Revision: An Evaluation.' *Canadian Public Policy* 14(2): 175–85.

Smith, Murray. ed. 1991. *Global Rivalry and Intellectual Property: Developing Canadian Strategies*. Montreal: Institute for Research on Public Policy.

Society of Composers, Authors and Music Publishers of Canada / Société canadienne des auteurs, compositeurs et éditeurs de musique (SOCAN). 1996. Submission to the House of Commons Standing Committee on Canadian Heritage regarding Bill C-32, An Act to Amend the Copyright Act. 30 August.

Statistics Canada. 1998. *Survey of Intellectual Property Commercialization in the Higher Education Sector*. Ottawa: Statistics Canada.

Subramanian, A. 1990. 'TRIPs and the Paradigm of the GATT: A Tropical and Temperate View.' *World Economy* 13(4): 509–21.

'Summary of Testimony.' In *The 5th Report of the Standing Committee on Industry*. (http://www.ic.gc.ca)

Taylor, Paul. 1993. *International Organization in the Modern World*. London: Pinter.

Taylor, Paul, and A.J.R. Groom. eds. 1988. *International Institutions at Work*. London: Pinter.

Thurow, Lester C. 1997. 'Needed: A New System of Intellectual Property Rights.' *Harvard Business Review* 75(3): 94–103.

Trebilcock, Michael, and Robert Howse. 1995. *The Regulation of International Trade*. London: Routledge.

Tupper, Allan. 1986. 'Federalism and the Politics of Industrial Policy.' In *Industrial Policy*, ed. André Blais, pp. 347–78. Toronto: University of Toronto Press.

Tyson, Laura D'Andrea. 1993. *Who's Bashing Whom? Trade Conflict in High Technology Industries*. Washington: Institute for International Economics.

United Kingdom, Department of Trade and Industry. 1995. *Trade and Industry 1995: The Government's Expenditure Plans 1995–96 to 1997–98*. London: HMSO.

United Kingdom Patent Office. 1990. *Framework Document 1990*. London: The Patent Office, 1990.

U.S. Information Infrastructure Task Force. 1995. *Intellectual Property and the National Information Infrastructure*. Washington: Department of Commerce.

U.S. General Accounting Office. 1993. *Intellectual Property Rights: U.S. Companies' Patent Experiences in Japan*. Washington; USGAO, GGD-93-126, July.

U.S. Patent and Trademark Office. 1993. *Planning Progress Report: Fiscal Years 1994–1998*. Washington: USPTO.

– 1994. *Strategic Plan 1996–2000*. Washington: USPTO.

– 1995. *Working for Our Customers: A Patent and Trademark Office Review Fiscal Year 1994*. Washington: USPTO

Vaver, David. 1995. 'Rejuvenating Copyright, Digitally.' In Department of Justice, Industry Canada, and Canadian Heritage. *Symposium on Digital Technology and Copyright*, pp. 1–20. Ottawa: Minister of Public Works and Government Services Canada.

Wade, Robert. 1990. *Governing the Market*. Princeton: Princeton University Press.

Wallerstein, M.B., M.E. Mogee, and R.A. Schoen, eds. 1993. *Global Dimensions of Intellectual Property Rights in Science and Technology*. Washington: National Academy Press.

Warshovsky, Fred. 1994. *The Patent Wars: The Battle to Own the World's Technology*. New York: Wiley.

Waverman, L., and S. Khemani. 1993. 'Strategic Alliances: A Threat to Competition?' Paper presented to Workshop on Competition in the Global Economy, University of California, 8–9 January.

Wegloop, Philip. 1996. 'Problems and Prospects of Bottom-up Policy Formulation: Towards User-Defined Innovation and Technology Policy.' *Science and Public Policy* 23(4): 241–9.

Weiss, Linda. 1998. *The Myth of the Powerless State: Governing the Economy in a Global Era*. London: Polity Press.

Westaway, Cynthia. 1997. 'Copyright Legislation: Ambushed by the Heritage Committee.' *CAUT Bulletin* 44(2): 1, 7.

Wilks, Stephen. 1993. 'Economic Policy.' In *Developments in British Politics*, ed. Patrick Dunleavy, pp. 220–41. London: Macmillan.

Wilson, A.H. 1970. *Background to Invention*. Ottawa: Science Council of Canada.

World Intellectual Property Organization (WIPO). 1994a. *WIPO Worldwide Symposium on the Future of Copyright and Neighboring Rights*. Geneva: World Intellectual Property Organization.

– 1994b. *Worldwide Forum on the Arbitration of Intellectual Property Disputes*. Geneva: World Intellectual Property Organization.

– 1995a. *Conference on Rules for Institutional Arbitration and Mediation*. Geneva: World Intellectual Property Organization.

– 1995b. *Governing Bodies of WIPO and the Unions Administered by WIPO*. Twenty-Sixth Series of Meetings, Geneva, 25 September to 3 October. Draft Program and Budget for the 1996–97 Biennium, p. 19.

– 1995c. *Governing Bodies of WIPO and the Unions Administered by WIPO*. Twenty-Sixth Series of Meetings, Geneva, 25 September to 3 October, pp. 99–102

– 1995d. *Intellectual Property Reading Material*. Geneva: World Intellectual Property Organization.

– 1995e. *WIPO: General Information*. Geneva: World Intellectual Property Organization.

– 1997. *Consultative Meeting on Trademarks and Internet Domain Names*. Geneva: World Intellectual Property Organization.

Wyatt, Geoffrey. 1986. *The Economics of Invention*. London: Wheatsheaf.

Yamin, F. 1993. 'Intellectual Property Rights and the Environment: The Role of Patents in the Conservation of Biodiversity.' LLM Dissertation, Kings College, London.

Yarbrough, Beth, and Robert Yarbrough. 1990. 'International Institutions and the New Economics of Organization' *International Organization* 44(2): 235–59.

Index